Fixed and Mobile Telecommunications: Networks, Systems and Services

2nd edition

Jan van Duuren
Peter Kastelein
Frits C. Schoute

ADDISON-WESLEY

Harlow, England • Reading, Massachusetts • Menlo Park, California • New York
Don Mills, Ontario • Amsterdam • Bonn • Sydney • Singapore
Tokyo • Madrid • San Juan • Milan • Mexico City • Seoul • Taipei

© Addison Wesley Longman 1996
Addison Wesley Longman Limited
Edinburgh Gate
Harlow
Essex
CM20 2JE
England

and Associated Companies throughout the world.

Cover designed by Designers & Partners, Oxford
and printed by The Riverside Printing Co. (Reading) Ltd
Typeset by CRB Associates, Norwich
Printed and bound by T. J. Press (Padstow) Ltd.

First printed 1996

ISBN 0-201-87754-6

British Library Cataloguing-in-Publication Data
A catalogue record for this book is available from the British Library.

The publishers wish to thank Airline Telecommunications and Information Services,
Neuilly-sur-Seine, for permission to reproduce Figure 2.5 in this book.

The publishers also wish to thank Philips Telecommunications Review, for permission to
reproduce Figures 7.11, 7.12, 7.13, 7.14, 7.15, 7.16, 7.17 and 7.18 in this book.

The publishers would also like to thank the International Telecommunication Union, for
permission to reproduce Figures 11.1, 11.2, 11.5, 11.8 and 11.9 in this book. The publishers
would like to point out that the choice of excerpts is entirely their own and ITU hold no
responsibility for the choice. The full text of each figure used may be obtained from the
ITU Sales Section, Place des Nations, CH-1211, Geneva 20, Switzerland.

Dedication

In remembrance of my father, Dr Hendrik C.A. van Duuren, inventor and designer of the first ARQ systems, enabling fault-free transmission, the prerequisite for data transmission.

Preface

This book is intended for all readers interested in the general aspects of telecommunication. It offers a concise overview of the history, present and future, of telecommunication. The emphasis is on the *networks, systems and standards* rather than on the detailed physics of information transfer on copper wires or satellite radio links.

The book is based on the course material written for use in the second and third year courses of the Telematics project at the Institute for Higher Professional Education, Hogeschool van Utrecht in the Netherlands and the valuable comments of the readers of that material. This project, which aimed at developing texts for training students in the complementary fields of telecommunication and computer science, arose as the result of close cooperation between education and industry.

The *course* was, therefore, geared as closely as possible to the real needs of the students' prospective employers. Further, the aim was to concentrate on equipment designed according to international and European standards rather than national standards.

The course was written to meet two goals: on the one hand as a general orientation for students who do not wish to specialize further in telecommunications and on the other as a basis for those who are planning to dig deeper into the subject later in their course.

From this double goal, there emerged a common desire to make the students familiar with the *terminology* used in the subject. This is an essential condition for being able to communicate with specialists later and to be able to understand the technical literature.

The first edition of the *book* was already intended for a somewhat wider audience. References to the literature were extended and a few advanced topics such as **Electronic Data Interchange (EDI)** were added.

For use at university level, the mathematical section was extended. A chapter on digital multiplexing was also added, which treats the topics of **Synchronous Digital Hierarchy (SDH)** and **Asynchronous Transfer Mode (ATM)**. To help self-study, each chapter had its own key terms section.

This second, updated version of the book is extended with a completely new elaborate treatment of **mobile communication**. Topics in this field such as **GSM, DSRR, DECT**, and **PHS** are covered. It is necessary to have some basic knowledge of ISDN, TDM, FDM and packet switching to understand these new topics. Those who do not have this basic knowledge will find this in the sections preceding the chapter on mobile communication.

The original material was properly sized to handle in a one-semester course. With the extensions of the material it is advisable to make a selection of the chapters and sections in case only one semester is available for the course. In this way the course can be tailored to the needs of colleges, universities and postgraduate seminars, and even of technically oriented marketing courses. The extensive list of key terms enables the reader to find the meaning of terminology encountered, but explained in other chapters.

Finally, I would like to thank all those who have contributed to the creation of this book. Peter Kastelein, lecturer at the Hogeschool of Utrecht, produced welcome criticism based on his long teaching experience. He also wrote Chapter 9 and part of Chapter 4. Frits Schoute, professor at the Delft Technical University, wrote Chapter 10, on performance analysis.

We thank all those who supported us in writing this book, in particular the publishers and their advisors and Bob van Loon and Frans Kluizenaar, who gave welcome comments on the new chapter on mobile communication.

Jan van Duuren
Huizen, The Netherlands
September 1995

Contents

Chapter 1

Introduction

1.1 Telecommunications

In electronics, the concept of telecommunications is generally used to denote the totality of techniques and circuits necessary for optimum information transfer via a given transmission medium, in the presence of noise and other possible forms of interference. In this book, a more restricted meaning is given to the term *telecommunications*. More specifically, we are concerned with the whole of the technology and procedures used to realize optimum information transfer via public facilities (such as the Public Switched Telephone Network (PSTN), the Packet Switched Public Data Network (PSPDN) and the Integrated Services Digital Network (ISDN)) or private facilities such as Local Area Networks (LANs). These networks all have standard interfaces. To use these networks it is necessary to know something about the services that are offered and the related standards for both the physical interface and the applicable procedures.

The whole complex of problems associated with the use of physical media for transmission, transmission technology, is so extensive that it cannot be treated here but is well covered in the literature. We do, however, describe how these physical media can be used for several simultaneous connections by the use of multiplexers.

The concept of information transfer is associated with the various categories of information shown in Figure 1.1. Traditionally, these categories have been approached completely differently from a communications point of view with, for example, their own networks, procedures and switching principles. There is an increasing tendency towards full integration.

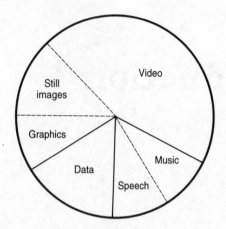

Figure 1.1   Division according to the nature of the information to be transmitted.

These differences will become steadily smaller. Investment in communications equipment in the networks is so large, and the increase in demand for communications so massive, that it is not possible to scrap older equipment in the short term. Thus, although new equipment is being introduced, only rarely do older systems disappear.

Figure 1.2 illustrates the main trend towards integration. However, it must not be concluded from this figure that the existing networks will have disappeared within a few years.

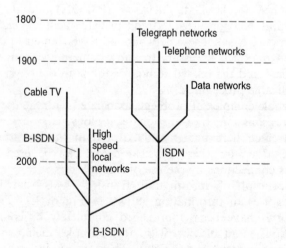

Figure 1.2   Integration of information transmission.

Integration is being facilitated by a number of developments, such as:

- the development of new switching principles such as packet switching and fast packet switching,
- the availability of the OSI Reference model for the definition of communication interfaces,
- the future availability of the ISDN and Broadband ISDN (B-ISDN).

In this book we survey the diverse aspects which are important from the communications point of view for information transfer using standard networks. Special attention is paid to the *terminology* used in this subject.

1.2   Communications in twelve chapters

The subject of communications is described in twelve chapters, and an overview can be seen in Figure 1.3.

After the introduction in Chapter 1, we describe in Chapter 2 the basic elements of telecommunication networks and illustrate these with

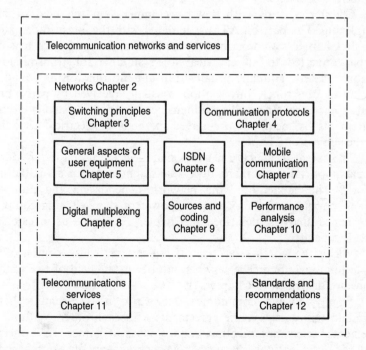

Figure 1.3   Overview of the book showing chapter contents.

some examples of networks. The networks require nodes that can switch the signals. The principles of switching are handled in Chapter 3, together with the switching equipment used in the nodes.

Information has to be exchanged between the connected equipment and the network to allow the desired connections to be set up and the required destination to be reached. Information also has to be exchanged between the nodes. This is based on the use of signalling protocols. Protocols are also necessary between the connected equipments. Several are described in Chapter 4. The internetworking protocols, **TCP/IP** and **X.75** are included in this second edition of the book.

The user can only make use of the network services offered by means of the connected user equipment, which forms the subject of Chapter 5. Because of the wide diversity of such equipment, we only cover the general aspects of user equipment in this chapter and limit ourselves to a few examples. More extensive treatment of the many sorts of user equipment can be found in the referenced literature.

A network currently of considerable interest, because it has now been introduced in many countries, is the ISDN. This is studied in detail in Chapter 6. Information on ISDN is important to understand the newest developments in mobile communication, described in the new Chapter 7.

Chapter 8 deals with new developments in the field of digital multiplexing. The part on ATM is updated with the latest information.

In Chapter 9 we describe how the information generated by sources can be converted to an electrical form suitable for transmission by electronic means. Humans usually transmit information as sound or a selection of keystrokes. Information is usually received by perception of sound or pictures. Reconciling human needs and the system's electronic requirements by means of pre-agreed methods of electrical encoding is also the subject of Chapter 9.

The extent to which a network can meet the users' requirements is of great importance; is there always sufficient capacity available in the network? The capacity of the network depends on the number of available circuits and the processing power of the switching equipment. Performance analysis, described in Chapter 10, assists us in calculating network capacity.

Via the networks, users are offered services which consist of more than technology alone. The services on offer in the field of telecommunications are described in Chapter 11.

Finally, in the communications world it is essential that the communicating parties make agreements with each other. Without such agreements, telecommunication cannot work. Chapter 12, concerning standards organizations, discusses how such agreements are reached and where they can be found.

Note to students

After studying a chapter, the list of *key terms* on p. 237 can be used to check whether the meanings of selected key terms have been remembered and, if not, the relevant text should be referred to. The terms themselves can be easily found in the text as they are in **bold** type.

1.3   Some definitions

As we have said, information on the many international and European organizations associated with telecommunications is the subject of Chapter 12. Because there are numerous references in chapters preceding this chapter to some of these bodies – CCITT, ITU and ISO – they are defined here for those readers who may not be familiar with them:

> **CCITT (Comité consultatif international télégraphique et télé-phonique)**, that is, the international consultative committee (for) telegraphy and telephony, is an organization within the **International Telecommunication Union (ITU)**. The CCITT specializes in wired, as distinct from wireless, telecommunications. CCITT has changed its name to **ITU-T**. Since many publications of older recommendations still carry the old name, CCITT, we still use it in several cases.
>
> **ISO (International Organization for Standardization)** is a worldwide standards organization, whose brief covers most fields of human endeavour (although not electronics or electrotechnology).

Mention should also be made here of **ASCII (American Standard Code for Information Interchange)**, a binary code to which several references are made in the book.

Chapter 2

Networks

2.1 Introduction

In this chapter a large number of concepts are treated that are related to the concept of networks. For further information, the reader is referred to the literature references at the end of the book. The emphasis in this chapter is on the *terminology*, which is essential for fruitful communication, not only between experts in the field of networks, but also for persons who have more incidental contact with the subject.

2.2 Network types

We distinguish between the **topology** and the **geography** when discussing types of network. Strictly speaking, the topology describes only the properties of the network that are independent of concrete properties, such as dimensions, the actual route that the cables follow and the number of pairs in a cable. Topology is thus an abstract concept, while the geography describes the reality of the network.

Topology is concerned with the interconnection pattern of the nodes in a network. This can be shown in tabular form, which is convenient for computer input, but it is more meaningful to use simple drawings in which **nodes** are connected by **links**. The total picture is called a **graph**.

In mathematical literature, there are many publications on **graph theory** but, up to now, it has not been of great significance for practical telecommunication networks. The terminology which has been developed is useful, however, even though some authors have made use of their own terms. We give a selection here; a number of basic network types are illustrated in Figure 2.1.

2.2.1   Networks without redundancy

The **point-to-point link** connecting two nodes is the simplest form of network. The number of links necessary to join two nodes is one, that is, one less than the number of nodes. To add a node to the network requires at least one new link. The minimum number of links needed to make a single connected network is thus $N - 1$ where N is the number of nodes. A network with this minimum number of links $(N - 1)$ is called a **tree**.

Special forms of tree networks are the **linear tree** and the **star**. A purely **hierarchical** network is equipped with the minimum number of links $N - 1$ and thus belongs in the tree classification.

2.2.2   Networks with redundancy

In practical networks, one would rather not have the absolute minimum of connections between exchanges. Although much attention is paid to making reliable connections, it is necessary to allow for connections becoming unserviceable. Therefore some **redundancy** is introduced into the network to improve **reliability**. A solution requiring only one extra connection is the **ring** network, in which the number of links is equal to the number of nodes. A ring network can be a good solution when there are relatively few nodes. A **fully connected** network, in which all nodes are connected by direct links, is, of course, much more reliable. An objection to this form of network can lie in the cost, especially for large numbers of nodes. Each of the N nodes must be connected with all other $(N - 1)$ nodes, calling for $N(N - 1)$ links. By placing a link from each node to each other node, $N - 1$ links leave each node but, since the other nodes also place a link, this results in two links between each pair of nodes. Thus the actual number of links required is half $N(N - 1)$:

$$L = \tfrac{1}{2}N(N - 1)$$

The addition of the Nth node to such a fully connected network costs $N - 1$ new links, which eventually becomes much too expensive, and is unlikely to contribute anything to an effective improvement in reliability.

In practice, therefore, many incompletely connected, or **mesh**, networks are to be found, in which the number of links lies between N and $\tfrac{1}{2}N(N - 1)$. The **triangulated** network is a special form of mesh

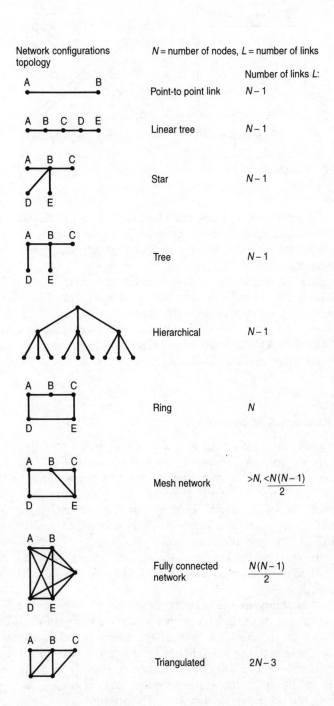

Figure 2.1 Network configurations.

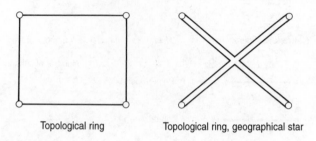

Topological ring   Topological ring, geographical star

Figure 2.2   Topological rings.

network. The addition of a new node to this type only costs two new links and thus does not become more expensive as the number of nodes grows. This explains why it is often used, whether or not in its pure form, for large networks.

Figure 2.2 clearly shows that a distinction must be made between the topology of a network and its geography; in this example, a topological ring is illustrated in the form of a geographical star. This can be found in practice, for example, in the token passing ring Local Area Network (LAN). It is left as an exercise for the reader to construct a geographical ring, topological star.

2.2.3   Examples of networks

Real networks are rarely built with a topology based on only one of the network types described above. Individual subscribers to a network are often connected with the minimum number of connections to the first node, in star form or with a linear tree – a **party line**. For the interconnection of a much smaller number of exchanges a more redundant form is chosen, such as fully connected or triangulated, depending on the size of the network. Because of financial considerations, there may be further local deviations from the chosen network type. The goal of a practical network remains high reliability for minimum cost.

The reliability of the network depends not only on the topology and the reliability of the links, but also on the reliability of the exchanges. Redundancy in the network makes it possible to select routes which bypass defective exchanges. Exchange failures are usually much less likely than circuit failure. For subscribers connected directly by a star network, exchange reliability is the main criterion, and is usually achieved by duplicating the central control system. The alternative, of duplicating the subscriber's network connection to separate nodes, is, of course, better but is rarely used because of its cost.

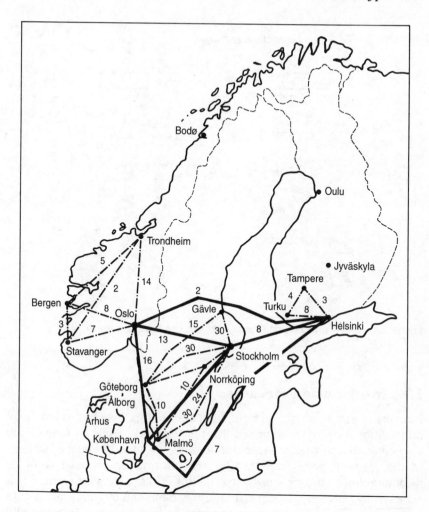

Figure 2.3   Scandinavia: Nordic public data network.

Figure 2.3 shows the fully connected network often used as the top level of the network for data networks, and the national data networks connected to it. Hierarchical networks have been commonly used for telephone networks, especially in the past. See Figure 2.4.

The network in Figure 2.5 is one in which the highest level is an almost complete mesh with the exchanges connected to it by a star network. This combination of network types is common in practice. In the Dutch telephone network, illustrated in Figure 2.6, an even more complicated combination of network types can be seen. Finally, Figure 2.7 shows an example of a higher level LAN with a topology consisting of a combination of linear trees.

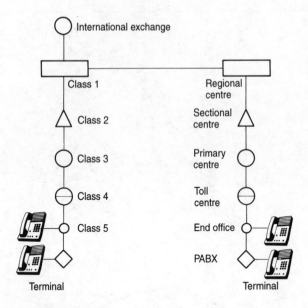

Figure 2.4   USA: national telephone network organization up to 1984.

2.3   Information streams

Networks are used in telecommunications for the transmission of information, which is supplied to the network from a **source** and communicated to one or more destinations, or **sinks**. Switching systems at the network nodes can transfer the information received from an incoming link to one or more outgoing links. In the simplest form, this is achieved by the through connection of incoming and outgoing circuits. In the earliest telephone exchanges, this was performed by an **operator** who connected a **cord** between the circuits of the two subscribers.

The information stream can be in one direction, which is adequate for telegram traffic, or a **two-way connection** may be required in order to hold a **conversation**. Incoming and outgoing information will often follow the same path through the network, but this is not essential.

The **one-way** information stream may be intended for one destination, but it can also be intended for a number of sinks (see Figure 2.8). This is called **multi-destination** traffic. If at the exchange it is necessary to give instructions regarding the destinations to which the message is to be sent, this is done by means of a **multi-address**. If the message is intended for anyone who wishes to receive it, then it can be sent to everybody and the receivers are left to decide whether or not they are interested. This is **broadcast** and is used, for example, on a cable television network. Police and meteorological messages are also suitable for broadcasting. There is

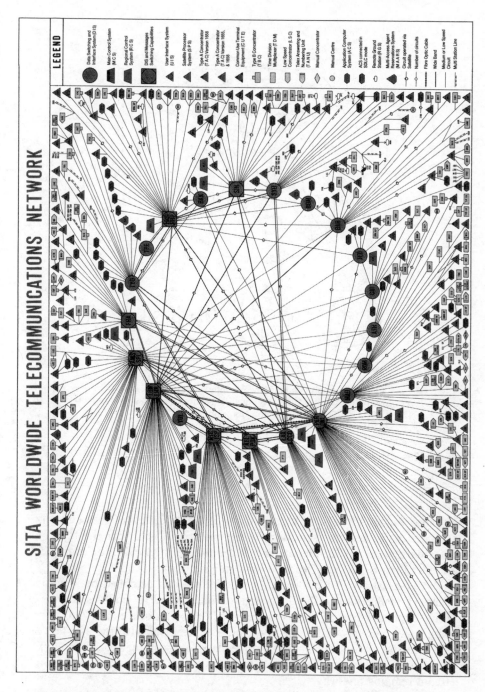

Figure 2.5 SITA network for airlines. (Source: Airline Telecommunications and Information Services. Société internationale de télécommunications aéronautiques. Neuilly-sur-Seine, 1991.)

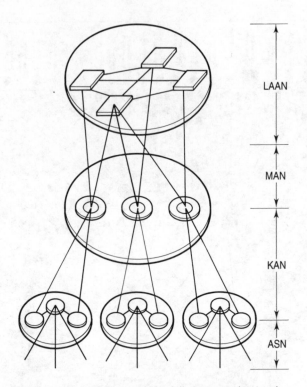

LAAN = Long distance network: fully connected network
MAN = Medium distance network: triangulated network
KAN = Short distance network: ring network
ASN = Subscriber star network: star network

Figure 2.6 The Dutch telephone network as an example of a multitype network.

no need for an address; at most a form of identification of the sender is included as a basis for selection by the receivers. Note that the type of information stream is independent of the type of network! For example, broadcasting is perfectly feasible on a ring network.

The last type of information stream that can be called one-way is **tributary (collection) traffic**, in which a large number of sources successively send information to a single sink. If this is clock controlled, it is completely one-way traffic; if, however, it takes place with the assistance of successive invitations to the sources sent over the network (**polling**), then a two-way connection is necessary. However, the main information stream remains one-way.

The technical provisions allowing information streams in both directions between two participants may be suitable for alternate working in only one of the directions (**two-way alternate**) or for concurrent

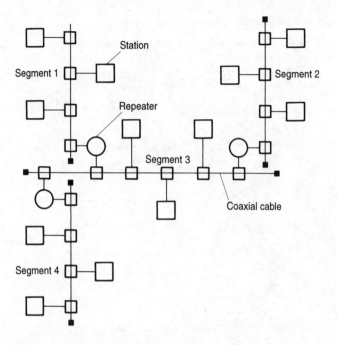

Figure 2.7 High level LAN; combination of linear trees.

traffic in both directions (**two-way simultaneous**). These are sometimes called **half duplex** and **full duplex**, respectively. Finally, it is possible to have conversations over a network with more than two participants, that is, a **conference**.

2.4   Communication channels

Channels are the basis of all communication networks. Modern transmission techniques make it possible to deliver many channels on a single transmission medium, such as coaxial cable, optical fibre or a satellite connection. This facility, called multiplexing, can be based not only on the use of different frequencies, but also on the use of different **time slots** for each individual channel. The latter method is referred to as **time division multiplexing** and is of major importance in digital transmission.

A modern form of multiplexing can be found in packet switching, in which one channel is used for the transmission of a large number of so-called **virtual circuits**. In a packet switch, information is relayed in the form of **packets** of several hundred bits, in order of arrival and not in fixed time slots. Identification of the virtual circuit to which the packets belong is carried in a **header** in the form of a **logical channel number**. This

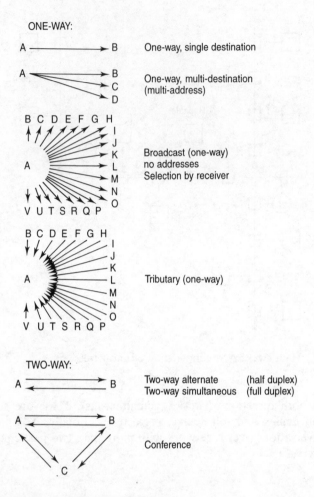

Figure 2.8   Traffic flows.

form of multiplexing requires the use of packet switches and cannot be considered separately from them.

For transmission over longer distances, it is necessary to insert repeaters at regular intervals to amplify weakened signals back to their original strength. The distance between consecutive repeaters depends on the transmission medium used. A great advantage of optical fibre is that distances as long as a hundred kilometres can be covered without the need for a repeater.

Not all the channels have to be used for the same network. For example, some of the channels on a link can be used for telephony while others are used for telex or digital television. It is, of course, necessary to have a channel of much higher capacity for television because, per unit time, many more bits of information have to be transferred than for almost any other type of traffic.

A **circuit** is the combination of two channels in opposite directions allowing bidirectional traffic between two points. A circuit that can be used simultaneously in both directions is also called full duplex. If it is only used in one direction at a time, because the terminal equipment does not allow anything else, this is called **half duplex operation**, which is the same as two-way alternate.

In most countries, the supply of circuits is controlled by **common carriers**, called **Public Telecommunication Operators (PTO)** by ITU, who have government permission to lay cables, install radio connections and allocate radio channels. In Britain, the role of common carrier is performed by, among others, BT. In the USA a number of recognized private operating agencies perform the role of telecommunications common carrier.

2.5 Nodes

Several channels meet at the nodes of a network. If there is just one incoming and one outgoing channel, then we have a simple through connection and not a node. The simplest form of node has at least two outgoing channels, as shown in the upper part of Figure 2.9.

2.5.1 Nodes with one-way traffic

The simplest operation at a node is to connect the outgoing channels to the incoming channel, converting it into a **distribution point**. It is sometimes necessary, for technical reasons, to amplify the signal but in most cases a simple through connection is sufficient. These types of node are to be found, for example, in the television distribution network.

If it is required to connect one of the incoming channels to one of the outgoing channels, and if the choice is to be easily changed, a **selector** is used. As long as only one incoming line is to be handled at a time, this does not cause any problems. However, if more than one incoming line must be connected, the problem arises that an outgoing line may be selected for more than one incoming line. If this is already **busy**, the desired information transmission cannot take place.

If it is essential to be able to select more than one outgoing channel, this can be indicated in the drawing by contacts in each outgoing line. It is thus possible to chose M out of N outgoing lines, the chance of selecting a busy line being even greater than in the previous example. To solve this problem, the node can be equipped with a means of storing the information until the outgoing channel is free, and a central control to

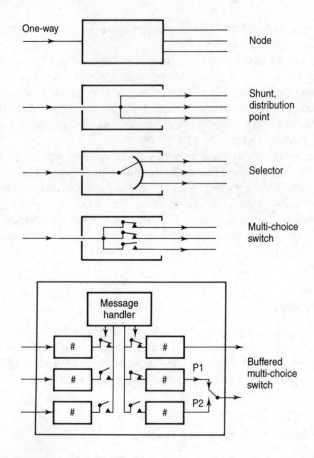

Figure 2.9   Nodes with one-way traffic.

ensure that the messages are placed in the appropriate queue for the outgoing channel. The node has now become a **message switch**. By creating several queues per outgoing channel, it is possible to allow high priority messages to overtake lower priority messages in the node.

2.5.2   Nodes with bidirectional traffic

The simplest configuration allowing bidirectional traffic is shown in the upper part of Figure 2.10. A bidirectional circuit is connected to a through circuit, which is also usually two-way. Information can be both received from and transmitted via the through circuit. A branch at a subsequent node on the through circuit will receive the same information as the branch at the node illustrated. This is called a **bus** circuit; it is also

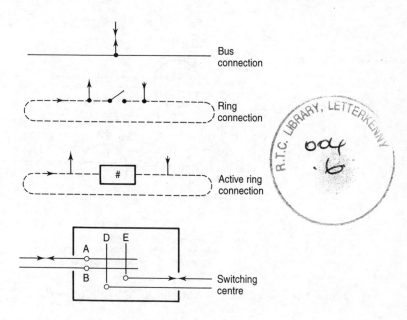

Figure 2.10   Nodes with two-way traffic.

sometimes called an **omnibus** circuit or a **party line**. The topology of a bus circuit is often a linear tree.

Use of a **ring** topology and a unidirectional channel causes the problem that information transmitted round the ring is received again a short time later at the transmitting node. If there is a through connection here the information continues to circulate round the ring – which is not the intention. In such ring circuits, the loop has to be broken during transmission. The transmitted information can still be received after travelling around the loop, permitting the operation of the loop to be checked. All subscribers on the ring receive the same information but, in contrast with a pure distribution network, each can also transmit information. Networks for the distribution of meteorological data are an example of a requirement for such facilities.

In Europe, the MOTNE meteorological network is based on the loop principle. Since leased lines are normally bidirectional (duplex) these can be used for two loops operating in opposite directions. In this way, 2 erlangs of information can be transmitted with only one duplex circuit. (The volume of traffic is 1 erlang for a fully loaded channel.) Just as for the bus, a method has to be found for the ring to regulate transmission on the loop. There are many possible ways of doing this. In the case of the MOTNE network (see Figure 2.11), it was decided to allocate fixed times at which each of the participants (meteorological services) can transmit their messages. The system also has provision, in urgent situations, for the

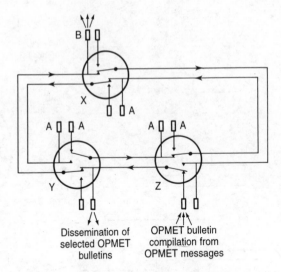

Figure 2.11 Simplified schematic of the MOTNE network.

transmission of high priority messages at other times. There is a continuous check that messages are not interrupted during transmission; by monitoring the loop, a node that has a high priority message for transmission can ascertain when a message has finished and thus choose a suitable moment at which to break in.

The task of coordinating the moments at which the various nodes are allowed to transmit can be simplified by including a memory function in the nodes. Traffic received round the loop can then be stored until a node's own transmission has finished. The addition of active elements, in this case memory, leads to the name **active ring connection**. It is again necessary to prevent messages circulating endlessly – a task for the transmitting node or, in cases where addressing is used, for the addressed node.

Examples of large-scale active ring systems are becoming rare. In the 1960s, United Airlines had a seat reservation system that operated an active ring system over the whole of the USA. Lower circuit costs and higher traffic volumes have made more redundant network forms possible, leading to increased network reliability. On a smaller scale, we can find active ring systems in the form of **token passing rings**. In this system, the memory enables a node to investigate whether a **token** is present, inviting the node to transmit information. If a token is found, the terminal is allowed to transmit its own information. The addressed node reads the information, after which the token is sent to the following connection on the LAN. Initially one token has to be inserted into the ring using a **master** node.

Finally, we come to the most common form of node, the **switching exchange**. The main task of the exchange is to make it possible to connect any circuit to any other circuit. In Figure 2.10, for example, A can be connected with either D or E. The node is so constructed that bidirectional traffic is possible over the chosen connection. This form of exchange, which employs **circuit switching**, is used on a very large scale in telephony. Telex also makes use of switching exchanges. Exchanges can be found in many sizes for switching anything from a few lines to tens of thousands of circuits.

2.6   Addressing, identification and numbering plans

In order to get the desired information stream to the right place, it is necessary to provide the nodes with suitable control information. In unidirectional systems, one usually speaks of the **addressing** of messages. The address information is usually at the beginning of the message in a **header**, which can additionally contain information that is useful for processing the message at the nodes, such as the **priority** level and possibly the **security** level. Information in the header is usually in the form of letters augmented with digits, that is, an alphanumeric string.

In telephony, a bidirectional system, an address consisting purely of digits was used to identify the called party. This is still more or less the case, but two symbols have been added, * and #. Moreover, checking that the correct subscriber has been reached is left to the users and accomplished by verbal exchange of the names of called and caller. For text-oriented services, such as telex and teletex, this exchange of names has been automated by the terminal apparatus sending on demand the preprogrammed telex **answerback code** and the teletex **terminal identification**. Telex and teletex also make use of digits to select the destination of a **call**. From these, the exchange in the node determines the connection needed to reach the required subscriber, thus choosing the **routing** in the node based on the selection data.

The addressing of message exchanges, and the numeric selection information for switching exchanges, is usually organized hierarchically. Part of the information is used to indicate a connection to the exchange within a village, town or business; where necessary, there is also an indication of the country in which the subscriber must be sought. In telephony, this is known as the **numbering plan**. For message traffic the addressing system is adjusted to the requirements of the system users and thus differs for different groups of users.

For international networks, international agreements are necessary about the addressing system and the numbering plan, and about their

implementation. In the case of public networks this is done within the
CCITT. For other networks, the organization using the network lays
down the rules to be used internationally.

2.7 Mobile subscribers

Subscribers who are connected to a network via a radio link have, in
principle, the ability to move within certain limits; they are not tied to a
fixed link. If they travel so far, for example, by car, that they move out of
the range of a fixed transmitter–receiver station, they are called mobile
subscribers. For communication to remain possible, they must periodically change over to working with a different fixed station. This creates an
extra problem for the network. In the case of subscribers connected by a
fixed line, the network knows via which exchange, and which exit of that
exchange, the subscriber can be reached. However, for a mobile
subscriber, this is no longer known with certainty. The subscriber moves
through areas, called **cells**, which are served by various fixed stations. For
this reason we talk of **cellular radio**. The allocation of frequencies which
may be used in the various cells has to be done with care, because the
many subscribers all have to share the same medium – long ago given
the somewhat unfortunate name of the **ether**. Fortunately, the range
of the high frequencies currently being used is so short that the same
frequency can be reused a few cells further on, but it does mean that the
fixed station being used changes very frequently.

Radio subscribers who remain in contact with a single fixed station,
as with **cordless telephones**, are normally not considered to be mobile
subscribers.

2.8 Public and private networks

Public networks are those which (on payment) are available to anyone
who wishes to make use of them and who has become a subscriber.
Private networks are only accessible to a limited group of users, and are
often optimized for those users. Private networks usually make use of the
transmission channels in the infrastructure created for the public network.
Private transmission means are usually not economically rewarding and
in some cases it is even illegal to install them. The switching equipment is
usually the property of the organization managing the network, but that
is not always the case. The most characteristic properties of private
networks are a limited user group and private management of addresses
and numbers. It is often possible to access the public network from a
private network, and a subscriber on a private network may be accessible
from the public network. It is, however, impossible for a public network

subscriber to communicate with another public network subscriber via private means. Business networks are considered as private networks. Government agencies also use private networks.

2.9 Routing in networks

The routes that can be taken by messages or calls depend largely on the type of network. Non-redundant networks offer no choice in the route to be followed from a given starting point to a given end point. The more redundancy in a network, the greater the number of possible routes that can be followed. Usually the shortest route through the network will be chosen and the switching apparatus programmed to follow it.

When faults occur in the circuits or exchanges, it is necessary to use an alternative route. A common strategy is for the alternative route to be preprogrammed and selected automatically when the exchange detects that the normal route is not available. This is known as **automatic alternative routing**.

If a circuit becomes overloaded, it is possible to use another, normally longer, route for part of the traffic. The rest can still use the original route. Here we are concerned with **overflow routing**.

There are many possible strategies for routing traffic through a network; for example, for a packet switching network, one can optimize for the minimum delay for an individual packet. The problem with many of the more complicated routing optimization systems is that, in times of network overload, they make extensive use of network management messages. This adds to the already high load on the network and results in the network becoming overloaded sooner. As a result, some advanced *online* optimizing systems have been abandoned in favour of *offline* calculation of optimum routing choices and preprogramming them in the control systems of the nodes.

Chapter 3

Switching principles and switching equipment

3.1 Switching principles

The principles of the most important forms of switching are described in this chapter, together with examples that illustrate the most important applications of these principles. The services using switches are studied in more depth in Chapter 11 (Telecommunications services). The switching principles discussed here are:

- circuit switching
- message switching
- packet switching
- fast packet switching
- local switching.

3.1.1 Circuit switching

In circuit switching, callers are usually connected to one called party although, exceptionally, there may be more than one. This circuit can be one-way, but a bidirectional connection is almost always provided by a circuit switch. Thus, after the circuit connection has been switched through, a two-way circuit is available. This direct connection means that the information offered at the input of a switch appears almost instantaneously in the same form at its output.

This is a basic difference from the forms of switching to be considered later, in which equality and simultaneity are not present.

Because of its properties, the circuit switch is well suited to the holding of conversations and its principal application is, not surprisingly, telephony. The circuit switch can also be considered for written conversations; the public telex service makes use of circuit switching.

3.1.2   Message switching

In message switching, incoming messages are stored in buffers. The message itself contains the information about where it is to be sent; a message can have more than one destination. The **message switch** cannot forward the message before it has received at least the **routing information**. There is thus always some delay between the switch receiving a message and its further transmission. Moreover, it may be necessary to delay the message even further if the outgoing circuits are busy.

The length of the **in-transit delay** depends on the network capacity and the related probability that the circuits are busy. Although, by ample dimensioning, the in-transit delay can be made so small that message switches could be used for two-way conversations, this is almost never done because the strength of the message switch lies precisely in the capabilities that are missing in the circuit switch. These possibilities arise from the fact that a **store and forward** technique is used, in which the inputs and outputs may be delayed and various forms of conversion may be applied to the data stream.

The possible conversions are in:

* time
* delivery order
* bit rate
* flow rate
* code
* protocol
* message format
* message composition.

By **conversions in time** we mean that the message can be forwarded at any desired time, not related to the time of arrival of the message. This property has the advantage for the sender that he is never confronted with a busy situation.

It is also possible to offer the receiver the opportunity to define when he wishes to receive the message. This is often the case with the related **Computer Based Messaging Systems (CBMS)** in which the data is retrieved from a **mailbox** at a time determined by the receiver (**store and**

retrieve). CCITT uses the term **Message Handling Systems (MHS)** for these systems. (See Chapter 11, Telecommunications services.) In addition to the message switching function, these systems offer assistance with message creation and filing.

Message transmission can take place immediately the system finds a free outgoing line. Expensive circuits between exchanges can be heavily loaded by choosing a capacity lower than that required for peak hour traffic. A peak hour load of three times the circuit capacity, that is 3 erlangs, is usually not a problem if the system is allowed to transmit the messages received during peak hour in subsequent hours. This is acceptable for many forms of traffic.

Where the former premise is not acceptable, use can be made of the **conversion in delivery order**. Higher priority can be given to some types of message, giving them preferential treatment for delivery. It is quite usual in message switching to have between three and eight levels of priority.

In a message switch, there is no reason to make the bit rates of the various circuits equal. On trunk circuits between exchanges, it is cheaper to use one high speed circuit than a number of low speed circuits; in this case we need **bit rate conversion**.

Some terminals can receive at a certain bit rate, but cannot do so indefinitely. This calls for a means of governing the flow rate. A message switch can in principle supply this **flow rate conversion** by means of **flow control** of the bit stream.

Code conversion has become necessary because of the many codes used in data communication and telecommunication (IBM, ASCII, CCITT ITA-2, CCITT IA-5, CCITT group 3 fax, to name a few). The standardization of protocols is similarly less than perfect, hence the requirement for **protocol conversion**.

Considerable divergence in the methods of composing message routing data is another aspect of non-standardization, for which the solution is **message format conversion**.

Finally, it is sometimes desirable to change the message contents, for example, by collecting the important points from several incoming messages into a single outgoing message. Termed **bulletin compilation** in meteorological networks, this **message composition conversion** can be performed in a message switch.

3.1.3 Packet switching

Like message switching, packet switching makes use of the store and forward technique. Although the message switch will split its messages into pieces (called **blocks**) in memory, to make efficient use of the memory, the message is still handled as a unit and the specified operations are carried out on the message as a whole. Priority handling can be taken as an example of this. Packet switches work with a **packet**, a unit of operation that is characterized by a fixed (or limited) length, which is normally shorter than the message length used in message switches. The CCITT term 'packet' is not used by ISO, which prefers the more general term **Network Protocol Data Unit** (**NPDU**), which is also used in environments not standardized by CCITT. Packet switches appear in many forms, of which the **datagram** version is similar to the message switch. Traffic is one-way and there is no suggestion of a connection. This type of packet switching is therefore called **connectionless**.

In this it differs from **connection oriented** packet switching, for which the CCITT specified the User Interface (DTE–DCE) in recommendation X.25, and is much more like circuit switching. In X.25, connections (**virtual calls**) are set up, used for a time for bidirectional data exchange and then broken down again. The major disadvantage of circuit switching, the chance of finding the called party engaged, is also a problem, as is the fact that the majority of conversions in message switching are difficult or impossible to implement. Only bit-rate conversion remains as a viable option. In this type of packet switch, an attempt is made to minimize the delay by generous dimensioning of the circuit capacity. As a result, the difference between it and circuit switching is very small. The advantage of bit-rate conversion is that many terminals with a limited bit rate (110–9600 bit/s) can communicate simultaneously with a computer, which can handle virtual-circuit communication with many such terminals over a single physical connection to the networks. This circuit can have a higher bit rate (9600–48 000 bit/s).

The connection oriented nature does not permit flow rate differences on one virtual circuit. If the traffic becomes too dense in the network, or at the receiving terminal, it is therefore necessary to be able to slow down the transmitting terminal. To achieve this, a **flow control** possibility is included in the packet switching communication protocol. On all connections between packet switches, and between switches and terminals, a **datalink** protocol is continuously executed. This has as its main task the correction of detected transmission errors by retransmission of an information **frame**. CCITT has standardized the LAPB protocol for this purpose. (See Chapter 4, Communication protocols.)

3.1.4 Fast packet switching

Specially developed for future broadband networks, **fast packet switching** is a form of packet switching based on the idea of connections and which, from a user's viewpoint, has characteristics very similar to connection oriented packet switches. An important difference is that bit speeds on the circuits in the network are too high to allow error corrections to be made at the link level. Moreover, efforts are made to keep the delays very short

3.2.1 Circuit switches

We stated earlier that in circuit switching a connection is created between two or more terminals. For circuit switched networks such as the telephone network it is usually necessary to be able to connect any terminal with any other terminal. The technical means of achieving this will be discussed later.

Once we have realized what it means to have to meet this requirement in a network of several million terminals, then we can see that the simple solution, shown in Figure 3.1, leads to an astronomical figure for the number of connection points (crosspoints) required. The number of crosspoints per subscriber (terminal) is equal to the total number of subscribers on the network. The total number of crosspoints is therefore equal to the square of the number of subscribers. Such a network would indeed ensure that every subscriber could call every other subscriber simultaneously, but that is quite unnecessary and we should look for other solutions.

Figure 3.2 indicates how the necessary number of crosspoints can be reduced by putting in only a limited number of links, equal to the required number of simultaneous connections, between two switching stages. Larger exchanges have several consecutive switching stages, in which the traffic from a large number of inputs is **concentrated** and **mixed** to allow each output to be reached from each input.

The largest part of the present telephone network still makes use of exchanges constructed using the **space division switching** technique described above. For the crosspoints, **electromechanical selectors**, **crossbar** switches or **reed** contacts are used. Today, because of their high switching speed, electronic components offer possibilities unrealizable with electromechanical components.

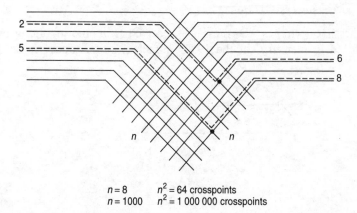

$n = 8$ $n^2 = 64$ crosspoints
$n = 1000$ $n^2 = 1\,000\,000$ crosspoints

Figure 3.1 Full crosspoint switching matrix.

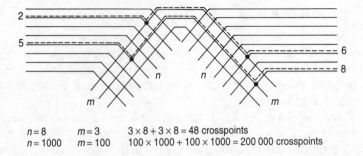

$n = 8$ $m = 3$ $3 \times 8 + 3 \times 8 = 48$ crosspoints
$n = 1000$ $m = 100$ $100 \times 1000 + 100 \times 1000 = 200\,000$ crosspoints

Figure 3.2   Reduction in the number of crosspoints by limiting number of links.

This property is used in **time division switching**, in which a periodic **sample** of the input (see Figure 3.3) is transferred to the desired output. This sample can represent an amplitude in the form of a pulse of a certain duration and voltage (Pulse Amplitude Modulation, PAM) or as a series of bits (Pulse Code Modulation, PCM). In this way, each crosspoint can be used for more than one connection path at different points in time, which again reduces the number of crosspoints. (See Figure 3.4.) This solution does cost extra provision per line, on both the input and output sides of the exchange. For PCM, a **codec** is necessary on the input side to convert the sample to a digital code. Digital time division switches use a slightly different principle, explained in Appendix A.

On the output side, an electronic circuit is required to convert the pulses received via the switching system back to an (analogue) signal. Exchanges using time division may also have multiple switching stages. Usually not all stages are of the time division type. There are also space division stages.

3.2.2   Message switches

For message switches, the messages received from the incoming circuits are stored in memory. In the 1950s, punched paper tape was used as a

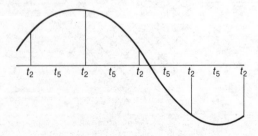

t_2 t_5 t_2 t_5 t_2 t_5 t_2 t_5 t_2

Figure 3.3   Input samples to be transferred to the required output, starting at t_2 and t_5.

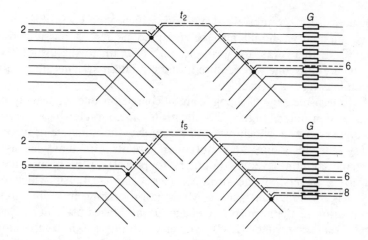

Figure 3.4 Time division switching principle.

storage medium. The CCITT ITA 2 telegraph code was generally used in the form of holes punched in five possible positions on the tape. (See Figure 3.5.) The small holes served only for paper transport.

In the simplest exchanges, the received tape was taken by operators in the exchange to one or more punched-tape readers for transmission via the outgoing circuits. This type of message switching exchange became known as a **torn tape centre**.

Europe played a leading role in the modernization of these exchanges. Siemens replaced the paper tape by magnetic tape; Philips introduced not only magnetic tape, but also magnetic-core memories shortly after they were developed by their Eindhoven Research Laboratories. This removed the necessity for carrying tapes, by switching between input and output memories.

At first, the routing instructions and priority indications had to be read from the message header by operators and given to the switching system. Further automation was only possible when the message originators were prepared to put the relaying instructions in a standard **message format**. At that time it was taken for granted that small

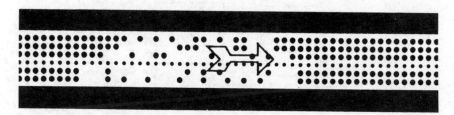

Figure 3.5 Punched paper tape.

divergences from the prescribed method, which gave no problems when handled manually, should also be accepted as far as possible by the machines. So there was, for example, no objection to the use of several spaces where only one was required. Some modern systems show serious shortcomings in this respect.

Modern message exchanges are all based on one, or usually more than one, computer. Figure 3.6 illustrates a computer-based message switching system in which we can recognize the subsystems used for handling the incoming and outgoing circuits. In many cases the subsystems contain several computers to process as necessary, the so-called lower layers of the protocol (see Chapter 4), of which error handling is an important aspect. Message processing, including routing and allocation to the appropriate **queue**, usually takes place in a separate **Central Processing Unit (CPU)**. Message storage for **in-transit storage** generally takes place in a common memory, usually electronic **Random Access Memory (RAM)**.

The transmitted messages are often saved for several weeks or months on a magnetic tape or disk. In some cases this is a legal requirement. For example, the Dutch Civil Aviation Authority (Rijksluchtvaartdienst) requires this on its networks to allow later investigations in the case of air traffic accidents. One of the uses of message registration is to show that the message switch was not to blame.

On receipt of a message, a message switching exchange takes over from the sender the responsibility for further transmission. This is a major difference from circuit switched systems, where the responsibility for checking the correct arrival remains with the sender.

With a message switch, the user must be able to trust the exchange to handle the message correctly and not lose it. For this reason, measures are taken in message switching exchanges to prevent loss of messages and to ensure that the transmission is completed.

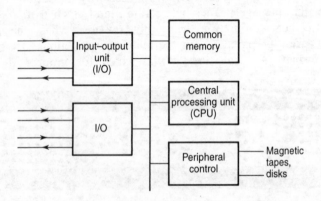

Figure 3.6   Schematic of a simple computer-based message switching exchange.

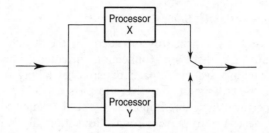

Figure 3.7 Principle of a duplicated message switching exchange.

Larger exchanges are usually fully duplicated. (See Figure 3.7.) In some cases incoming traffic is accepted by both halves of the system, but only one half is responsible for normal transmission. Only if that half fails is transmission taken over by the other half. In order to know which messages must be taken over, the **online** part of the system keeps the **offline** part informed about the processing of its messages. Peripheral equipment, such as disks and tapes, must also be duplicated. The simplest arrangement for handing over messages is to make these equipments switchable between the online and offline parts of the system.

3.2.3 Packet switches

As far as hardware is concerned, packet switches are very similar to message switches. In connection oriented packet switches, however, the responsibility for the message is not taken by the equipment; the sender retains the ability to check whether the dialogue with the called party has been broken off too soon. Storage of the accepted traffic is not a normal requirement, since the responsibility lies with the sender and thus the equipment can never be blamed if a message does not arrive. An extra requirement, however, is that of **flow control**. This is a software requirement and has little influence on the hardware.

Another requirement of packet switches, especially those used in public networks, is that they may have to switch enormous volumes of traffic, because data networks using packet switches not only transport *messages* but also, in conversations with computers, sometimes have to transfer huge *files*. This places high demands on the **throughput capacity** of these exchanges.

Terminals that are not capable of working with a packet protocol are connected to packet switching exchanges via a **Packet Assembly/Disassembly (PAD)** unit, which may be centralized or distributed. These units convert data from a number of connected terminals (usually asynchronous) into packets and transmit these packets via an X.25 connection to the packet switch.

3.2.4   Fast packet switches

Fast packet switches are primarily intended for the switching of broadband links and are therefore connection oriented. For very small broadband switching systems, space division switching is not a bad choice because the crosspoints only have to pass on the bit stream; there is no need to perform switching functions at speeds related to the bit rate. It is, however, necessary to prevent connections mutually interfering with one another. For larger broadband switches, the quadratic or almost quadratic increase in the number of crosspoints can become a problem. Fast packet switches have been developed to overcome this.

Normal time division, in which a sample of 8 bits (ISDN) is transferred and a destination is read from memory, is quite practical at 64 kbit/s or 2 Mbit/s with the present speed of electronic switches. It is, however, a different story if we have to work with broadband circuits of 150 or 600 Mbit/s. The limitations in memory read/write speeds force us not to access the memory too often. Therefore it is necessary to handle and switch greater numbers of bits as a unit. These units are called **cells** and should not be too short. On the other hand, in order to keep switching delays within the users' requirements, they should not be too long either. The cell length currently being chosen is 48 + 5 bytes; 48 bytes of information to be transferred and a header of 5 bytes. The choice for the data field in the cell is a compromise between an American proposal of 32 bytes and a European proposal of 64 bytes. The development of fast packet switches is still at an early stage.

3.2.5   LAN equipment

The connecting element in a LAN is a common medium, such as a coaxial cable, several copper wires or an optical fibre. In broadband LANs, modems are used to allow the terminals to communicate at the required carrier frequency. In addition to any necessary modems, all terminals have an electronic circuit for implementing the LAN access protocol (see Chapter 4). Circuits are also necessary for selecting the data destined for an individual terminal from that received for all terminals operating on the same frequency band. These circuits are usually contained on a **LAN card** in the terminal. **LAN repeaters**, **LAN bridges**, **LAN routers** or **LAN gateways** are sometimes used for LAN coupling.

In LAN repeaters, only the lowest, physical layer of the LAN protocol is handled, usually in the form of a signal amplifier, and data from the higher layers is passed on transparently. This is usually sufficient for the coupling of two LANs and terminals from the same supplier. The most complex coupling system for a LAN is the gateway. This is required for translation of layers above layer 3, which would be needed, for

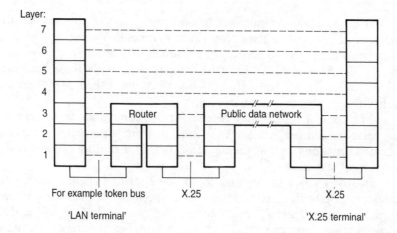

Layer:

For example token bus   X.25   X.25

'LAN terminal'   'X.25 terminal'

Figure 3.8   Example of the use of a router, shown in a layered model.

example, for coupling to a system that does not fully meet the ISO standards. The bridge is an intermediate form that can carry out transformations on level 2, while the router is one that can transform up to layer 3. (See Figure 3.8.) Routers and bridges also pass on higher layer protocols transparently. It is necessary for these protocols to be based on the same standards and to use the same options on both sides.

3.3   The control system of switching equipment

The intelligence of a switching system is located in the **control system** of the switching system, which receives and interprets the commands sent to the system from various sources. Important sources for such commands are the users (subscribers) of the system.

Switches operating in a network also receive many commands from adjacent switching systems with requests to extend the call further (for example, in the case of circuit switching) or to relay the information to a following destination (as in the case of message switching), see Figure 3.9.

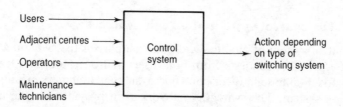

Figure 3.9   The control system's inputs and output.

Other sources of commands to the control system are the operators who provide services to the users. Users can contact these operators to request information or to be switched through to a certain department. In some cases users may be brought into contact with these operators automatically, for example, in a PABX when the called party was not reached (busy, absent or non-existing).

The control system may receive further commands from maintenance personnel, to perform test functions, or from supervisors to perform dedicated functions such as the implementation of routing changes or the provision of statistics.

In many cases the command to the control system contains the request to establish a connection to a specified number or to relay information to a specified destination. The control system will deduce which functions have to be performed and carry out the steps required to satisfy the request. The details of this procedure differ for the various types of switching systems. In all cases, the control system needs to know which users are connected to its system by a direct line and the characteristics of these connections (directory number, terminal capabilities, restrictions), as well as how the indirectly connected destinations can be reached. This may require quite an extensive database.

Where a system is provided with a **central control system** the operation of the switching system depends completely on the proper functioning of the control equipment. This frequently leads to the requirement of redundancy, for example, in the form of duplication of the control system hardware. This means the control system needs a more complicated structure so that it can perform a number of functions to enable dual operation and automatic recovery actions when one of the hardware parts has failed.

In the case of more distributed types of control system a number of functions should be available in the control system to take appropriate measures for the detection of faults and their recovery.

The main task of the control system is to instruct other parts of the switching system to establish the required communication. Different types of switching systems have their own ways of achieving this goal.

3.3.1   The control system of circuit switches

The control system of circuit switches is the part of the switching system that interprets the requests from both users and operators and translates them into suitable signals for controlling the switching network inside the switching system. The switching network then provides for the through connection of circuits to establish the desired connections in the communications network. Three phases can be distinguished:

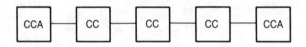

Figure 3.10   Functional model for the ISDN circuit-mode bearer service call control.

- call set-up phase
- connected phase
- call clear phase.

In the connected phase all circuit switched systems offer full duplex connections between parties. Depending on the type of switch the connections can be used for telex, data or voice-band information exchange.

The protocols to establish and clear connections differ for different types of networks (telex, circuit switched data, telephone, ISDN) but all show similar characteristics. As an example we will take the call set-up of circuit switched calls in the ISDN (see also Chapter 4). The general principles of the ISDN call set-up and clear procedures are described in CCITT Recommendation Q.71, which uses the help of a functional model. This functional model (see Figure 3.10) contains two functional entities, the **Call Control Agent (CCA)** entity and the **Call Control (CC)** entity.

The CCA is in direct contact with the users and is capable of translating their wishes into a standard protocol that can be understood by all switches in the network. In other words, the CCA represents the users as an agent in their negotiations for temporary connections in the network.

CC functionality can be found in all switches of the network. It can establish, manipulate and release connections based upon the request of a CCA.

Both the CCA and CC functions are carried out by the control system of most ISDN switching systems. Only in higher network levels are switching centres dedicated to CC functionality to be found. Figure 3.11 illustrates the exchange of control information needed to setup an ISDN circuit-mode bearer service connection where the call can be successfully completed (no busy condition for party B).

3.3.2   The control system of message switches

A characteristic of the message switch is that it takes over the responsibility for correct delivery of a message from the sender as soon as it has arrived in the switch. In many cases this can mean that the sender is not

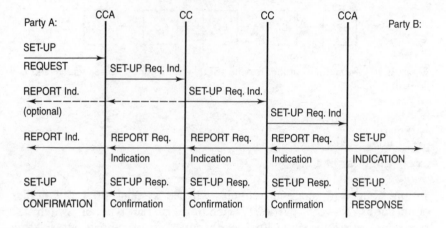

Figure 3.11 ISDN control information exchange for a successful circuit switched bearer service call set-up.

bothered by the rejection of a message, even when apparent faults are detected in the communications header (containing the addresses and other instructions) of the message. Usually the control system software or the service operators can understand what the intention of the sender was when he composed the header. The control system software for message switches is made **tolerant** of minor mistakes such as additional spaces where one space would suffice. Certain addresses, such as LONDRES instead of LONDON, may be accepted automatically although the user's instructions may ask for the latter spelling. More difficult problems are automatically referred to a service operator. Certain misspellings may be unacceptable since it may not be clear what the intention was. Messages containing these types of faults will either be returned to the sender or will be corrected by the service operator after consultation with the sender.

Computer-based messaging systems (CBMS) as well as the new X.400-based message handling systems (MHS) are less tolerant than the older message-switching systems. This difference may stem from the fact that most CMBS and MHS systems handle messages of less urgency than the older message-switching systems. The transit time requirements of older message-switching systems, used heavily in aviation and defence networks, did not allow senders to be penalized for their mistakes by additional delays.

The control system of the message switch may analyse the information in the message header and deduce the correct outgoing circuit or circuits on which the message should be relayed. It must also detect the priority indication and then register the message in the proper queue with respect to destination and priority.

In the case of message switching no instructions to a switching network are needed, as there are no connections. The handling of input messages is completely separated from the output of messages, hence, there may be a large time difference between them, at least for low priority messages. The *minimum* time difference is the time to receive and analyse the header and attach the message to the outgoing circuit queue. It is not absolutely necessary that the total message is received before the outgoing transmission is started. Generally, however, the outgoing transmission is not started before the message has been completely received in view of the difficulties that may arise when the incoming transmission is slower than the outgoing transmission.

The control system must make sure that one or more copies of the message with the properly updated headers are stored in the system for later relay. This storage is called **in-transit storage**. For much later retrieval there may exist requirements for **short-term shortage** (a few hours) or **long-term storage** (a few months). The control system has to administer the stored messages and must be able to retrieve them.

3.3.3 The control system of packet switches

We will limit this section to the description of packet switches of the connection oriented type with CCITT X.25 interfaces. We will assume that these switches use similar connection oriented packet level protocols internally in the network. (*Note*: X.25 is limited to the description of the DTE–DCE interface, so does not specify internal network protocols.) The control system must handle **Virtual Calls** (**VCs**) as well as **Permanent Virtual Circuits** (**PVCs**). We first concentrate on VCs. The information needed to establish a call to the requested destination is contained in a separate packet called the **call request** packet, sent by the calling party (see also Chapter 4). The control system analyses this information and deduces the proper outgoing circuit. The call request information is now forwarded to the next centre on the path to the addressee. The last centre on this path will ascertain that the called terminal is free to accept the call and return an indication that the call can be accepted. The calling subscriber receives a **call connected** packet from the switch to which he is connected (see Figure 3.12).

The control systems of the centres register the identity of the incoming and outgoing logical channels to be used for the relay of the packets on this successfully established connection.

The calling terminal will send further packets in the **data transfer phase**. These packets do not contain the full address of the destination, nor its origin, as was the case with the call request packet. They only contain a logical channel number, a numbering of sent and received packets (see Chapter 4) and, of course, that part of the information that

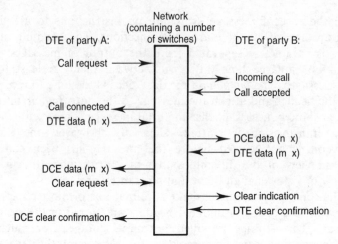

DTE: data terminal equipment; DCE: data circuit terminating equipment

Figure 3.12   Exchange of packets for the set-up and clear of a virtual call.

had to be transferred. The control system will analyse the received logical channel number and consult its tables of established connections in order to find the corresponding outgoing channel number to be attached to the packet and the proper outgoing circuit to be used. Packets flowing in the opposite direction on the connection will be treated similarly.

When one of the parties wants to end the conversation he sends a **clear request** packet. The network will now send a **clear indication** to the other party. The terminal of this party should respond with a **DTE clear confirmation**. Finally, the first party receives a **DCE clear confirmation** from the network.

The handling of PVCs is no different from the handling of VCs during the data transfer phase. However, the user is not given the possibility to set up and clear calls. The virtual connection for a PVC is set up once by a service operator and remains available for the user until he ends his subscription for this particular PVC. This service thus provides almost the same service as a leased channel. However, in most countries customer charges are based on a fixed sum independent of traffic volume for a leased channel, while for PVCs the charges are usually based on the number of packets transferred.

3.3.4   The control system of fast packet switches

Protocols for fast packet switches are still in the early phases of specification by CCITT, so it is not possible to describe the control system of these switches. It is highly likely, however, that the control system will not show significant differences from the control system of regular packet switches.

3.3.5   The control system of LANs

The control system of LANs is a good example of **distributed control**. Although many types of LANs require some form of central control (a master function), in addition to the distributed functions, this can be assigned to one of the participants in the LAN. In the case of malfunction another participant can take over the master function.

    The network configurations of most types of LAN do not provide for alternative routing and the number of outgoing circuits in a node is minimal, so the routing function in the LAN control equipment is simple. The other control functions are quite different for each type of LAN. Many LANs are of the connectionless type and do not require a call set-up and clear procedure.

Chapter 4

Communication protocols

4.1 Introduction

As soon as networks appeared, a need arose for a means of indicating which subscriber one wished to contact. Protocols were developed to meet this need.

In telegraphy, these protocols consisted mainly of a number of rules for the format of the telegram header. The essential point is to indicate unambiguously the destination or destinations of the telegram. Registration of the sender is also necessary for use by the receiver.

In telephony, with its circuit switched network, a somewhat different procedure was necessary. At first, this procedure consisted of being wished 'Good morning' or 'Good afternoon' by the operator and passing on the name of the subscriber one wished to contact. This procedure had a user friendliness that was almost completely lost in later automation. There were few strict rules; one could give a number, a name, or even a profession. The message: 'I need the doctor' or: 'There is a leak in my house' was sufficient to get the required connection. After this procedure, which consisted of a conversation with **intelligence** in the network, there followed a further exchange between caller and called to establish each other's identity. Only then did the real conversation begin.

In the case of modern, automatic circuit switched networks, the procedures have evolved from unstructured dialogues to strictly regulated **protocols** which have, in some cases, become extremely complicated because of the many functions that have been added. The **model** of the procedures of earlier telephone conversations is still recognizable in

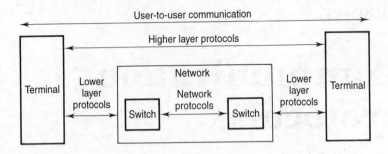

Figure 4.1   Simple communication model.

the simplest model for modern circuit switched communication. The terminology has, however, been somewhat modified. (See Figure 4.1.)

The protocols between terminal and network, which are intended to achieve the build up of the desired connection, are called **lower layer protocols**. Internally in the network, between the switches themselves, a protocol is also needed for the creation of the connection from switch to switch. This is a **network protocol**. In telephony both protocols are referred to as **signalling**.

Protocols between two terminals (see Figure 4.1) are called **higher layer protocols**. The information contained in these is passed on **transparently** by the network from one terminal to the other; the switches do nothing else with the information.

Finally, there is **user-to-user communication**, which is the real goal of the network so far as the users are concerned. This information is used by neither the network nor the terminal, but simply passed on. The user's conversation in telephony is a good example.

The goals of a model include making the various functions clearly recognizable, capable of independent specification and, by the assignment of names, easy to discuss. A model is thus an aid to protocol design. Sometimes there is a danger that the model will become a goal in itself, to which the logic and efficiency of the protocol being designed are very much of secondary importance. The application of a model developed for a specific type of communication, such as computer-to-computer packet switching, to another situation, such as message switching, LANs or ISDN, also raises the question as to how sensible this is. Nevertheless, international standardization has chosen this route and it is almost unthinkable now that it will not continue to be followed. The model referred to is the **Open Systems Interconnection** (**OSI**) model of the International Organization for Standardization (ISO).

The OSI model and selected communication protocols are described in the following.

4.2 Reference model for Open Systems Interconnection (OSI)

4.2.1 The model

Although we assume that the reader is already acquainted with the OSI model of the ISO, we offer a brief resumé to refresh the memory.

The **Reference model for Open Systems Interconnection**, referred to as the **OSI model**, achieved international standard status (ISO 7498) in 1983. CCITT has adopted the standard as Recommendation X.200. In the meantime, much effort is being put into giving substance to the protocols.

For the lowest layers, this work has resulted in a number of usable standards. For the higher layers, many different protocols have turned out to be necessary; only a few of them have been finished and it is highly likely that even these will have to be revised in the near future. CCITT Recommendation X.25 belongs to the first category and fulfils a very large part of the functions of the OSI model layer 3. It also indicates a choice of options, **Link Access Procedure B** (**LAPB**), from an ISO standard (ISO 7776, HDLC) for the next lower layer 2.

The OSI model is based on a **layered architecture** which has a general formulation. The functions to be performed in order to set up, execute and end a communication are split into groups. These groups, or **layers**, have been organized as logically as possible, although the original choice of the ISO remains fairly arbitrary. The layers were chosen so that a hierarchical relationship exists between the functions; those in a higher layer in the model make use of, and can only operate properly with the help of, those in the layer below. Thus a layer (for example, layer N) makes use of the functions of the layer below it (layer $N - 1$) and offers services, the **(N) service**, to the next higher layer (layer $N + 1$). A function in layer N is called an **(N) entity**. Entities in the same layer are called **peer entities**. The boundary between two layers where the (N) service is offered to an $N + 1$ entity is called the **(N) Service Access Point** (**NSAP**) (see Figure 4.2). There can be more than one NSAP on a boundary between two layers. ISO calls the 'boundary' an **interface**. CCITT interprets 'interface' as a physical interface, which is represented in the OSI model as a vertical line between two systems.

ISO has chosen a layered structure with seven layers, of which three are access functions to the communications network and contain the **relay system** function. These pass on the information transparently for the other four layers, via the communications network, to peer entities in the other terminal (see Figure 4.3). In each layer, relations are maintained between the entities on one side with peer entities on the other side by means of a **peer protocol**. In Figure 4.3, ten peer protocols are

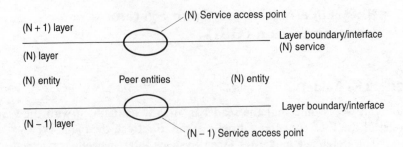

Figure 4.2   Principle of the OSI 'layered architecture'.

shown – four higher layer protocols and two sets of three lower layer protocols.

Thus the main information flow in the layered model goes from end user A downwards through all layers. A physical medium is used (for example, copper wire) from the terminal to the network. The lower layer protocols inform the network about the required destination. Then the network is crossed, and the terminal is again reached via a further physical medium. After all layers have been passed, the information finally reaches end user B. Information exchange in the opposite direction is also possible.

In this model, any form of circuit switched or virtual circuit switched datanet can be used for the communication network (relay system). Even a LAN, or several networks in series, can be used as a communication network. A message switching network is not recognized by ISO as a communication network (which exists in, at most, the lowest three layers). ISO sees message switching as an application layer function.

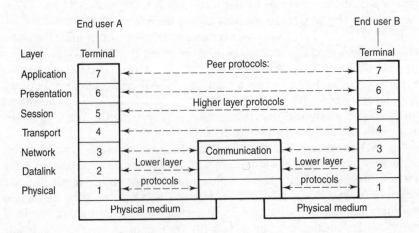

Figure 4.3   OSI layered model.

So, according to the ISO specification, a message switching network cannot be used as the relay system in the model.

From the telecommunications point of view, this is a somewhat strange idea: message switching communication that is seen as an application offering a transmission service to other functions in the same layer, yet not in a higher layer. However, from the point of view of an application programmer, message switching is also an application layer function.

The latter point of view has prevailed in ISO and CCITT. It has, however, resulted in the specification of many sublayers in the application layer, in order to be able to fit message handling into the OSI model.

Terminals that operate according to OSI specifications are called **open systems**. The *open* refers to the idea that systems should be able to communicate with each other whoever their manufacturer might be. Alas, there are now too many possibilities in the OSI-ISO protocols; inter-working problems are still possible, even if both parties adhere to the ISO specifications but have chosen different options. This problem is being tackled at European level, for example, by limiting options in so-called **functional standards**.

The **Protocol Control Information (PCI)** necessary for the execution of protocols in each layer is passed on in **headers**, each layer having its own header. The information passed from one terminal to the other thus has headers for all six layers above the physical layer. Information is passed on from layer to layer in **Protocol Data Units (PDU)** (see Figure 4.4). The PDU is named after the layer in which it is created, from the PDU of the next higher layer, by the addition of the PCI header. The

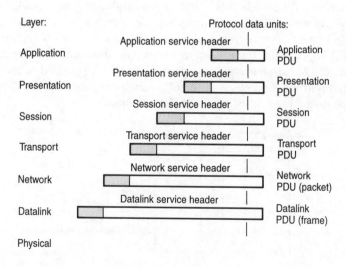

Figure 4.4 Protocol data units and headers.

presentation PDU is thus created by the addition of a PCI header to the *application PDU* and is then passed to the *session layer*.

Communication between layers, that is, between the higher **service user** layer and the next lower **service provider** layer, occurs (usually in software) by means of **service primitives**. The latter can be divided into **requests**, **indications**, **responses** and **confirmations**. (See Figure 4.5.)

A request to a lower layer (N) results, in another system, in the corresponding indication of the layer (N) to the higher layer. This is the way in which a message transfer takes place from system A to system B in the peer protocol. A response usually follows a request and is received as a confirmation.

4.2.2   The layers

Each layer has a number of fixed tasks which result from the layered construction of the OSI model. Thus there are always interfaces with the layers immediately above and below, with the associated formation and processing of headers.

For almost every layer, there may be several service users in the layer above wishing to make use of its services. This common usage of the lower level services is known as **multiplexing**. In this situation, there are several $(N + 1)$ connections making use of one **(N) connection**.

It is desirable to divide the information into blocks, or **segments**, of limited length primarily to assist with error detection; the process is called **segmenting**.

On the other side this leads to **reassembling**. The model does not exclude the possibility that a different segment length is chosen in each layer. In order to reassemble and deliver the blocks in the correct order, it is useful to number them and to check the numbers on receipt. This process is called **sequencing**. **Flow control** can also be applied in each layer, and it might be necessary to **reset** some data, such as the sequence numbers to be used, after a failure, for example.

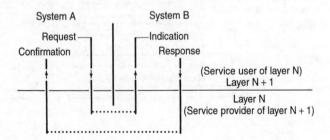

Figure 4.5 Service primitives.

A number of functions, of which we now give a few examples, are specific to a particular layer.

The **application layer** is layer 7 in the OSI model. This layer has to be able to cooperate with many different applications (above layer 7). This results in there being a great variety of protocols in layer 7, including:

- OSI Virtual Terminal Service
- OSI File Service
- OSI Management and Job Transfer Service
- CCITT X.400 series: Message Handling System (MHS)
- CCITT X.500 series: Directory System

The functions required for data exchange between specific application processes are found in layer 7, provided that these are not so general that they belong to one of the lower layers.

The **presentation layer**, layer 6, makes it possible to convert information with a specific proprietary coding and form, **syntax**, into a standardized form, **transfer syntax**, for transfer to another open system. On the receiving side, layer 6 then takes care of converting the information into one or more forms of encoding suited to the requirements on that side.

The presentation layer is very useful for pure **connection oriented** information transfer. For document transmission by the message handling system in which the connection runs from one MHS node to another MHS node and switching takes place in the node, the presentation layer is less useful. The reason is that it is often required to use more than one form of presentation in one document, in order to be able to transmit mixed text and graphics. For this reason, the application layer includes provisions for identifying the presentation used and any necessary conversions can take place in this layer. This is described in a **document architecture**. ISO recognizes, for example, the **Office Document Architecture (ODA)**. A document may consist of some parts which are encoded, for example, as group 3 fax (photos), ISO 646 (text) and PCM (speech).

The **session layer**, layer 5, makes it possible to use one physical connection for several simultaneous logical connections. Multiplexing is thus an important function of layer 5. The control of a dialogue with, for example, limitation to **two-way alternate** is also possible.

The **transport layer**, layer 4, has the task of resolving a number of shortcomings that arise in the lower layers containing the communication networks. This layer provides end-to-end solutions, the need for which is largely dependent on the nature of the network used. For this reason, there are a large number of possibilities. The transport layer allows us to choose from five classes of protocols: Class 0 to Class 4. The layer can also take care of the choice of the most suitable service from the underlying network services for a given situation, and take into account limitations in the networks such as bandwidth and quality.

The **network layer**, layer 3, translates the wishes of higher layers for the set-up, holding and breakdown of connections over communication networks of various types. Important functions are **routing** of the **network connections**, multiplexing of the network connections and flow control.

Before the OSI model was defined, CCITT had already standardized the X.25 network access protocol for packet switched data networks. With a small adjustment, the packet level protocol (PLP) of X.25 fits nicely into layer 3 of the model. The LAN protocols of the American **Institute of Electrical and Electronics Engineers (IEEE)** are less easily adapted. The OSI model originally only allowed connection oriented protocols, while LANs were **connectionless**. Currently ISO also has a **Connectionless Network Service (CLNS)** in addition to the **Connection Oriented Network Services (CONS)**. Both are described in ISO standard 8348.

The **datalink layer**, layer 2, has as its main task the correction of any errors that occur on the transmission path. These errors can arise as a result of interference by adjacent connections (crosstalk), current surges on electricity cables or atmospheric interference. Datalink protocols sometimes allow the possibility of **multipoint operation**. The best known protocol in this layer is the **High Level Datalink Control (HDLC)**. CCITT Recommendation X.25 uses for its level 2 a version of this called LAPB; see Section 4.3. In LANs, the datalink functions can be found in two sublayers; see Section 4.4.1.

The **physical layer**, layer 1, provides the physical and procedural means to transport the bits. CCITT X.25 prescribes Recommendation X.21 as the physical interface for public data networks. When using a telephone line, conversion is necessary from digital signals (bits) to signals in the speech frequency band. The **modem** that performs this task is thus also part of layer 1.

Finally, information transfer takes place over a **physical medium** which may be not only a copper pair, a coaxial cable or an optical fibre, but also a radio or satellite link.

4.3   High level datalink control (HDLC), CCITT/ITU-T LAPB

The HDLC protocol is a **bit oriented protocol**. Before HDLC, most of the datalink protocols were **character oriented**. A datalink protocol with error correction usually works with the data segmented into blocks or **frames**. Apart from the transfer of user information, there is also a requirement for the transfer of signalling information, **control information**, to be able to signal back, for example, that a frame has been received containing transmission errors. It is also necessary to have some means of indicating the beginning and end of a frame.

In character oriented protocols, this was solved by reserving a number of the possible bit combinations for signalling functions, the remaining combinations being used for the transmission of letters, digits and symbols. ASCII and CCITT IA 5 are examples of codes using this technique.

There were objections to the limitation of the use of bit combinations in some cases; the resulting data transfer was not fully **transparent**.

Bit oriented protocols are transparent. A trick was necessary in order to achieve this; all bit combinations are to be available for bit transfer and thus there are no combinations left for signalling information. The minimum necessary for signalling is one special token. If this has been reserved, then the other signalling functions can be indicated by bit combinations at fixed places following this one token. In HDLC, the special token is called the **flag**, and is used to give the division between frames. The same token, the flag, bit combination 01111110, is placed both before and after the frame. The requirement that all bit combinations may be used in the frame has not yet been met; the bit combination of the flag may not occur in the frame. This is solved by investigating if the information offered contains the bit combination 011111. As soon as this combination is discovered, the value 01111110 with six 1s is prevented from arising by inserting an extra 0; this is called **bit stuffing** or **bit insertion**. By applying the inverse process at the receiving side, the original information in the frame can be recovered. The shortage of 8-bit combinations is solved, on the transmission circuit only, by the temporary use of a 9-bit combination.

Most of the signalling information has a fixed place in the **frame**, called the **control field**. An **address field** is also included in the frame for use in multipoint working. The information to be transferred is placed in the **information field** (see Figure 4.6). In order to make error detection possible, a **Frame Check Sequence (FCS)** is added.

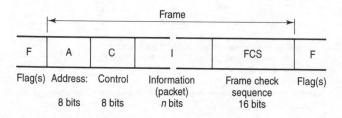

Figure 4.6   HDLC frame.

One or more flags can be sent between the frames. The beginning of a frame is characterized by the absence of the flag pattern and the receipt of another bit pattern.

HDLC has three sorts of frames (see Figure 4.7):

- I-frames: information frames
- S-frames: supervisory frames
- U-frames: unnumbered frames.

The U-frames are mainly used for selecting between various options, called **modes**. CCITT LAPB, applied in X.25, uses the **Asynchronous Balanced Mode (ABM)**. This is a version of HDLC in which both ends of the link are equal in the protocol; there is thus no master–slave relationship. At most, one could say that both sides behave as the slave of the transmitting side during the time that they are receiving information. The U-frame, with the command **Set Asynchronous Balanced Mode (SABM)**, is used to get into the AB mode. The same command can be used as a **reset** to escape from a situation with an undefined position, for example, after an equipment error, to permit restart from a defined position (counters zero).

The S-frames are used for **commands** and **responses**, in which the serial number of the next good I-frame to be received is registered, for example, to show that the indicated I-frame has not yet been properly received. This is the case with the **reject (REJ)** command. **Receive Not Ready (RNR)** is used to indicate that the receiving side is temporarily unable to receive frames. **Receive Ready (RR)** is used to indicate that a frame has been received without errors. It contains the number of the expected next frame, thus acknowledging receipt of all previous frames.

In Figure 4.8, the encoding of the control field applies to **basic operation** in CCITT LAPB. There is also an **extended mode**, in which the

Control field bits	1	2	3	4	5	6	7	8
I-frame	0		N(S)		P		N(R)	
S-frame	1	0	S	S	P/F		N(R)	
U-frame	1	1	M	M	P/F	M	M	M

N(S)   Transmitter send sequence number (bit 2 = low-order bit)
N(R)   Transmitter receive sequence number (bit 6 = low-order bit)
S   Supervisory function bit
M   Modifier function bit
P/F   Poll bit when issued as a command, final bit when issued as a response (1 = poll/final)
P   Poll bit (1 = poll)

Figure 4.7   LAPB control field format.

Format	Command	Response	Encoding					
Information transfer (I)	I (information)		0	N(S)			P	N(R)
Supervisory (S)	RR (receive ready)	RR (receive ready)	1	0	0	0	P/F	N(R)
	RNR (receive not ready)	RNR (receive not ready)	1	0	1	0	P/F	N(R)
	REJ (reject)	REJ (reject)	1	0	0	1	P/F	N(R)
Unnumbered (U)	SABM (set asynchronous balanced mode)		1	1	1	1	P	1 0
	DISC (disconnect)		1	1	0	0	P	0 1
		DM (disconnected mode)	1	1	1	1	F	0 0
		UA (unnumbered acknowledgement)	1	1	0	0	F	1 1
		FRMR (frame reject)	1	1	1	0	F	0 0

Figure 4.8   CCITT LAPB – basic operation.

control field has 16 bits and the sequence numbers have 7 bits instead of 3. This field length increase is important for connections with a long delay, such as **satellite** links; extended mode is only used in these connections.

The I-frames have two numbers in the control field. In addition to the **Receive Sequence Number, N(R)**, which is also contained in the S-frame, a number is given to each transmitted frame with the **Send Sequence Number, N(S)**. References to this number in the S- and I-frames are given in the other transmission direction in the N(R) field.

The numbers in the frame make it possible for the sending side to transmit several frames without waiting for a confirmation of their good arrival (with an RR). The numbering makes it possible to indicate up to which I-frame the reception has been error-free. The number of I-frames that may be sent without waiting for confirmation of arrival can be defined in the HDLC procedure by a parameter called the **window size**.

Flow control is possible with the use of the RNR command, which stops the flow, and the RR command, which restarts it. The window mechanism can also be used for flow control purposes. A well-known PC communication protocol is the X-modem protocol. This protocol operates similarly to HDLC.

4.4   IEEE 802 protocols (LAN)

4.4.1   Common channel access and OSI

For the use of the so-called **common channel media**, such as LANs, community antennas, cable television networks (CATV) and packet radio networks, the access protocols of layer 2 (datalink layer) and layer 1 (physical layer) can differ considerably from the previously discussed HDLC protocol. In these media, the access mechanism differs from the HDLC LAPB protocol, which is intended for use mainly with connection oriented point-to-point links in a Wide Area Network (WAN) – in particular between DTE and DCE.

Within the scope of this chapter we shall limit ourselves to the Group 802 LAN protocols, specified by the IEEE Project 802 Committee on Local Area Networks on the basis of proposals worked out by various industrial companies. These protocols have been largely taken over now by ISO and published as an **International Standard (IS)** or as a **Draft International Standard (DIS)**.

The mutual relationship between these protocols, and their relationship to the two lowest levels of the OSI model, can be imagined as that shown in Figure 4.9.

The datalink layer, used by a large number of LANs, consists of two sublayers: the **Logic Link Control (LLC) sublayer** and the **Medium Access Control (MAC) sublayer**. The LLC protocol is compatible with all existing MAC 802 protocols. The MAC protocol to be used is thus determined by the type of LAN. The IEEE MAC standard at the same time specifies the appropriate physical layer.

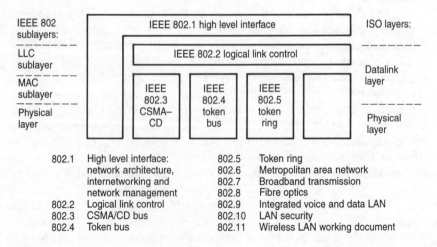

802.1	High level interface: network architecture, internetworking and network management	802.5 Token ring
		802.6 Metropolitan area network
		802.7 Broadband transmission
		802.8 Fibre optics
802.2	Logical link control	802.9 Integrated voice and data LAN
802.3	CSMA/CD bus	802.10 LAN security
802.4	Token bus	802.11 Wireless LAN working document

Figure 4.9   Relationship between the IEEE Project 802 Committee standardization and the OSI model.

4.4.2 The LLC standard (ANSI/IEEE 802.2–1985 and ISO/DIS 8802/2)

The protocol functions as a service provider for the network layer (layer 3 of the OSI model). At the service access point it also behaves in a manner comparable to the HDLC protocol.

The LLC protocol performs all functions for which the datalink layer is responsible, provided that they are independent of both the medium and the LAN access method used. The protocol offers three different types of service:

- *Type 1 Operation*: Unacknowledged connectionless service (error detection but no error correction and no flow control);

- *Type 2 Operation*: Connection oriented service (with error correction based on HDLC ABM and with flow control);

- *Type 3 Operation*: Acknowledged connectionless service (with a limited amount of error correction but without flow control).

For the execution of the various services, the LLC has an **LLC Protocol Data Unit (LLC PDU)** with three different formats for the control field as shown in Figure 4.10c.

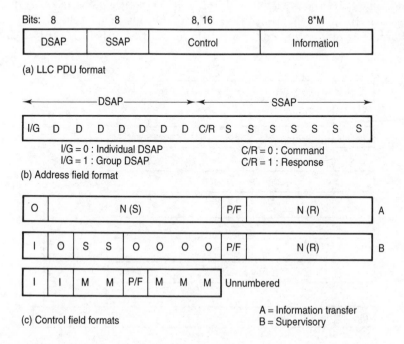

Figure 4.10 LLC protocol datalink formats.

The LLC PDU format includes the **Destination Service Access Point (DSAP)** field and the **Source Service Access Point (SSAP)** field. Type 1 and type 3 services make exclusive use of the unnumbered control field format, while the type 2 service uses all three formats.

4.4.3   The CSMA/CD standard (ANSI/IEEE 802.3–1985)

Carrier Sense Multiple Access/Collision Detect (CSMA/CD) is a method which is similar to, but not fully compatible with, the various versions of the **Ethernet LAN**. The relationship between the various functions specified by this standard is indicated in Figure 4.11.

The **transceiver**, the access from both the sender and the receiver to the physical medium, is responsible for:

- generating the carrier sense signal for the MAC sublayer;
- detecting **garbling** and generating the jamming signal for the medium and the collision detect signal for the MAC sublayer;
- generating and receiving frames.

The **encoder/decoder** provides line encoding and decoding, and generation and removal of the **preamble** with the **Start Frame Delimiter (SFD)**, which together form a synchronization field of 64 bits. This field consists of alternate 1s and 0s and ends with 1011 as follows: 101010 ... 1011. Also,

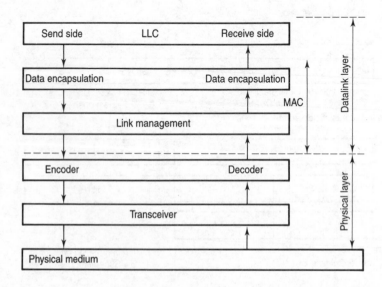

Figure 4.11   The various functions in the CSMA/CD protocol.

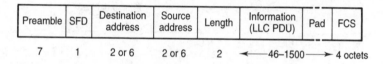

Preamble	SFD	Destination address	Source address	Length	Information (LLC PDU)	Pad	FCS
7	1	2 or 6	2 or 6	2	◄——46–1500——►		4 octets

Figure 4.12 CSMA/CD frame format.

by means of a **pad**, the minimum length of the frame is achieved for purposes of collision detection.

Link management is responsible for the correct functioning of the access mechanism; the **carrier sense** and **collision detect** signals are used for this purpose. **Data encapsulation** and **data decapsulation** provide a frame format, with the exception of the preamble, as shown in Figure 4.12.

They are also responsible for the execution of an error detection mechanism, using the **Frame Check Sequence (FCS)**, for the higher levels of the interface protocol and for error correction where necessary (see Section 4.4.2).

The physical layer of the CSMA/CD standard has various transmission options, such as broadband and baseband, coaxial cable and unshielded twisted pairs, various transmission rates and line encodings – such as Manchester coding and Differential Phase Shift Keying (DPSK). These will not be discussed further here.

4.4.4 Token ring access method and physical layer specifications (ANSI/IEEE 802.5–1985 and ISO 8802/5)

In this protocol use is made of a **token**, as shown in Figure 4.13.

The **Starting Delimiter (SD)** differs from all other data by a so-called **Violation (V)**, a deliberate infringement of the line encoding used in this protocol. The **Ending Delimiter (ED)** is also formed by such violations. However, in the SD these violations are encoded in combination with 0 codes, while in the ED they are encoded in combination with both 0 and 1 codes. In Figure 4.14 both fields are specified, together with the **access control (AC)** field.

The **Priority Mode (PM)** (3 bits, 8 levels) is contained in the AC field of the token. If the priority of a station given in the LLC protocol data unit is greater than or equal to a certain value, the station receiving

Starting delimiter SD	Access control AC	Ending delimiter ED
1 octet	1 octet	1 octet

Figure 4.13 Token format.

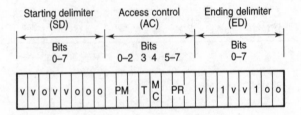

Figure 4.14 Specification of the token.

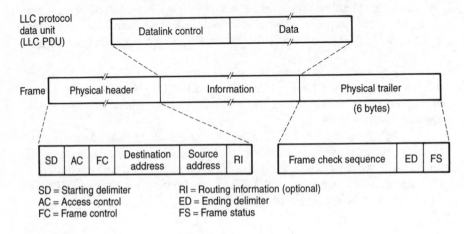

SD = Starting delimiter   RI = Routing information (optional)
AC = Access control   ED = Ending delimiter
FC = Frame control   FS = Frame status

Figure 4.15 The format of IEEE 802.5 frames.

the token can convert it into a frame. This requires not only the conversion of the **token bit (T)**, but also the addition of a number of fields and, for example, the information in the LLC PDU together with a few further possible changes – such as the last two bits of the ending delimiter (the intermediate frame I-bit and the error detect E-bit). See Figure 4.15.

4.5   CCITT X.25 (PDN)

CCITT Recommendation **X.25** describes the interface and access protocols for **Data Terminal Equipment (DTE)** operating in packet mode, connected via a **Data Circuit Terminating Equipment (DCE)** to a **Public Data Network (PDN)**. Although the X.25 interface is mainly used by computer systems, display terminals and personal computers are usually connected to it indirectly via a **Packet Assembly/Disassembly (PAD)** facility, which translates the essentially simple terminal protocols to the more complicated X.25 protocols.

X.25 contains three layers of the OSI model:

- layer 3 is the X.25 Packet Level Protocol: **X.25 PLP**
- layer 2 is the LAPB HDLC protocol already described
- layer 1 is the physical interface, one of three possibilities based on the CCITT Recommendations X.21, X.21 bis and V.24 in so far as these describe the interface.

4.5.1 X.25 PLP

The X.25 PLP defines **packets**, which are transferred in the information field of the HDLC frames. There are many types of packets, an overview of which is given in Table 4.1.

Table 4.1 Packet types.

Packet type		Service*	
From DCE to DTE	*From DTE to DCE*	*VC*	*PVC*
Call set-up and clearing			
Incoming call	Call request	X	
Call connected	Call accepted	X	
Clear indication	Clear request	X	
DCE clear confirmation	DTE clear confirmation	X	
Data and interrupt			
DCE data	DTE data	X	
DCE interrupt	DTE interrupt	X	
DCE interrupt confirmation	DTE interrupt confirmation	X	
Flow control and reset			
DCE RR	DTE RR	X	X
DCE RNR	DTE RNR	X	X
	DTE REJ	X	X
Reset indication	Reset request	X	X
DCE reset confirmation	DTE reset confirmation	X	X
Restart			
Restart indication	Restart request	X	X
DCE restart confirmation	DTE reset confirmation	X	X
Diagnostic			
Diagnostic		X	X
Registration			
Registration confirmation	Registration request	X	X

* VC = virtual cell; PVC = permanent virtual circuit.

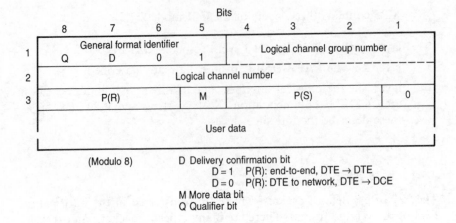

Figure 4.16   DTE and DCE data packet format.

Data packets are used for data transfer. The structure of the packet is shown in Figure 4.16. In addition to the 4 bits necessary to distinguish the packet from other types of packets (**general format identifier**), there is the **logical channel group number** which, together with the **logical channel number**, forms a binary number used to identify all the packets belonging to a single **Virtual Circuit (VC)**.

Thus on one physical circuit it is possible to have many VCs, up to a maximum of 4 K, the binary number of 12 bits, which is over 4000. The number is defined on the DTE–DCE interface. The same number is not used at the other side of the connection or internally in the network since, on its way through the network, the packet constantly gets other channel numbers. The relationship at each node is pre-determined during the call build up. The number of virtual connections in the network is thus not limited to 4000.

The send numbering P(S) and the receive numbering P(R) of the packets is usually passed on unchanged by most networks. By using a window and delaying the confirmation of good reception with a following P(R) by the receiving terminal, the latter can control the flow of new packets over the network. This is called **flow control**. The **more data bit (M)** makes it possible to mark a number of packets as belonging together. One use of this is to allow recombination of a packet which has been split up for one network section when packet networks with different maximum packet lengths are coupled together.

The procedure to build up a required connection, or **virtual call**, begins from the terminal (DTE) by the transmission of a **call request packet** (see Figure 4.17). In this, the DTE addresses of both caller and called party are registered. The requirement for the use of special party facilities can also be indicated in this packet. To give an impression of the sort of

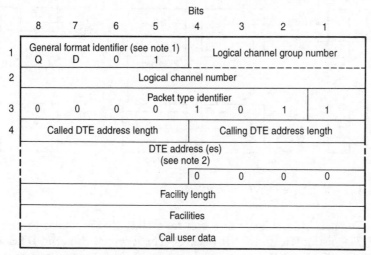

Figure 4.17 Call request and incoming call packet format.

facilities available, Table 4.2 lists the special facilities in X.25. When a call is set up, the called DTE receives an **incoming call packet** containing the same address information as that in the caller's call request packet.

The called DTE normally answers with a **call accepted packet**, which the caller receives in the form of a **call connected packet**. Cleardown of the call takes place in a similar manner and makes successive use of **clear request**, **clear indication**, **DTE clear confirmation** and **DCE clear confirmation**. See also Table 4.1.

Permanent, non-selected connections, or **Permanent Virtual Circuits** (**PCV**s), do not require any call build up or cleardown from the terminal. Packets specific to the virtual call are not then used by the DTE.

Table 4.2 X.25 special facilities.

Flow control parameter negotiation (packet size, window size)
Throughput class negotiation
Closed user group selection
Closed user group with outgoing access selection
Bilateral closed user group selection
Reverse charging
Fast select
Network user identification
Charging information (several types)
Selection of Registered Private Operating Agency (RPOA)
Called line address modified notification
Transit delay selection and indication

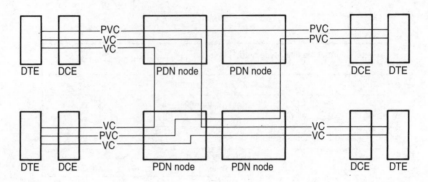

Figure 4.18   X.25 layer 3: VCs and PVCs.

The packet level has a flow control facility that is similar to that in the HDLC using RR and RNR packets. The terminal can send **DTE RR packets** and **DTE RNR packets**, while the DCE side can give flow control commands in the form of **DCE RR packets** and **DCE RNR packets**.

While one type of reset command was sufficient for HDLC, at the packet level we need more. This is because reset can relate either to a DTE interface, and therefore to all VCs (logical channel numbers) passing through it, or to a single VC corresponding to one destination.

In the latter case, one speaks of a **restart**. Moreover, the packet protocol differentiates between packets sent by the DTE and the DCE and makes use of the receive confirmation to define four types of restart packet: **restart request, restart indication, DTE restart confirmation** and **DCE restart confirmation**. There are also four types of packet for the reset (see Table 4.1).

Figure 4.18 shows layer 3 for a network example containing PVCs and selected VCs. The VCs in layer 3 between the DCE and the PDN node will generally be handled by one physical circuit having one layer 2 with one HDLC protocol.

Traffic between nodes can be so high that the VCs make use of several physical circuits. The CCITT has specified a **Multilink Protocol (MLP)** for layer 2 to deal with this situation; the capacity of the links is divided evenly over all active virtual circuits (PVCs and VCs).

4.6   CCITT signalling system no. 7 (PSTN and ISDN)

The goal of **CCITT Signalling System No. 7 (SS No. 7)** was to offer an internationally standardized signalling system for the interconnection of computer controlled telephone exchanges. The system was to be suitable for the handling of call build up, management information and maintenance messages – including those for what were then future systems, such as ISDN and circuit switched data networks. In the meantime, many

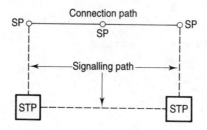

Figure 4.19 SS No. 7 signalling path.

countries have installed systems using SS No. 7 signalling, although these are often national versions. The system is optimized for the use of 64 kbit/s channels for signalling, although it can operate on analogue channels with lower bit rates. Satellite links can also be used.

SS No. 7 is a **common channel signalling system**, that is, a single common channel is used for signalling relating to connections on many other channels. This is in contrast to the majority of older systems, in which signalling and speech used the same channel.

SS No. 7 also makes it possible to choose the path to be used by the signalling completely independently of that for data or speech; the signalling is thus not necessarily **channel associated**. SS No. 7 uses its own channels through the network, and together they form the SS No. 7 signalling network.

The sources and destinations of SS No. 7 messages are the **Signalling Points (SP)**. A node in the signalling network capable of switching SS No. 7 messages from one link to another is called a **Signalling Transfer Point (STP)**. See also Figure 4.19.

4.6.1 The SS No. 7 CCITT/ITU-T recommendations

CCITT started specification of SS No. 7 in 1976. Although large parts have reached reasonable stability, in particular the specifications of the three lower layers, the work is far from finished. The 1988 CCITT *Blue Book* contains about 1000 pages relating to SS No. 7 signalling. Table 4.3 gives an impression of the existing recommendations.

4.6.2 SS No. 7 and the OSI model

The specification of SS No. 7 was originally based on connection oriented telephony requirements. CCITT started work on the specifications in 1976 before ISO had commenced work on the OSI model.

With an eye on the requirements at that time, a four-level model was chosen. The lowest three levels, which form the **Message Transfer**

Table 4.3 CCITT recommendations relating to SS No. 7.

Introduction to CCITT signalling system no. 7	Q.700
Message transfer part (MTP)	Q.701–704, Q.706–707
Telephone user part (TUP)	Q.721–725
Supplementary services	Q.730
Data user part (DUP)	Q.741 and X.61
ISDN user part (ISDN-UP)	Q.761–764, Q.766
Signalling connection control part (SCCP)	Q.711–714, Q.716
Transaction capabilities (TC)	Q.771–775
Operations maintenance and administration part	Q.795
Signalling network structure	Q.705
Numbering of international signalling point codes	Q.708
Hypothetical signalling reference connection	Q.709
PABX application	Q.710
CCITT SS No. 7 test specification (general)	Q.780
MTP level 2 test specification	Q.781
MTP level 3 test specification	Q.782
TUP test specification	Q.783
Monitoring and measurement for the CCITT SS No. 7 network	Q.791

Part (MTP), are used for a number of **user parts**. Levels 1 and 2 of SS No. 7 correspond to layers 1 and 2 of the OSI model.

For the benefit of two recently defined user parts, the **ISDN User Part (ISDN-UP)** and the **Transaction Capabilities (TC)**, the CCITT has attempted to modify the architecture of SS No. 7 to the OSI model by the introduction of a functional module called the **Signalling Connection Control Part (SCCP)**, which offers an OSI network service to the higher user parts. The layer 3 OSI model network service is offered here by a level 4 SS No. 7 module. See also Figure 4.20.

Thus, the OSI layers and SS No. 7 levels coexist in SS No. 7.

4.6.3 Message transfer part

The MTP consists of three parts, called levels, as follows:

- MTP level 1: the **signalling data link** (ITU-T Recommendation Q.702);
- MTP level 2: the **signalling link** (ITU-T Recommendation Q.703);
- MTP level 3: the **signalling network**.

MTP level 1 covers the physical and electrical media for the datalink, the means of accessing this link and possibly the means of set-up and

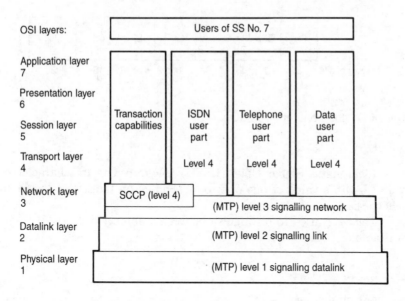

Figure 4.20 Architecture of CCITT SS No. 7.

breakdown. In a digital environment, 64 kbit/s channels will be used for this.

MTP level 2 makes use of the level 1 datalink as a carrier and to guarantee reliable transmission of the bits. MTP 2 is fully comparable to OSI layer 2 and LAPB. MTP level 2 does offer faster detection of problems with the datalink, by carrying out a continuous check on the link with **Fill-in Signal Units** (**FISU**) even when there is no data to be transported. See Figure 4.21.

In the FISU, the **Forward Sequence Number** (**FSN**) and the **Backwards Sequence Number** (**BSN**) are comparable to the N(S) and N(R) of LAPB or HDLC. The check bits (CK) have the same role as the frame check sequence (FCS). The **Length Indicator** (**LI**) indicates the number of octets between the LI and the CK and is therefore 0 for this type of unit. The **Backward and Forward Indication Bits** (**BIB** and **FIB**) are used in repeated transmissions.

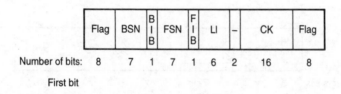

Figure 4.21 Structure of an FISU.

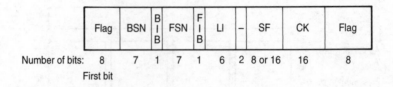

Figure 4.22 Structure of an LSSU.

Link Status Signal Units (LSSU) (Figure 4.22) are characterized by an LI with a value of one or two, depending on the size of the **Status Field (SF)**.

The SF is used to distinguish between a number of types of LSSU, for example:

- out of service

- out of alignment

- processor outage

- normal.

For the transmission of the signalling message itself, the **Message Signal Unit (MSU)** is used (Figure 4.23). The **Signalling Information Field (SIF)** contains the information for the higher layer 3 of the MTP. The LI is now two or more. Table 4.4 gives an impression of the types of message used by SS No. 7.

4.6.4 User parts

The user parts specified by CCITT (see also Figure 4.20) are:

- **Signalling Connection Control Part (SCCP)** gives the higher layer (SS No. 7 level 4) or layers (ISO layers 4–7) both a connection oriented and a connectionless network service.

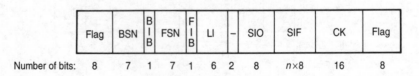

Figure 4.23 Structure of an (MSU).

Table 4.4 CCITT SS No. 7 message types.

Address complete	Facility accepted
Answer	Facility reject
Blocking	Facility request
Blocking acknowledgement	Forward transfer
Call modification completed	Information
Call modification requested	Information request
Call modification reject	Initial address
Call progress	Loop back acknowledgement (national use)
Circuit group blocking	Overload (national use)
Circuit group blocking acknowledgement	Pass-along
Circuit group query	Release
Circuit group query response	Release complete
Circuit group reset	Reset circuit
Circuit group reset acknowledgement	Resume
Charge information (national use)	Subsequent address
Confusion	Suspend
Connect	Unblocking
Continuity	Unblocking acknowledgement
Continuity check request	Unequipped Circuit Identification Code (CIC) (national use)
Delayed release	User-to-user information

- **Telephone User Part (TUP)** provides the necessary signalling functions between telephone exchanges for the build up of national and international calls.

- **Data User Part (DUP)** does the same for data connections between circuit switched data exchanges.

- **ISDN User Part (ISDN-UP)** handles the signalling for both telephone and data connections in the ISDN. In a number of cases the SCCP is used for this function.

- **Transaction Capabilities (TC)** always use the SCCP, making use of the connectionless part. Exactly which services are to be provided by TC is still under review. Database access making exclusive use of the SS No. 7 signalling network, and not of the connections in the switched network, is one of the probable functions.

It is to be expected that, in the future, still more user parts will be necessary – for example, for maintenance purposes. These user parts can be added later without problems.

4.7   Internetworking protocols

For the coupling of packet oriented networks (packet networks and LANs) we need **internetworking protocols**. We discuss two widely used internetworking protocols: **X.75** and the **Internet Protocol (IP)**.

X.75 is the protocol used to couple two X.25 based networks. When the national public data networks reached their maturity, the need to extend the operation over the borders of the countries became apparent. X.25 specifies the interface between the terminal (DTE) and the network. To interface two networks we need a protocol between two equal parties, two networks. This requires a **symmetrical protocol**. There is no justification to design an asymmetrical protocol! X.25 is a protocol for duplex operation and is therefore already of a symmetrical nature for a large part of the specification. But the parties are not equal. The terminal is, for instance, not supposed to be able to provide network information and the network side cannot provide terminal details. So, X.25 is not symmetrical.

X.75 is a protocol that uses only symmetrical parts of X.25 and contains some specific network-to-network additions to the protocol. The main goal of X.75 is to extend the VCs of the one connection oriented X.25 based network with VCs of the other connection oriented X.25 based network. Thus, the user gets one VC passing two networks. By coupling more networks of the same type, the VC can pass several networks. This makes international operation of the public data networks feasible. Several private X.25 based packet networks can be coupled in the same way with X.75. Unlike X.25 X.75 does not support PVCs, only virtual calls.

The situation becomes more difficult for the coupling of networks of many different types. The IP is designed for the coupling of networks such as LANs of different manufacturers and packet switched networks. The IP functions at the interface of two networks. The choice was made for a connectionless, datagram protocol. Individual packets each carry their destination and origin address and follow the route that seems most suitable at that time. Particularly for a military network this is an advantage since routes may be out due to war handling.

The possibility that packets of the same message follow different routes to the same end destination introduces the risk that occasionally packets are received out of sequence. In some unfavourable cases packets may be lost unnoticed. This introduces the need for an end-to-end protocol that corrects these types of problems. The end-to-end protocol used in the core of the worldwide computer network, the internet, on top of the IP, is the **Transmission Control Protocol (TCP)**. TCP is a transport layer protocol. Together the two protocols IP and TCP are referred to as **TCP/IP**. For more details on TCP/IP and other internetworking protocols see the selected literature at the end of this book.

Chapter 5

General aspects of user equipment

5.1 Introduction

Although the term **user equipment** in everyday conversation can include everything from coffee percolators to cars, its meaning in the tele-communications world is limited to the telecommunication equipment used directly by the subscriber. The term **peripheral** is also employed for this purpose. The remaining equipment, the links, transmission equipment and switching equipment, is referred to as the **infrastructure** (see Figure 5.1). The user equipment thus consists of the terminals by which the end users gain access to a telecommunications network.

The situation is rather more complicated for large organizations (see Figure 5.2): between the public infrastructure and the user terminals there is a private telecommunication system, comprising, for example, a business message switching system and a cable network. Some common carriers refer to this business equipment as user equipment, although many within the organization see it as their infrastructure and regard the terminals as being peripheral equipment.

User equipment, then, consists of two types of apparatus:

- terminals
- equipment for private infrastructure.

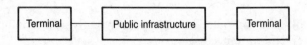

Figure 5.1 User equipment connected to the public infrastructure.

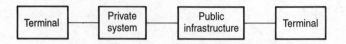

Figure 5.2   Private system connected to the public infrastructure.

5.2   General functional aspects of terminals

In the past, terminals had the single function of providing people with access to a telecommunications network. The primary concern was the human interface. Later, many other functions, designed to simplify the use of the telecommunications equipment, were added to the terminal. In the case of the telephone, this consisted of adding the ability to repeat previously dialled numbers and to select frequently used numbers by pressing a single button. For text oriented terminals, it was the ability to store and edit data.

The latter development caused the terminal to take on a marked resemblance to the original word processor, which had not been designed for use in telecommunications. By equipping the word processor with a communications interface, however, the differences between telecommunications text terminals and communicating word processors disappear, and we obtain a multifunctional workstation.

One further step leads to the use of an even more universal piece of equipment, the Personal Computer (PC), as a terminal.

In addition to its greater functionality, an advantage of using the PC in this way is the lower price, made possible by the large numbers in which these universal. non-telecommunications specific terminals can be produced. A disadvantage is that the 'human interface' (the keyboard) does not have a sufficient number of individual keys to cope with the multitude of operations possible. This leads to the use of overlays to enable access to more functions. However, in some cases this is still insufficient and key combinations (using, for example, 'Alt' or 'Ctrl' along with another key) are required to enable operations without a specific key to be performed. The use of **overlays** around the keys, and of **soft keys**, improves the situation a little but it remains a problem for beginners and incidental users trying to familiarize themselves with the keyboard. Software with graphical human interfaces, for example Windows, has improved this situation. There is still room for future improvements in this area.

Finally, the computer can act independently as a terminal, making human intervention unnecessary.

5.3   General functional aspects of equipment for private infrastructure

Private infrastructure is sometimes viewed by suppliers of public infrastructure as an extension of the public networks, just as the terminal was originally viewed exclusively as a network terminal by the network suppliers. From within larger businesses, the picture is exactly the opposite; the public infrastructure is seen as an extension of the private infrastructure, particularly where the private infrastructure cannot itself meet the needs economically.

In the first view, the use of public standards for private communication is justified. For the interface between the two infrastructures, that is also the most practical solution. For internal business communication, however, it has long been the case that many more facilities are offered than are available on the public networks. It is also reasonable to allow more diversity, since all businesses do not have the same infrastructure requirements; for some, specific facilities may be desirable.

There are, for example, special facilities in business exchanges for hotels. In the field of text and data communication a number of organizations have their own standards and facilities for the use of priorities, multiple addresses, user-friendly address codes and so on. Complete uniformity can be undesirable in this area.

Conversion of the current system to systems that have exclusively implemented public standards can thus also have drawbacks. It is, of course, necessary to strive for the removal of *unnecessary* differences wherever it is economical to do so. When communicating with other businesses that work internally to their own standards, it is also preferable to use international standards.

There is a growing trend for public digital networks to supply special facilities for private networks; these facilities are known as **virtual private networks**.

5.4   Connection conditions for peripheral equipment

In a large number of countries the carriers have for many years enjoyed a monopoly on the supply of user equipment. Recently, however, drastic changes have taken place, and in almost all European countries the tendency now is to keep the infrastructure in the hands of the carriers but to deregulate the supply of user equipment. In these countries, a supplier must meet the conditions laid down by government controlled agencies. In the UK the Telecommunications section of the British Standards

Institution draws up the regulations that have to be met for equipment approval. Connection of non-approved equipment to the public network is forbidden. In many countries outside Europe, the situation is not so clear.

5.5 Reliability

High equipment **reliability** is one of the important factors for achieving satisfaction among the equipment users. Reliability can be expressed as the average time between two failures, the **Mean Time Between Failures (MTBF)**. For the usability of the equipment, the time that equipment is unserviceable after a failure, the **Mean Time To Repair (MTTR)**, is also of importance. The MTTR includes any waiting time before an actual repair can begin. The average time that the equipment is available (MTBF) as a percentage of the total time (MTBF + MTTR) is called the **inherent availability** (A_i). Inherent refers to the fact that the equipment is technically available. Even if it is technically available, it may still not be usable for non-technical reasons, such as logistics (for example, out of paper). The **operational availability** (A_o) can thus be considerably shorter than the technical or inherent availability. This can be represented by formulae as follows:

$$A_i = \frac{MTBF}{MTBF + MTTR}$$

$$A_o = \frac{MUT}{MUT + MDT}$$

In the last formula, MUT is the **mean uptime** and MDT the **mean downtime**.

The introduction of programmable equipment has created a new problem; software can be lost when a failure occurs. Software can consist of programs or data. In both cases **recovery**, to the situation existing before the failure, is necessary. To what extent this is possible depends on the measures taken either within the equipment itself or by the user to allow rapid recovery – the **backup** facilities. Backup is usually achieved by periodically copying essential data to one or more independent storage media. For programs which are not subject to regular change, it is possible and sensible to record them in a storage form that is very unlikely to fail or be subject to human error, such as **Read Only Memory (ROM)**. ROM can be obtained in several forms including **Programmable Read Only Memory (PROM)**. **CD-ROM** also belongs to this category.

For backup we make use of multiple storage of data, or **redundancy**. To increase the availability of the equipment, it is also possible to apply hardware redundancy by duplicating the most vital parts. This is usually not considered necessary for terminating equipment but for central equipment, such as a business exchange where one failure could deny hundreds of users access to the central services, redundancy is applied to essential system parts. This duplication is only of use if sufficient measures have been taken to prevent failures in one part causing failures in the other. This leads to a requirement for separate power supplies for the two halves.

5.6   User friendliness

The satisfaction of the users will depend to a large extent on the so-called **user friendliness** of the equipment and what their expectations are. Users who work several hours a day with a piece of apparatus will have no difficulties, even with equipment that has a very user *un*friendly design. They learn to live with it and may even be proud of the fact that they can work with the equipment and others cannot.

For users who make only sporadic use of that same equipment, or of the same facility, its user unfriendliness becomes very apparent. This category of user often has to work with various types of equipment and many different facilities. For them the ease of operation of the equipment is of great importance and the success of equipment in this **casual user** market will ultimately depend on its user friendliness. Equipment for which the user manual has to be consulted in order to work with it will either not be used at all or only a limited number of its facilities will be used. For casual users, standardization of the **human interface** is of great importance.

Standardization of user interfaces leaves much to be desired. In the case of telephones, for example, CCITT has defined some standards, but these are limited to the most frequently occurring matters such as the positioning of the number buttons. Alas, ISO has decided on a totally different layout for the number pads of data keyboards. Efforts are being made to eliminate the differences. Because the telephone users' group is so large, preference is being given to the CCITT standard.

```
   1   2   3            7   8   9

   4   5   6            4   5   6

   7   8   9            1   2   3

   *   0   #                0

      CCITT                  ISO
```

The user interface is also the subject of a number of national standards, such as the German DIN 66234 and the Dutch NEN 3002. At European level, the European Computer Manufacturers' Association (ECMA) has made recommendations in *ECMA 126* entitled: 'Ergonomics – Requirements for Colour Visual Display Devices'.

It takes a long time to become fully acquainted with user unfriendly equipment; users should therefore undergo special training. This is rarely done, mainly because of cost considerations, with the result that much time is spent trying out the equipment, making errors, losing data and interrupting other people to get help. This is the true cost, not usually visible, but becoming increasingly significant as equipment offers more and more facilities. As the trend is towards incorporating more and more facilities, increasing attention will need to be paid to aspects of user friendliness.

Some common failings of the human interface are:

- Reporting that an error has occurred without giving any indication of what remedial action is required or what has caused the error.

- No confirmation that an action has been carried out.

- Too little use of graphical information or colour.

- Lack of consistency in the use of abbreviations, names and symbols.

5.7 Safety

As ordinary telecommunications users, we do not usually need to be concerned about our personal safety. Equipment sold to the public has for years had to meet national safety requirements. In the framework of making European standards uniform, there is now a European standard, ENV 41 003, entitled: *Particular safety requirements for equipments to be connected to telecommunication networks*. More generally, there is the European standard EN 60 950, derived from the international norm IEC 950, entitled: *Safety of information technology equipment including electrical business equipment*.

5.8 Precautions against misuse

There are two types of misuse against which precautions need to be taken. The first is misuse of the equipment by unauthorized people; the second is misuse of transmitted, received or stored information.

The use of terminals, such as telephones, by unauthorized persons for private calls at the expense of a business can be reduced by introducing a mechanism into the business exchange which restricts usage. For example, it can be determined whether international calls may be set up from a particular terminal. If this facility is blocked, a call can still be made via the operator. The exchange can also be equipped with **abbreviated dialling**. A terminal for which international calls are blocked can still use an abbreviated code to allow access to the international numbers of importance to the organization. It is also possible to block all non-local calls during certain periods to limit misuse, for example, by cleaning personnel.

Misuse of telecommunications facilities by unauthorized persons can also be prevented by fitting locks. With telephone sets this is not very effective, because it is too easy to replace the telephone by another without a lock, and make use of the connection.

Use of **passwords** is of less practical significance than one might think because of the difficulty of keeping them secret. They also present an extra burden to the bona fide user.

ISDN offers a service known as Calling Line Identity Presentation (CLIP). This supplementary service offers a means of identifying which terminal has made a call. Depending on the identity, it can be decided to block access to a database, for example. This can be done by taking measures in the computer holding the database. Modern business telephone and data exchanges have a similar facility.

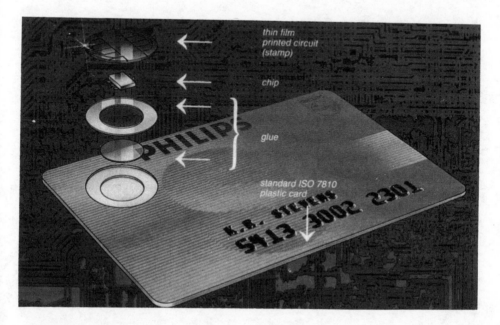

Figure 5.3 Smart card.

The standard (analogue) public telephone network does not have any facility for identifying the caller. For many years, the simple method of (non-automatic) calling back to the caller has been used. If the caller has given a wrong number to keep his identity secret, then the call back will not reach him. This method can also be automated, by means of either special hardware or software in the database computer or in the communications exchange.

Increasing use is being made of the **smart card** (see Figure 5.3) which can be used for the identification and registration of a user. This card can also play a role in the protection of information by providing a key for the encoding of information.

Chapter 6

Integrated services digital network (ISDN)

6.1 Introduction

The question 'what is ISDN?' cannot be answered clearly and simply in a single sentence. ISDN is a complex worldwide phenomenon that is capable of being seen from many points of view.

6.1.1 Integrated digital network

The **Integrated Digital Network** (**IDN**) was a first step in the direction of an integrated services digital network. This first step consisted of the gradual replacement of FDM transmission multiplexers using analogue technology, by TDM multiplexers using digital technology.

In the USA, these first transmission systems provided 24 digital channels, of 64 kbit/s each, by multiplexing a 1.5 Mbit/s bit stream. These systems are known as **T1 carrier systems**. The 64 kbit/s signals were used for the transmission of PCM coded speech and also for **in band** signalling by periodically 'stealing' a bit from the PCM signal. By choosing the least significant bit of the PCM signal for this purpose, no problems were experienced in practice. For data at 64 kbit/s, this stealing is not acceptable and, for this reason, its use in the USA was limited to 56 kbit/s. This data speed can be used if all least significant bits (that is, 1 in 8) are given up. The mixed use of channels for speech (or data) and signalling was normal in the analogue systems of that time. In Europe the choice was made of a 2 Mbit/s carrier and 32 channels, of which two were reserved for test and common channel signalling purposes. The conversion of the network to digital traffic has continued with digital multiplexers for higher bit rates. Only recently have identical values been used worldwide for the highest bit rates after agreement was reached within CCITT on the **Synchronous Digital Hierarchy (SDH)**. The lowest standardized bit rate, SDH level 1, is 155.520 Mbit/s. (See Chapter 8.)

6.1.2 Digital switching systems

A logical consequence of using digital technology in the transmission network was the introduction of switching systems based on digital technology. Initially, digital switches were introduced for the circuit switching of the 64 kbit/s B-channels. This allows a certain amount of integration; it is not necessary to demultiplex the multiplexed signals down to separate physical circuits before carrying out the switching function. The exchange must be capable of switching **bytes**, called a PCM **sample** in the case of telephony, from a certain **time slot** on the incoming line to another slot on the outgoing line, determined by the call build up. This allows a basic ISDN function, the **circuit mode, 64 kbit/s unrestricted, 8 kHz structured bearer service** to be offered. This is not, however, a full function ISDN exchange. ISDN also has packet-mode bearer services for which the exchange can be equipped. Moreover, ISDN is not limited to 64 kbit/s based services. Fast packet switching based on a carrier of over 150 Mbit/s is being considered for broadband ISDN.

6.1.3 Terminal connections

Another area affected by implementation of the ISDN is that of digital terminal connections. Although initially almost all telephones connected to the digital network were analogue using analogue signalling on the local line, ISDN also offers digital connections, making it possible to integrate various other services. The digital interface offers **basic access** via a so-called D-channel and two B-channels in time multiplex. The D-channel is primarily intended for signalling, but can also be used for transmitting and receiving data packets. The B-channels can be used independently of each other for circuit switched connections of diverse nature (voice, data, text, fax) and even for packet-mode bearer services.

6.1.4 ISDN services

Finally, integration can be seen in the services that can be offered by ISDN; existing services, such as data and telex services, will at some stage be capable of technical integration into the ISDN. It is, however, questionable whether this will be either economical or practical. It is probable that the existing services will continue to work separately for the next few years, and that use of the facilities offered by ISDN will only be incidental. New services, such as **bearer services**, **teleservices** and **supplementary services**, which have been developed specially for ISDN, can be offered as soon as there is sufficient demand and the service providers, the PTTs, decide to start the appropriate service. In Europe, several decisions have already been taken (Anonymous, 1991), as discussed in Sections 6.8, 6.9 and 6.10. For more information see CCITT (1989a).

6.2   Reference model

A reference model or **reference configuration** is a drawing in which the relationship between **functional groups** and **reference points** is depicted (CCITT, 1989b). A reference model does not show how system parts must be physically implemented, but makes it possible to come to agreements about the cooperation of functional groups. It also makes it possible to lay down specifications, for example, at the datalink layer, and only later to decide at which reference points in the system these will be applied. CCITT does, however, limit itself to the specification of interfaces to already specified reference points. In an actual implementation, a reference point may well be in the middle of a subsystem so that no physical interface can be recognized. At a certain reference point, a choice can be made from many interface specifications.

CCITT has recommended a reference model for the user connection to ISDN. See Figure 6.1.

Figure 6.1(b) shows an alternative reference configuration for the case where a terminal TE2 is used which has a non-ISDN interface. The terminal is connected to a reference point R and a terminal adapter TA is used to connect it to the ISDN.

The terminal TE1 includes all the functions needed for it to be connected directly to the ISDN interface. This terminal can be a telephone, a data terminal or, for example, an integrated workstation.

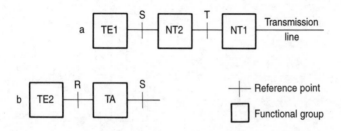

Figure 6.1   CCIIT reference model for the ISDN user connection.

Network Termination 2 (NT2) is the group of functions capable of connecting several ISDN interface terminals. An ISDN business exchange (ISPBX) (see Figure 6.2) or an ISDN LAN can perform the NT2 functions. Network Termination 1 (NT1) is the group of functions required for terminating the user's connection line. One function of NT1 is to provide the multiplexing of the B- and D-channels on the line.

6.3   Interfaces, layers

A number of specifications have been drawn up by CCITT for use at the S or T reference point. These specifications are according to the OSI model. For layer 1 the specifications are for the **basic user–network interface** (2B + D) in Recommendation I.430 and for the **primary rate user–network interface** in Recommendation I.431. The primary rate user–network interface offers the possibility of 30 B-channels and one D-channel on a 2048 kbit/s carrier (referred to as 2 Mbit/s) or, following the American standard, 23 B-channels and one D-channel on a 1544 kbit/s carrier (1.5 Mbit/s). The primary rate user–network interface can be used with a more limited number of channels with a higher bit rate (H-channels) on the same carriers.

At the S reference point, it is possible to connect a maximum of eight terminals on a basic user–network interface (2B + D). (See also Figure 6.2.)

Specifications also exist for layers 2 and 3 (although the layer 3 specifications are not yet complete), and refer to the signalling. After a circuit switched connection has been established, ISDN is transparent to the user on the B-channels for the layer 2 and higher level protocols. When using the packet mode, the user must follow the recommendations for layers 2 and 3.

The reference model has no reference points in the local transmission circuit (see Figure 6.1). CCITT originally defined the reference point U for this purpose. However, because the conclusion has been reached that it is desirable to allow a free choice of transmission system in

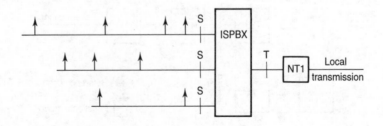

Figure 6.2   In-house network based on an ISPBX.

different countries, and that this should not therefore be specified by CCITT, the U reference point has been dropped. It is hoped that this will prevent recurring requests for standards at this point. By having the same specification at the S reference point it is possible to use the same terminals in different countries.

Signalling system DSS 1 has been specified for the user–network interface. This protocol is discussed in Section 6.5. Signalling system SS No. 7 is recommended by CCITT for use between two ISDN exchanges. This protocol has been described in Chapter 4. Both protocols have a layered structure.

For the broadband system planned for the more distant future, protocols derived from the above are specified by ITU-T.

6.4 Local transmission

It must be possible to install ISDN terminals several kilometres from the exchanges. Moreover, to avoid high introduction costs, the connection must be over existing copper-pair cables. Finally, there is the desire to use the same pair of wires for both transmission directions so as to be able to use the existing wires for as many connections as possible.

This is not a simple problem as two 64 kbit/s B-channels and a 16 kbit/s D-channel are required in both directions. With several extra bits for synchronization and signalling at the physical level, we need at least 160 kbit/s in both directions. Because the attenuation on copper pairs rapidly increases with frequency, it is necessary to organize transmission so that only a limited bandwidth is required, despite the relatively high bit rate.

ISDN requires a full duplex (2B + D) connection. There are two possible ways of achieving this with only two wires:

(a)   alternately transmitting in the two directions with at least double bit rate: the so-called **ping pong** method;

(b)   taking special measures and transmitting in both directions simultaneously: the so-called **echo cancelling** method.

(Note that the use of separate frequencies for the two directions is also possible in principle, but offers no advantages.)

Method (a) (Figure 6.3(a)) uses a greater bandwidth and therefore suffers greater attenuation. In practice, this means that signals received over distances of 2 to 3 km are hardly greater than interference and noise. It is only possible to achieve a reasonable bit error rate of 10^{-7}, for example, over a shorter distance than with method (b).

have a bit rate of 64 kbit/s in both cases, but the D-channel also has a 64 kbit/s bit rate in this case. Instead of B-channels, the primary rate user–network interface may also make use of higher bit rate channels, for example five H0 channels of 384 kbit/s. The number of channels involved must be capable of being multiplexed on a carrier of 2048 kbit/s, or 1544 kbit/s in the USA.

6.5.1   DSS 1 layer 2, datalink layer

At the S reference point, several terminals can be handled over the datalink, in contrast to X.25, which allows only one terminal at the network connection. This leads to the requirement that it must be possible to send frames to all terminals simultaneously (**broadcast**). When broadcasting, an acknowledgement message from all receivers is undesirable; the procedure must be modified for this feature. The DSS 1 layer 2 protocol LAPD is similar to the X.25 LAPB, but does have some clear differences. Figure 6.4 illustrates a Format A frame, which contains only a control field and no information field.

A frame with an information field is called a Format B frame. (See Figure 6.5.)

As with LAPB, the control field can have three formats: the I, U and S formats.

In addition to the types of commands and responses in LAPB, RR, RNR, REJ and DISC, LAPD also contains the following types from the LLC protocols: **Unnumbered Information (UI)** and **Exchange Identification (XID)**. In place of the LAPB command SABM, LAPD has the command **Set Asynchronous Balanced Mode Extended (SABME)**. (See also Table 6.2.)

6.5.2   DSS 1 layer 3, network layer

The term **layer 3** is used by CCITT to indicate the procedures described in Recommendations Q.930, Q.931 and Q.932:

- Recommendation Q.930 (= I.450); ISDN User–Network Interface Layer 3 – General Aspects

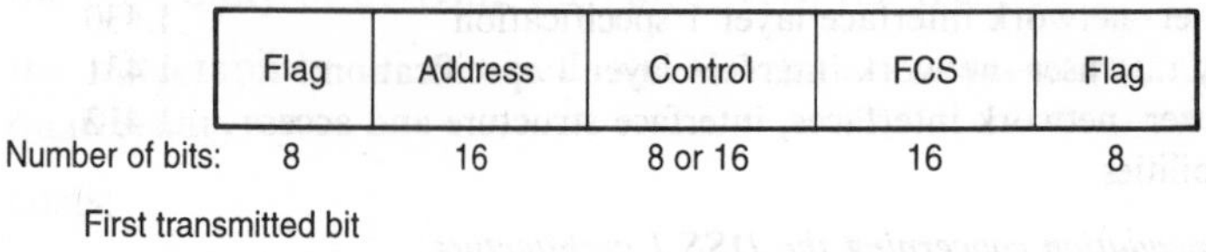

Flag	Address	Control	FCS	Flag
8	16	8 or 16	16	8

Number of bits:

First transmitted bit

Figure 6.4   Structure of an LAPD Format A datalink frame.

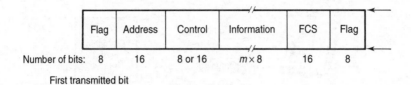

Number of bits: 8   16   8 or 16 $m \times 8$ 16   8

First transmitted bit

Figure 6.5   Structure of an LAPD Format B datalink frame.

- Recommendation Q.931 (= I.451): ISDN User–Network Interface Layer 3 – Specifications for Basic Call Control
- Recommendation Q.932 (= I.452): Generic Procedures for the Control of ISDN Supplementary Services

The layer 3 procedures offer the means to set up, hold and cleardown **network connections** between **communicating application entities** on ISDN. They also provide the access to a number of basic procedures for use with the **supplementary services**. Although the recommendations are fully described in CCITT books they are not yet completely stable, that is to say that they still may be subject to modifications, hopefully small.

The layer 3 protocol, of course, makes use of the DSS 1 layer 2 service. The layer 3 protocol offers subscriber equipment the opportunity to exchange signalling messages with the control equipment of the exchange.

A subscriber connection protocol has an asymmetric character principally because the functions of the two ends of the connection are different. The desire to apply layer 3 protocols between two exchanges,

Table 6.2   CCITT LAPD commands and responses.

Application	Format	Commands	Responses
Unacknowledged and multiple frame acknowledged information transfer	I: Information transfer	I: Information	
	S: Supervisory	RR: Receive ready RNR: Receive not ready REJ: Reject	RR: Receive ready RNR: Receive not ready REJ: Reject
	U: Unnumbered	SABME: Set asynchronous balanced mode extended UI: Unnumbered information DISC: Disconnect	DM: Disconnected mode UA: Unnumbered acknowledgement FRMR: Frame reject
Connection management	U: Unnumbered	XID: Exchange identification	XID: Exchange identification

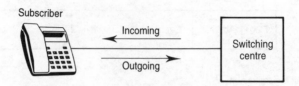

Figure 6.6   Definitions of 'incoming' and 'outgoing' in ISDN.

for example, between a public ISDN exchange and a PABX, has led to the desire to make the layer 3 protocols as symmetrical as possible. It remains possible, however, for the subscriber to make an independent, thus asymmetric, choice for the two directions from the possibilities offered by the protocols.

It is thus useful to agree as to what is meant by *incoming* and *outgoing* in layer 3 specifications. Figure 6.6 clarifies this and defines the terms from the subscriber's point of view. A large number of different messages are required for signalling. Table 6.3 gives a summary of the message types defined for a circuit switched connection. There are similar lists of message types for packet switched connections and for temporary connections necessary for signalling, but which are not directly associated with a particular connection. The latter are called **temporary signalling connections**.

Table 6.3   Message types for circuit switched connections.

Call establishment messages	Alerting
	Call proceeding
	Connect
	Connect acknowledge
	Progress
	Set-up
	Set-up acknowledge
Call information phase messages	Resume
	Resume acknowledge
	Resume reject
	Suspend
	Suspend acknowledge
	Suspend reject
	User information
Call clearing messages	Disconnect
	Release
	Release complete
Miscellaneous messages	Congestion control
	Facility
	Information
	Notify
	Status
	Status inquiry

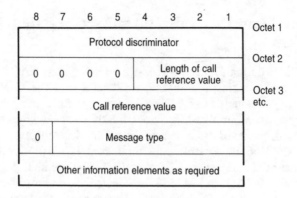

Figure 6.7 Format of the signalling message.

The format of the messages always begins with the same elements; thereafter, the format differs per message type. Figure 6.7 illustrates the format.

The four fixed elements are:

- The **protocol discriminator**. One of the values is used to indicate a Q.931 subscriber signalling message. Other values are reserved for national versions of the signalling protocol. Use of X.25 can also be indicated here; this is required if the D-channel is used for sending and receiving data, in which case the ISDN creates a packet switched connection. For data exchange, the B-channel can also be chosen – in which case the data will be circuit switched, so far as the ISDN is concerned. It is not certain that every exchange will offer both options in the future; there is, therefore, no guarantee that every subscriber connection will be able to use X.25 over the D-channel.

- The **call reference value**. Because more than one connection can be handled on the signalling channel, an identification given with the call reference is required for each connection.

- The **length** of the field in which the identification is given is defined by four bits in the second octet. See Figure 6.7.

- The **message type**. There are 7 bits available for indicating the message type, so 128 different types can be distinguished. One bit is reserved, to allow for future extension of the message field. By giving this bit the value 1 instead of 0, the other 7 bits can then be reserved, for example, for a length indication of the message type field that is then included in the following octets. This extension method has not yet been defined, although the necessary bit has been reserved. Table 6.3 shows the number of message types. Each type is assigned a binary value, laid down in CCITT Recommendation Q.931.

6.6   Broadband ISDN digital subscriber signalling system

Protocols for broadband ISDN are still in the first phase of development. CCITT is working on this at world level and the **Commission of the European Communities (EC)** is similarly working at the European level. However, an impression can already be gained as to what technology will be used in a future broadband connection. Although an interim solution is possible, the final goal is currently to use **fast packet switching** in the form of the CCITT specified **Asynchronous Transfer Mode (ATM)**. ATM can be viewed as a simplified form of packet switching. ATM also supports the concept of virtual circuits as in X.25 based packet switching. The term **Virtual Channel (VC)** is used for this. Different VCs being carried on the same physical circuit can be distinguished from each other by the **Virtual Channel Identifier (VCI)** which is included in the **header** of each packet, which is called a **cell**.

A difference from X.25 based packet switching is the omission of error detection or correction of the transmitted information at link level. As a consequence, ATM data transfer is put into layer 1 of the OSI model. After the set up of a connection in broadband ISDN, the higher layers are no longer operative in the exchange, just as is the case with a circuit switched 64 kbit/s connection. Error detection and correction can be provided on an end-to-end basis if required.

A separate virtual channel is allocated for signalling. Layer 1 for signalling is otherwise identical to that for data transfer.

The cell length has now been defined to be 48 octets for the data and 5 for the header. This is a compromise between the American wish for 64 octets and one European counter-suggestion of 32. The user connection will have a uniform bit rate of about 150 Mbit/s on a coaxial cable electrical interface. The principle of fast packet switching allows any lower speed to be chosen for the actual data transfer. If there is no data to be transferred, **empty** cells can be used to maintain synchronization between the sending and receiving sides.

At the bit rate that has been chosen, optical fibre is the only real possibility for covering distances of more than a few hundred metres. The optical fibre transmission system will have the same coaxial cable electrical interface as the user's side. For shorter distances, coaxial cable is sufficient.

Signalling also makes use of cells. The VCI indicates whether a cell contains signalling information. These cells are sent to the control computer of the broadband exchange. The higher layers of the protocols for circuit set up and cleardown will be as similar as possible to those of the **narrowband ISDN**, that is, to DSS 1.

6.7   Specification methods for CCITT/ITU-T recommendations for ISDN services

CCITT has laid down in Recommendation I.130 how the ISDN recommendations for 'Basic and Supplementary Services' are to be structured. A number of concepts are defined, which must be known before the various recommendations can be understood. The specification tasks were divided into three stages:

- The service aspects: **stage 1**. This describes the specifications from the user's viewpoint.

- The functional network aspects: **stage 2**. This describes the functions that have to be performed in the ISDN network in order to provide the user with the services described in stage 1.

- The network implementation aspects: **stage 3**. These specifications contain the details, such as protocols and message formats, that are necessary for performing the functions described in stage 2.

Level 1 is the description of the division into stages, as in Recommendation I.130. Within a *stage* a further subdivision is made into **level 2** and **level 3**. (See also Figure 6.8.) Level 2 defines the descriptive method to be used in each stage, such as the use of plain **prose** in stage 1 and the use of structured description languages such as the CCITT **Specification and Description Language** (SDL) in stage 3. The detailed specifications for the ISDN services are thus only to be found in the level 3 specifications.

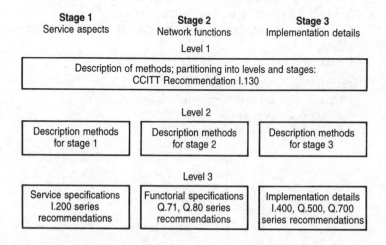

Figure 6.8   Structure of the CCITT recommendations on ISDN services.

6.8   Bearer services

ISDN **bearer services** provide information transfer functions between access points situated on the reference points T, S or R (see Figure 6.1) and are all concerned with the lower layers 1 to 3 (see Figure 6.9). Each bearer service can be seen as a combination of choices from a number of properties, or **attributes**, offered by ISDN.

These attributes can be divided into three groups:

- **information transfer attributes**,
- **access attributes**,
- **general attributes**.

The access attributes specify the signalling system being used and the channel structure (for example, 2B + D or 30B + D). General attributes cover such matters as commercial, operational and quality aspects. Figure 6.10 gives an impression of the information transfer attributes available in ISDN. Other attributes are to be found in the CCITT recommendations (CCITT, 1989b). CCITT specifications are available, or in preparation, for the following bearer services:

- Circuit mode bearer services (Recommendation I.231):
    - 64 kbit/s unrestricted, 8 kHz structured,
    - 64 kbit/s, 8 kHz structured, usable for speech,
    - 64 kbit/s, 8 kHz structured, usable for 3.1 kHz audio,
    - Alternate speech/64 kbit/s unrestricted, 8 kHz structured,
    - 2 × 64 kbit/s unrestricted, 8 kHz structured,
    - 384 kbit/s unrestricted, 8 kHz structured,
    - 1536 kbit/s unrestricted, 8 kHz structured (mainly for use in the USA),
    - 1920 kbit/s unrestricted, 8 kHz structured.
- Packet-mode bearer services:
    - virtual call and permanent virtual circuit,
    - connectionless (in study phase),
    - user signalling (in study phase).

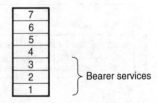

Figure 6.9   OSI layers used for bearer services.

Possible values of attributes								Information transfer attributes:
Circuit						Packet		1. Information transfer mode
Bit rate (kbits/s)						Throughput		2. Information transfer rate
64	2 × 64	384	1536	1920	Other values for further study	Options for further study		
Unrestricted digital information	Speech	3.1 kHz audio	7 kHz audio	15 kHz audio	Video		Others for further study	3. Information transfer capability
8 kHz integrity	Service data unit integrity		Unstructured		TSSI *		RDTD **	4. Structure
Demand	Reserved		Permanent					5. Establishment of communication
Unidirectional	Bidirectional symmetric		Bidirectional asymmetric					6. Symmetry
Point-to-point		Multipoint		Broadcast				7. Communication configuration

* TSSI = Time slot sequence integrity
** RDTD = Restricted differential time delay

Figure 6.10 Possible values of bearer service information transfer attributes (according to CCITT *Blue Book* Recommendation I.120).

- Additional packet-mode bearer services (all in study)
  - frame relaying 1,
  - frame relaying 2,
  - frame switching,
  - X.25 based additional packet mode.

An additional framework is defined for the above services in CCITT Recommendation I.122.

For broadband, no bearer services have been defined as yet, although a start has been made on the specification of broadband services.

In Europe, the following circuit mode bearer services have been available since 1992:

- 64 kbit/s unrestricted, 8 kHz structured

- 64 kbit/s, 8 kHz structured, usable for 3.1 kHz audio.

Other circuit-mode services and packet-mode bearer services may be offered in a number of countries.

6.8.1   64 kbit/s unrestricted, 8 kHz structured bearer service

This circuit-mode bearer service can be used for a wide variety of applications; there are no restrictions on the input bit patterns and the bits are delivered unchanged. This is termed **bit integrity**. Groups of 8 bits, octets, are transferred through the network at a frequency of 8 kHz. This service is most suited to the transmission and circuit switching of digital data.

CCITT recommendations allow several information transfer options including:

- *demand*/reserved/permanent,
- *bidirectional symmetric*/unidirectional,
- *point-to-point*/multipoint.

The options in italics have been available since 1992 in many European countries. Only the B-channel will be available for access; the D-channel will be used exclusively for signalling.

6.8.2   64 kbit/s, 8 kHz structured, usable for 3.1 kHz audio bearer service

This service only guarantees the transmission of frequencies offered within a 3.1 kHz band; it does not guarantee the reproduction of the same bit patterns. There may, for example, be an analogue section included in the network between the ISDN exchanges.

This bearer service is primarily intended for the transmission of data signals which have been converted by modems within the 3.1 kHz band. Group 3 fax also falls within this category. The limitations referred to in Section 6.8.1 are also valid here: a circuit-mode service for information on the B-channel and similar information transfer options.

6.9   Teleservices

ISDN **teleservices** provide services to terminal users and their terminals. Teleservices involve all the layers of the OSI model, not only the lower ones. (See Figure 6.11.) They make use of the same attributes of the lower ISDN layers but can make their own choice from these attributes, which may differ from those for the implemented bearer services.

Teleservices choose not only information transfer, access and general attributes, but also **higher layer attributes**.

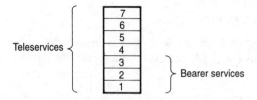

Figure 6.11 OSI layers used for teleservices.

For the time being, CCITT has limited itself to the following ISDN teleservices:

- telephony
- teletex
- telefax group 4
- mixed mode
- videotex
- telex.

In Europe at least the first of these is implemented in most of the countries.

6.9.1 Telephony

An audio bandwidth of 3.1 kHz is used for the telephone service. Use is made exclusively of the bidirectional mode. The service may utilize various signal processing methods, such as analogue transmission, echo cancelling and lower bit rate encoding. Recoding from μ-law to A-law PCM and vice versa, or into ADPCM, is also allowed within the network. The B-channel is prescribed for the transmission of user information (speech); for signalling, use is made of the DSS 1 signalling system on the D-channel

6.9.2 Teletex

The teletex service uses the unrestricted 64 kbit/s value, either in circuit mode on the B-channel or in packet mode on the B- or D-channels. The higher layers follow the rules specified for teletex (CCITT Recommendations T.60, T.61, T.62, T.70). Also specified are the ISDN supplementary services which may be used for teletex. There is also the possibility to interwork with teletex terminals connected to a CCITT recommended ISPBX.

6.9.3   Telefax group 4

The telefax group 4 service also makes use of the unrestricted 64 kbit/s values, but only on the B-channel. The service recognizes three classes of terminals:

- class I: a terminal which can both send and receive facsimile coded messages;
- class II: a terminal that can also receive teletex and mixed mode teletex messages;
- class III: a terminal that can also generate and transmit the aforementioned messages.

For telefax 4, interworking with terminals connected to an ISPBX is also recommended. The protocols to be used for telefax are to be found in the CCITT T Series Recommendations.

6.10   Supplementary services

ISDN supplementary services are described in the CCITT I.250 series. Table 6.4 gives an overview of the supplementary services and, in so far as they are specified by CCITT, the services to which they can be applied.

A few of the supplementary services specified by the CCITT were expected to be operational in the European ISDN from 1992, while a number of the other services were to be introduced shortly afterwards, depending on their expected popularity with the users. The supplementary services expected in Europe during 1992 were:

- **Calling Line Identification Presentation (CLIP)**,
- **Calling Line Identification Restriction (CLIR)**,
- **Direct Dialling In (DDI)**,
- **Multiple Subscriber Number (MSN)**,
- **Terminal Portability (TP)**, which has not yet been described as a supplementary service by the CCITT.

6.10.1   Calling line identification presentation (CLIP)

The CLIP supplementary service (CCITT I.251.3) offers the possibility to the called ISDN subscriber of determining the ISDN number of the calling subscriber, for example, on the display of his terminal. In addition to an ISDN number of up to 15 digits, a sub-address can also be given in order to identify an application in an associated processing system, for example.

Table 6.4 Overview of ISDN supplementary services and their application to ISDN services.

Supplementary services	Circuit-mode bearer services			Teleservices				
	64 kbit/s unrestricted demand	64 kbit/s speech demand	64 kbit/s 3.1 kHz demand	Telephony	Teletex	Telefax 4	Video tex	Mixed mode
Direct dialling in	X	X	X	X	X	X	X	X
Multiple subscriber number	X	X	X	X	X	X	X	X
Calling line identification presentation	X	X	X	X	X	X	X	X
Calling line identification restriction	X	X	X	X	X	X	X	X
Connected line identification presentation	X	X	X	X	X	X	X	X
Connected line identification restriction	X	X	X	X	X	X	X	X
Malicious calls identification								
Sub-addressing								
Call transfer	X	X	X	X				
Call forwarding busy	X	X	X	X				
Call forwarding no reply	X	X	X	X		X		
Call forward unconditional	X	X	X	X		X		
Call deflection								
Line hunting	X	X	X	X				
Call waiting	X	X	X	X				
Call hold	X	X	X	X				
Call completion on busy	X	X	X	X				
Conference calling	X	X	X	X				
Three-party service	X	X	X	X				
Closed user group				X	X	X	X	X
Private numbering plan								
Credit card calling								
Advice on charge	X	X	X	X	X	X	X	X
Reverse charging	X	X	X	X	X	X	X	X
User-to-user signalling	X	X	X	X	X	X	X	X

6.10.2   Calling line identification restriction (CLIR)

The CLIR supplementary service (CCITT I.251.4) enables the calling party to prevent disclosure of his identity. This service makes it possible to keep an ex-directory number secret.

6.10.3   Direct dialling in (DDI)

Direct dialling in (CCITT I.251.1) enables the setting up of a direct connection to a subscriber on an ISPBX without intervention of the operator.

6.10.4   Multiple subscriber number (MSN)

Similar to DDI, the multiple subscriber number supplementary service (CCITT I.251.2) offers the possibility of addressing one of a group of terminals connected via an ISDN interface. The difference is fairly minor, mainly a question of the number of digits. The MSN supplementary service will work with the same number of digits for all connections for differentiation among the subscribers. It can be expected in practice that this will usually be limited to a difference in the last digit only, for those connected to the same termination.

DDI is intended for the connection of both small and large ISPBX exchanges, in which the number of digits to be used by the ISPBX for terminal selection will depend on its size. Per termination, the number of possible subscriber numbers will thus be determined by the number of digits allowed for selection in the ISPBX. For the MSN supplementary service, on the other hand, there will be a fixed number of digits for terminal selection per service provider.

6.10.5   Terminal portability (TP)

Terminal portability is described as a draft **European Telecommunications Standard (ETS)** under ETSI number T/NA1(89)17. Terminal portability allows the transfer of a terminal from one connection point to another on the same ISDN basic interface during a **conversation**. This cannot take place during the call build up phase. It is possible not only to move a terminal, but also to replace the terminal by another one on the same contact point and then continue the original communication.

Chapter 7

Mobile communications

7.1 Introduction

In the section on networks we explained the main differences between mobile subscribers and subscribers connected by wire. This chapter gives further, more detailed information on radio communication, satellite communication and on specific systems for mobile communication that are the focus of attention today. Separate sections are devoted to two of them, DECT and GSM.

Where the use of wire is impossible or clumsy the use of electromagnetic waves offers a good solution. **Electromagnetic waves** travel through air, our atmosphere and even through the vacuum of space. The best-known representative of electromagnetic waves to us is **light**. We are able to receive the electromagnetic waves of a specific wavelength range by our sensors, our eyes. Thus, we are familiar with most of the properties of electromagnetic waves: waves travel in straight lines, they can be reflected, they can be bent by inhomogeneous media and they can be attenuated by certain media.

The main drawback of the use of radio waves is that the same medium must be used by all participants. With wired communication each group of participants or even each participant can use his own wire. Not only the wanted participants use the common medium but even unwanted sources emit signals on the medium. Examples of these are lightning, sparks caused by electric trains and radiation from interstellar sources.

One method to distinguish different communications is by using different **carrier frequencies**. The actual signal is transmitted as a modulation of the carrier frequency. Further, it is possible to agree on the allocation of certain periods of the day that this same carrier frequency is used by different users. For signals with a low power or otherwise restricted range, it will be possible to reuse the frequencies at a safe distance. All these methods require a strict set of rules and careful allocation of frequency bands to interested parties (for example, aviation, defence, radio and TV broadcast) and assignment of frequencies and periods to individual communications. The international rules are agreed upon in the **International Telecommunications Union (ITU)** in Geneva and European matters are handled by the **European Radiofrequency Office (ERO)** in Copenhagen. All frequencies are registered by the **International Frequency Registration Board (IRFB)**.

Radio broadcasts are addressed to all parties that may receive the transmissions. These receivers could be stationary (**fixed stations**) as well as mobile. In this chapter, however, we concentrate on mobile subscribers that want to communicate with a particular party.

7.2   Propagation of electromagnetic waves

For all types of waves, mechanical waves in violin strings, acoustic waves in air or waves in electric conductors, the formula for the relation between wavelength (λ), frequency (f) and speed of propagation through the medium (V) is the same:

$$\lambda = \frac{V}{f}$$

The **speed of propagation of electromagnetic waves in free space** (C) is 3×10^8 m/s, so for electromagnetic waves the formula becomes:

$$\lambda = \frac{C}{f}$$

The **wavelength** (λ) is the distance the wave travels during one full cycle of the oscillation. Electromagnetic waves consist of two components, an electric field and a magnetic field. The moment of maximum electric potential coincides with the moment of minimum magnetic energy. The vector of the electric field is perpendicular to the vector of the magnetic field and both are perpendicular to the direction of travel of the wave (Figure 7.1).

The spectrum of frequencies and wavelengths of radio waves ends where infrared waves start (Table 7.1).

The propagation properties of electromagnetic waves are dependent on the frequency. We know that light waves do not pass without high attenuation through most physical objects like walls of houses, whereas

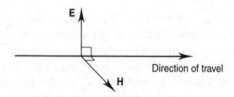

Figure 7.1 Electromagnetic wave vectors.

long radio waves are only slightly affected when passing through the same wall. For light waves it makes a vast difference to pass a wall or a window; for radio waves the difference is minor. On the other hand light is not significantly disturbed by wire netting, whereas certain radio waves are stopped by it. However, the free space characteristics are in principle the same. Waves originating from a point (or at least an object orders of magnitude smaller than the distances we consider) spread along straight lines and thus the distance between these lines grows in proportion to the

Table 7.1 The spectrum of electromagnetic waves.

Frequency	Abbr. name	Name	Wavelength	Name
3–30 kHz	VLF	Very low frequency	100–10 km	
30–300 kHz	LW	Long waves	10–1 km	Kilometric waves
300–3000 kHz	MW	Medium waves	1–0.1 km	
3–30 MHz	SW	Short waves	100–10 m	
30–300 MHz	VHF	Very high frequency	10–1 m	Metric waves
300–3000 MHz	UHF	Ultra high frequency	100–10 cm	
3–30 GHz	SHF	Super high frequency	10–1 cm	Centimetric waves
30–300 GHz	EHF	Extreme high frequency	10–1 mm	Millimetric waves
1000–300 000 GHz		Infrared light	300–0.7 μm	
Around 500 000 GHz		Visible light	0.7–0.4 μm	
Above 1 000 000 GHz		Ultraviolet light	0.4–0.000 01 μm	

distance from the point of emission. The energy of the wave spreads over
an area, in a plane perpendicular to the direction of travel, that grows
with the square of the distance. Consequently, the energy that is available
per square metre (energy density) decreases with the square of the
distance. Since the energy is proportional to the square of the electric
field strength, the voltage decreases proportionally to the distance itself.
The **attenuation** is measured in **decibels (dB)** (one tenth of the rarely used
bel) and is defined as follows:

$$\text{Attenuation} = 10 \log \frac{Pt}{Pd} \text{ (dB)}$$

where *Pt* is the power radiated from a source, for example the transmitting antenna, in a certain direction, and *Pd* the power received at a
distance, for example by a standard antenna. Thanks to the log definition
of the attenuation, decibels can be added to calculate total attenuation,
for example, of the antenna and the free space path. It is useful to
remember that a power ratio of 2 corresponds with an attenuation of
3 dB, and doubling of the free space distance implies a power ratio of 4,
or 6 dB attenuation.

Table 7.2 gives some more precalculated results. Just as a cable,
free space is characterized by its characteristic resistance, this being
120π ohms. The strength of the electric field (*E*) in V/m follows
from:

$$E^2 = P \times 120\pi \quad (P \text{ in W/m}^2)$$

Table 7.2 The relation between power ratio and decibels.

Power ratio	Voltage ratio	Decibels	Remarks
1.00	1.00	0	No attenuation
1.02	1.01	0.1	
1.26	1.22	1	
1.58	1.26	2	
2.0	1.41	3	Power ratio 2 = 3 db
2.51	1.58	4	
3.16	1.78	5	
3.98	2.0	6	Power ratio 4 = 6 db
5.01	2.24	7	
6.31	2.51	8	
7.94	2.82	9	
10	3.16	10	(log 10 = 1)
100	10	20	(log 100 = 2)
1000	31.62	30	
10 000	100	40	

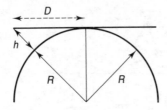

Figure 7.2   Line-of-sight.

7.2.1   Line-of-sight

Light follows an almost perfect straight line and thus the curvature of the earth limits the view of the light source on a part of the globe without mountains. This **line-of-sight (LOS)** can be approximated with the help of Pythagoras $(A^2 + B^2 = C^2)$ (Figure 7.2).

$$D^2 + R^2 = R^2 + 2RH + h^2$$

where

> D = distance between transmitter and receiver in km
> R = radius of the earth, being 6375 km
> h = height of the source of emission (or alternatively the receiver) in km

When h is small compared with D, generally a fair assumption, then h^2 can be ignored. Thus

$$D^2 = 2 \times 6375h = 13\,750h$$

For radio waves with frequencies near to those of light this calculation is close to reality. For lower frequencies the waves follow a curved path, bent slightly downwards towards the earth. This is caused by the index of refraction of the normal lower atmosphere (troposphere), which decreases with height.

For UHF waves we can calculate the practical line-of-sight by substituting 4/3 times the earth's radius in the formula. With long waves the line-of-sight disappears since the waves can follow the curvature of the earth. This makes long waves suitable for long distance communication.

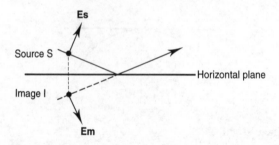

Figure 7.3   The reflection of a vertically polarized wave at a horizontal plane.

7.2.2   Reflection of radio waves

The **reflection** of radio waves is similar to the reflection of light waves. Both are electromagnetic waves and have much in common. Radio waves as well as light waves can be **polarized** in a certain direction or the polarization can be circular. Polarization plays a role during reflection of waves. The polarization of a wave is called vertical when the electric field oscillates in a vertical plane. When this type of wave hits a horizontal reflecting plane, the mirror, at a small angle (see Figure 7.3) then the wave continues its path after the reflection as if it originated from a point (I) at the same distance under the mirror as the real source (S) is above the mirror. The vertical electrical field vector (**Es**) at the source is mirrored as well (**Em**). This constitutes a 180 degree phase shift of the electrical component of the wave after reflection.

With **horizontal polarization** the reflection on a horizontal plane does not alter the phase of the electrical component since the electrical vector is parallel to the mirror and remains parallel. This is as you see a mirror image in a mirror. Of course the same phenomena occurs with a vertical reflecting plane. Vertically polarized waves do not change the phase of the electrical field whereas horizontally polarized waves do.

7.2.3   Interference of radio waves

A receiving antenna will generally not only receive the direct wave straight from the sending antenna but many more signals. Particularly, when these other signals are of the same frequency but opposite phase, the signal strength will decrease and may even decrease so much that the signal becomes weaker than other disturbing signals, the noise. Since mobile radio should provide its service everywhere and the environment, with mountains, buildings, and moving objects, is a given factor, it is not easy to avoid the adverse effects of **interference** completely.

Interfering signals of exactly the same frequency in most cases originate from the same source but reach the receiver along different paths. This is the case when reflecting objects are located near the path of the direct connection. In the case that all the objects, including the sending antenna and the receiving antenna, do not move, the received signal may be improved by the reflections, or may be weakened or even undetectable. The moment at least one of the parties moves, the path differences change and alter the situation favourably or unfavourably. AM speech connections show this alteration by changing loudness of the speech at the receiver. This is called **fading**.

Although the additional paths to the receiver cause a lot of trouble, they are helpful in the case that the direct path is interrupted by, for example, a building. Now the connection can only be kept in operation by the waves received through reflections. These reflected waves may very well be of comparable strength and thus cause heavy fading during moving.

Radio waves transmitted by a vehicle moving towards or away from the receiver will not receive exactly the same frequency as that of the transmitter. This effect is called the **Doppler effect**. The Doppler effect is well known for its influence on sound waves. The frequency of the sound heard from an approaching source of noise is higher, and that of the disappearing source, lower. This is easily noticed for fast moving vehicles like aeroplanes and racing cars. The same phenomena is present with radio waves. The influence of the Doppler effect with high speeds, such as with low earth orbit (LEO) satellites, cannot be ignored in the receiver design. With personal communications from a handheld set the speed is generally too low to cause any detrimental influence on the frequency stability. With fast cars some care must be taken in the design to allow for the change of frequency caused by the Doppler effect. The formula for the received frequency F_r when a transmitter is moving with a speed V towards the receiver is as follows:

$$F_r = F[1 + V/C]$$

In this formula C is the speed of the propagation of the radio wave, and here is taken equal to the speed of light. The frequency shift $F_s = F_r - F = F \times V/C$. So for higher frequencies the frequency shift becomes larger. This can be a reason to opt for a system with a large bandwidth for the transmission of a number of channels in TDM instead of a system with a number of small bandwidth channels each carrying one channel.

Interference of radio waves of different transmitters operating on the same frequency is called **co-channel interference**. The shortage of frequencies and the increasing demand for mobile communication forces the adoption of a small **reuse distance** when operating at the same frequency. With analogue transmission even a rather weak signal from a remote transmitter (compared to the wanted signal) disturbs speech considerably. Using digital transmission is favourable in this respect.

7.3   Long distance radio communication

The generation of stable high frequencies was a technological problem in the previous century. With heavy electromechanical generators, very similar to electric power generators for the mains supply, radio waves with frequencies up to a few hundred kHz, but with high power, were generated. Today we call the high frequencies of that time very low and low frequencies.

After **Marconi** made the first radiotelegraphic connection over the Atlantic in 1901, it took only nine years to see the first mobile receiver in an aircraft. In World War II submarines received their instructions, even submerged in the ocean, over large distances by **long wave radio**. The number of low frequency channels that exists is however very limited, so growth of long wave communication was severely restricted and could not meet the demand.

Further developments with electronic solutions for the generation of frequencies allowed the use of **medium waves**. They became very popular for radio broadcasts.

Trials with still higher frequencies showed that reception of the transmissions became impossible at distances somewhat further than the line-of-sight. This decreased the hope that **short waves** could be used to bridge the same distances as long waves. Amateurs, however, discovered that their transmissions were received very far beyond the horizon and indeed not close to the line-of-sight. How could this be explained?

7.3.1   Short wave communication (HF)

Studies and tests proved that long distance reception of **short waves** (10–100 m, 3–30 MHz) depends entirely on sky waves reflected from the **ionosphere**. This is a region high above the earth's surface where the rarefied air is sufficiently ionized to reflect or absorb radio waves, depending on the free-electron density. This electron density depends on the position of the sun and the emission of UV light by the sun.

To make things still more complicated, **sunspot** activity with an 11-year activity cycle influences the UV radiation. And at least four different layers, each at its own height, can be distinguished: the **D-layer** at 50–90 km, the **E-layer** at about 110 km, the **F1-layer** at 175–250 km and the **F2-layer** at 250–400 km.

Waves that approach the layers with a high angle pass the layer without reflection; only waves at a shallow angle reflect back to earth, and they reach the earth far beyond the line-of-sight. (See Figure 7.4.) This is the explanation for the zone around the line-of-sight without reception.

The earth has reasonably good reflection properties for short waves. This results in a second upward wave, which again will be

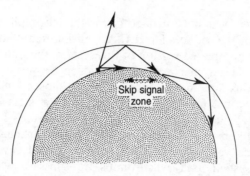

Figure 7.4 Simplified schematic explanation of the zone without reception.

reflected downward. This process can go on several times. We speak of a **multi-hop connection** in these cases. Under favourable conditions it is even possible to receive HF signals around the globe. An advantage of the HF band over the longer waves is that it offers much more frequency space for transmission channels than the lower frequency ranges. The range 3–30 MHz offers 27 MHz total bandwidth whereas the 3–30 kHz range offers only 27 kHz. The disadvantage of the HF frequencies is the bad transmission quality and dependence on conditions in the troposphere.

With high power the quality can be better, but it will still be necessary to change to a more favourable frequency from time to time. For speech, with its large information redundancy, HF offers periods of sufficient quality to understand the speakers. For hi-fi music the quality is not sufficient.

7.3.2 Telegraphy on HF channels

With HF telegraph transmission for teleprinting equipment, the quality is not sufficient to offer a service to the public. A person who pays for a service should get uncorrupted and completely readable information for his money. The public needed a better service, so a new method to handle telegraphy on HF channels was introduced in the USA. A 7-unit telegraph code was designed, by J.B. Moore and R.E. Mathes, known as the **Moore code**. This code is an error-detecting code of the **constant-ratio** type: 3 out of the 7 bits are 1 (or 0 if wanted in a particular channel). This code gives 35 usable combinations. Since teleprinters use a 5-unit code with 32 combinations, this leaves 3 combinations available. When an error was detected, the receiving side printed a special error symbol in place of the character received in error. An operator was later asked to repeat those telegrams that were unreadable because they contained too many errors.

This system was not satisfactory for the telegraph service, nor for the customers of the service. Dr H.C.A. van Duuren of the Dutch PTT invented a fully automated version of this system, the **Automatic ReQuest (ARQ)** system. This system was also based on a constant-ratio code of seven bits, but this time the combinations were chosen such that an easier translation between 5-unit code and 7-unit code was feasible. This code was internationally accepted by the ITU, CCIR (Rec. 342-2) and CCITT (Rec. S.13) and known as **International Telegraph Alphabet No. 3 (ITA3)**. The system was very successful since it combined several important features. The system used synchronous transmission whereas all telegraph systems based on 5-unit code used asynchronous transmission. This removed the problem of the creation of a series of errors when one start bit of the asynchronous system was corrupted during transmission. Further, it allowed the efficient use of the transmitters by combining four telegraph channels into one channel with time division multiplexing. This had the extra advantage that burst errors are spread over the telegraph channels, thus causing only single errors in each channel as long as the burst is not longer than four signals.

Further, detection of the quality of the received signals was introduced. Thus, characters containing suspect signals could be declared to be faulty.

In some situations two antennas could be used for so-called **diversity reception**, which allowed use of the least suspect signal. The detection of corruption of the received character results in an immediate automatic request for repetition. In view of the transmission delays, at least three characters should now be repeated. In modern data transmission terminology the block length is thus one character and the window size is three. The system operates with a fixed window size. A header per block is not needed so the transmission is highly efficient. All the error control methods together resulted in a system that provided HF telegraph channels of equal or better quality than landlines. In 1947 the first error-protected HF telegraph circuit was started between Amsterdam in the Netherlands and Berne in Switzerland.

The switched telegraph network for the public, the telex network, needed international circuits. A version of the van Duuren ARQ system allowing telex signalling (with two of the three extra combinations) was used for quick international extension of the telex network. This version of the system is known as the **TOR (Telex Over Radio) system**. TOR systems were also installed for mobile stations aboard ships. The ARQ system needs a full duplex connection. For ground stations it was general practice to use widely dispersed sites for reception and for transmission. This prevents heavy interference between both directions of a full duplex connection. On a ship this is not feasible. The **simplex TOR** was developed using alternate transmission and reception (on a per character basis) to solve this problem. This **simplex TOR** was, in addition, provided with the possibility to send forward error correcting codes. This mode of operation is used in cases where transmission is prohibited (in many harbours) so error requests cannot be sent, or in cases where sending error requests is unwanted (in the case of broadcast messages).

7.3.3 VHF communication

The still higher frequencies of the VHF range (30–300 MHz, 1–10 m wavelength) are not reflected in the ionosphere so are not suitable for direct long distance communication. Here, the line-of-sight is the limit. Only with high power, using scattering of the rays by objects or particles in the air, is it possible to extend the range of VHF transmissions to a maximum in the order of 1000 km. We call this **extended range VHF**. The development of telecommunication satellites in space created new possibilities for long distance communications. This is the subject of the next section.

7.4 Satellite communication

Satellite communication uses frequencies that can pass through the ionosphere without high attenuation and without reflection. The centimetric waves in the range 3–0 GHz are suitable for this type of communication. At much higher frequencies, rain and snow severely attenuate propagation in the troposphere. The free space attenuation in the centimetre range is so high that it is not sufficient to mount a passive reflector on the satellite: high amplification before the signals are returned to earth is essential. This causes a second problem. When even a very small fraction of the high powered transmission from the satellite is received by the highly sensitive receiver in the same satellite, this causes continuous oscillation. This problem is solved by using different frequency ranges for transmission and reception at the satellite.

7.4.1 Geosynchronous satellites

The first communication satellites started around 1962 with channels for telephony and for TV broadcast. They were of the geosynchronous type. **Geosynchronous satellites** rotate around the earth above the equator with a rotation speed of one revolution per day. This has the effect that they appear to be stationary when seen from an earth station. Consequently, they are also referred to as **geostationary satellites**. The fact that they appear to be motionless is very convenient because it eliminates the need to reposition the receiving and transmitting antennas.

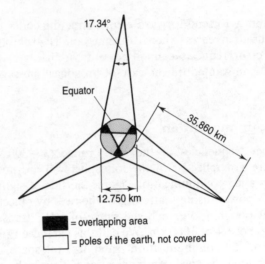

Figure 7.5   The footprints of geostationary satellites.

Geosynchronous operation is only possible at a height of about 36 000 km above the equator. Only three satellites are needed to almost completely cover the earth's surface. See Figure 7.5. Only areas at the north and south poles are not covered. The area covered by the satellite and reached by its radio beams is called the **footprint** of the satellite on the earth.

Initially only low power was available in the satellites. This implied the use of large-size parabolic antennas of more than 10 metres in diameter at the ground stations. A few years later the available power in satellites increased and smaller ground station antennas of about 1 metre in diameter could be used; they are called **Very Small Aperture Antennas (VSAT)**. This made it possible for larger organizations to install private networks with their own VSAT earth stations. They rented either channels in the satellite or a whole **transponder**, a set of directional antennas and an amplifier in the satellite.

In 1982 the **International Maritime Satellite Organization (Inmarsat)** service became operational. Inmarsat was originally exclusively intended for communication of several ground stations with ships at sea, for the improvement of safety. This service operates in the **L-band (1.5–1.6 GHz)** and **C-band (4–6 GHz)**. Although a geosynchronous satellite is stable, the earth station on a ship is not. The antenna (often a 90 cm parabolic antenna) is mounted on a stabilized platform and is provided with autotrack facilities. This enables the antenna to remain pointing at the satellite despite ship movements. The **Inmarsat C service** is capable of serving earth stations on trucks driving all over the world. With higher power in the satellite and the use of a limited bandwidth the antenna size could be significantly reduced. An omnidirectional antenna can be used for small bandwidth applications (low speed text, data or very efficiently coded voice), thus avoiding the complication of a stabilized platform. For road and maritime traffic applications the communications facility is usually integrated with a system that provides accurate (about 20 m accuracy) information on the position of the vehicle on earth by use of a **Global Positioning System (GPS)**. For aircraft the use of mobile communication poses more problems than for road vehicles. The installed antennas must not increase the drag of the aircraft. This requires very specialized antenna designs and the gain of these antennas is not optimal. This causes the received signals to be rather error prone, and adequate error control methods must be applied. A further problem is the shift of the frequency due to movement of the aeroplane. This so-called **Doppler effect** is much more pronounced than with surface vehicles. It requires adequate measures in the electronic equipment. The harm from multipath effects by reflected additional waves reaching the moving receiver in road vehicles or ships is less harmful than the reflections received by an aeroplane from the ground. They cause 50–200 Hz fading at normal flight speeds.

7.4.2 Medium earth orbit (MEO) and low earth orbit (LEO) satellites

The use of **Medium Earth Orbit** (MEO) and **Low Earth Orbit** (LEO) satellites (see Figure 7.6) for mobile communications is planned for operational introduction around the year 2000. The advantages of medium and low orbit satellites are:

(1)   The attenuation of the free space path is considerably lower because of the much smaller distance to the earth. Thus antennas at earth stations do not need to be directional, and are suitable for mobile applications; also, the power required in the transmitters is much lower. This lower power is an essential requirement to enable the use of radio handsets. Higher power requirements would result in the need for large and heavy batteries, not very convenient in a handset. It is also not certain that it is completely safe to operate with high powered transmitters in handsets so close to the human brain.

(2)   The footprints of the satellite antennas are smaller. Many more satellites with many more footprints are needed to cover the earth. Since the MEO or LEO satellites do not necessarily rotate in the plane of the equator it is possible to serve the polar zones. Beams with non-adjacent footprints can reuse the same set of frequencies. This increases the capacity significantly.

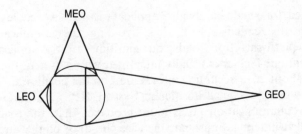

Figure 7.6 MEO and LEO satellites.

Since a larger capacity is required to service the increasing demand for mobile radio, and this demand cannot exclusively be answered by terrestrial solutions, it will be necessary to introduce MEO and/or LEO satellites.

There are, however, several obstacles. For each altitude it is possible to calculate the corresponding satellite rotation speed needed to keep it in the circular track around the earth. With lower flying satellites the stronger gravitational force can only be compensated by a larger centrifugal force, resulting from a higher rotational speed. With this higher rotational speed the period necessary to perform one cycle is reduced from 24 hours for the Geosynchronous Earth Orbit (GEO) satellites to less than two hours for LEO satellites. The relation is given in graphical form in Figure 7.7.

The high speed of the satellite implies a necessity to hand over standing connections to other satellites quite frequently. This hand-over occurs between two paths that differ in length. It requires complicated actions, in most cases including the selection of different frequencies or time slots. It is not acceptable that a satellite which should

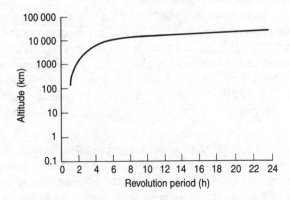

Figure 7.7 The relation between altitude and cycle time of satellites in a circular track.

Table 7.3 1995 proposed plans for a mobile satellite service.

Name/ organization	Number of satellites/ satellite type	Number of orbit planes	Altitude (km)	Modulation method	Multiplexing method
InmarsatP/ Inmarsat	10 MEO				CDMA
Odyssey/ TRW	12 MEO		10 354	QPSK	CDMA on 4 FD channels of 4.83 MHz bandwidth
Globalstar/ LoralQualcomm	48 LEO	8	1401	QPSK	CDMA on 16.5 MHz bandwidth
Iridium/ Motorola	66 LEO	6	784	QPSK	FDMA and TDMA
Teledesic/ Craig McCaw	840 LEO				CDMA

QPSK = Quadrature Phase Shift Keying
CDMA = Code Division Multiple Access
FDMA = Frequency Division Multiple Access
TDMA = Time Division Multiple Access

take over the connection is busy on all its channels and thus cannot accept the handover during the connection. From statistical calculations it follows that the average traffic load should be kept low to be able to guarantee a handover without problems. The lower the altitude of the satellite, the higher the speed and consequently the stronger the Doppler effect. Thus LEO satellites will need technically sophisticated solutions to overcome the above problems. They also require the largest number of satellites and ground stations.

Five companies have offered solutions to the **Federal Communications Commission (FCC)** in the USA since 1990 to become licensed for a **Mobile Satellite Service (MSS)**. Two of them offered MEO solutions, three LEO systems. Some of the characteristics of the systems offered are given in Table 7.3.

The bandwidth that is internationally allocated to the MSS is rather restricted; 1.610–1.6265 GHz and 2.4835–2.5 GHz are available. To use the available bandwidth efficiently all proposed systems opt for digital transmission and **Quadrature Phase Shift Keying (QPSK)** as the modulation method. QPSK uses four different phase positions in its transmission, leading to a double bit rate in about the same bandwidth compared with modulation systems with only two different positions.

The **Bit Error Rate (BER)** in the given situation of low power transmitters, multipath effects and high attenuation is not very low. A minimum of **Forward Error Control (FOC)** is needed: depending on the application and on the position on earth, other error control methods may be needed.

The most widely advocated multiplexing method to derive the required channels is **Code Division Multiple Access (CDMA)**. CDMA uses a set of frequencies in a sequence. The choice of current channel is dictated by a code, only available at the sender and receiver. CDMA is frequently used in the USA for terrestrial mobile systems. For these terrestrial systems CDMA was an optimum choice, since it is one of the few systems that can be introduced in a frequency band that is already used by several others and where no own-frequencies are available. CDMA is chosen in military applications because it uses many frequencies in sequence so it cannot be disturbed by malicous interference on a particular frequency, nor can it be tapped without first breaking the code. For all applications it is important that the multipath effects are quite different for the several frequencies used. This offers the advantage that the connection is never continuously disturbed by a serious multipath problem. Of course one cannot expect a very good quality (low BER) circuit with this system, unless stringent error detection and correction is applied.

All proposed systems plan to interface to terrestrial networks, in particular the **Public Switched Telephone Network (PSTN)**. Traffic between mobile stations, often handheld Mobile Sets (MS) that operate through different satellites and ground stations are connected via the PSTN. Only Iridium can perform direct satellite-to-satellite communications. For this purpose it uses 25 Mbit/s datalinks between satellites operating in the frequency band 22.55–23.53 MHz. These high frequencies can be used since the waves do not pass through the troposphere, with its very high attenuation at these frequencies. Not only regular traffic is handled on these datalinks but also coordination between satellites for the handovers and set-up of calls. The Iridium system needs very sophisticated equipment in the satellites for these functions. The possibility to bypass the terrestrial network may be seen as a political drawback by governments that do not want bypassing of their national telecom organizations. All other proposers stress the fact that they want to complement the terrestrial services and not to compete with them. The satellites cannot stop their rotation at national borders, so international agreements will be necessary. Iridium may therefore have to face international opposition.

A major technical problem is that it will not be possible to combine the FDMA/TDMA multiplexing of Iridium with the CDMA multiplexing method of the other systems within one frequency band.

7.5 Medium distance mobile communications

The restriction in distance due to the line-of-sight limitation with VHF and UHF frequencies is not only a disadvantage; it can be an advantage since it gives the possibility of reusing the same frequencies in another area outside the line-of-sight without any mutual interference. Restriction of the power of the transmitter can further reduce the acceptable reuse distance.

Medium distance mobile radio communications can be used in two different ways. It can be used for operations restricted to an area covered by the medium distance communications or it can be used to access a longer distance communications network that may extend worldwide if required. This longer distance network can be a private network or a public network. Following the sequence of events as they took place historically, we start with the medium distance mobile communications for operations in a restricted area, and with systems that use a private network to extend the area of operations. All these systems are intended for use by a limited group of persons, not by the general public. The name **Private Mobile Radio (PMR)** is used for these systems.

7.5.1 Private mobile radio (PMR)

A very high demand for mobile radio exists in the area of command and control of a group of mobile people with a common operational goal. This goal can vary from the extinguishing of a fire, the saving of human life, catching criminals, to collecting and delivering freight or passengers.

Common to all these activities is that they need coordination and are restricted to a group of persons active in a limited area. Generally the use of speech is preferred. It is an advantage that all group members are informed about the situation, so all mobile stations may receive information from a control station as well as answers from mobile stations. In this situation the simple technique of a system with only one frequency for transmitted and received information is adequate. Such a system is called a **simplex system**. Only one transmitter should send at a time and one person could be in charge to coordinate the use of the single common frequency. At the moment of transmitting, the own receiver should be switched off to prevent too strong a signal at this receiver. For these reasons the hand-held microphone includes a send–receive switch that has its rest position in the receiving mode of operation.

From a regulation point of view these systems are simple. Since they operate in a restricted area there is no need to specify the equipment nationally or internationally: it is only necessary to give rules to prevent interference with other users and to assign frequencies to the different operators. A consequence is that the number of different technical solutions for PMR in the world is very large. Most systems are designed for operation in an area with a radius of less than 30 km. Originally all systems were of the analogue type. Digital PMR systems will not play a major role before the year 2000.

The shortage of available frequencies and increasing demand for PMR forces the development of systems that use the available frequency band more efficiently. A step in the direction of more efficient use is the assignment of a **group** of frequencies to a larger number of operations or a large group of users, but coordination of the use of the frequencies becomes more difficult. Human coordination is generally simplified by the assignment of one frequency as the control channel. This system is acceptable for communications without urgency, and is used in **Citizens' Band (CB)** but is not acceptable for operations requiring very urgent communications. Human coordination has its advantages but cannot offer very high efficiency.

The next step is automation of the coordination of the use of the frequencies, systems using this automated control being known as **trunking systems**.

Trunking systems

Users in a system using trunking can gain access to every channel assigned to the system and therefore can use channels that are temporarily not used by other user groups. When the assignment system operates efficiently, this offers a better **Grade-Of-Service (GOS)** to users, even at high system loads. The GOS is the probability that a particular call cannot be established, and is the same as the ratio of the number of calls that cannot be established to the total number of attempts to make a call, measured during a long period. The difference between the efficiency of a trunking system and the use of single frequencies is rather striking. This can most effectively be shown by some examples of calculations, using Erlang tables.

Whereas mobile terminals in simplex systems operate on one single frequency for sending and receiving, trunking systems use a choice of several different frequencies for sending and receiving in the mobile station. Trunking systems can be divided into two types: decentralized and centralized systems. Two typical examples of these types of systems are described below.

Decentralized trunking systems handle the automated control completely in the mobile stations (MS). The MS equipment is continuously tuned to the reception on a particular channel, the control channel. An MS that wants to start a conversation places a call on this channel and scans the other channels to find an unused channel. The call on the control channel contains the identification of the calling equipment, the identification of the group to which the caller belongs and the number of the channel that has been found free. Other MSs analyse the received identity

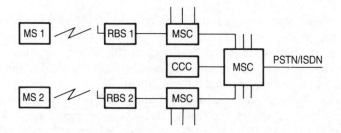

Figure 7.8 A typical simple trunking system with centralized control.
MSC   Mobile Switching Centre; CCC   Computers Control Centre

of the group to which the caller belongs. When they belong to the group, they all switch to reception on the indicated channel.

Centralized trunking systems control the traffic by central computer facilities. Central control offers important advantages. The network can be extended to cover many sites, each with its own **Radio Base Station (RBS)**. The traffic between sites is handled on a network connecting the RBSs, in most cases by land lines. This system organization enables MS 1, operating with RBS 1 (see Figure 7.8) to establish a call to MS 2, operating with RBS 2. A further possibility is that MS 1 travels to the area covered by RBS 2 and can now contact RBS 2 to establish a call.

The centralized control can handle the calling MS in all areas provided that is the wish of the user. It is more difficult to handle a call **destined** for an MS that travels from area to area. Mobile stations that travel from their home area to other areas are called **roamers** in the host area. The central control registers the fact that a roamer placed a call in a particular area and uses this knowledge to send the call for the roaming MS through the RBS that the MS contacted the previous time. When the MS detects that the signals on the control channel of its home RBS have become very weak it may switch to the control channel of the next RBS and place an automatic call to this RBS, to inform the central control of the need to handle further calls through this host RBS. Centralized trunking systems can be extended to cover a whole nation. These systems are generally somewhat more complex, and include hundreds of RBSs, many regional control stations and a national control station. For handling traffic between areas they make use of a complete private telephone network with several circuit switches. Such networks have different tariffs for subscribers that only use the facilities of one particular area, of a larger region, or of the whole country. It is understandable that a certain degree of standardization of the equipment in such a large system is required. The UK standard **MPT 1327** became popular outside the UK.

Most trunking systems use duplex operation between the **control station (CS)** and an MS, using one frequency from control station to MS and another from MS to control. This allows for quick response to commands from the control station and eliminates switching from receiving to sending and vice versa. Generally the system uses special control channels for the exchange of control information for the assignment of frequency channels to individual calls.

Most present systems use digital signalling (typically with fast frequency shift keying at 1200 bit/s) and analogue speech on 25 kHz, or newer systems on 12.5 kHz channels in frequency bands allocated differently in the various nations. In the UK the former black-and-white TV channel **Band Three (174–225 MHz)** was used to cater for 140 frequency channels for the nationwide trunked **Advanced Mobile COmmunication Network (AMCON)** in 1987.

For the future a group in the **European Telecommunications Standards Institute (ETSI)** has prepared a new standard for trunked PMR based on fully digital signalling, voice and data handling. The system will have many similarities with the **Global Mobile System (GSM)**, aimed at the public mobile service, but will offer many special features that are available in present-day analogue PMR systems. The system, the **Trans-European Trunked RAdio (TETRA)** system, aims at larger cell size, entailing lower frequencies than GSM, and handling according to several priorities to cater for emergency services. It also provides for group calls, general broadcast and conferencing. To be able to introduce the new system in the present frequency bands, alongside existing analogue systems, the bandwidth of the channels is chosen at 25 kHz. To attain more channels in the same bandwidth the 25 kHz band will be used to provide four channels in time division. Similar to GSM, the TETRA system will also give access to public networks.

7.5.2   Public land mobile networks (PLMN)

Public networks, in particular the PSTN, want to give their subscribers access to mobile stations and mobile subscribers access to the non-mobile ones. The technical provisions needed are similar to those required in the private mobile networks. A difference is that public services should be offered to a whole nation and should preferably not be offered exclusively to a small group of users in a small area. So these public systems aim at coverage of the whole country, or at least a high percentage of it. This requires large investment, long before the number of subscribers is large enough to generate sufficient income to pay for the actual costs. To keep investments low, public networks started with a low number of large cells and gradually evolved to smaller cells with many more transmitters. The trend towards smaller cell sizes coincides with the trend to higher frequencies. The limitation of the number of frequency channels available for the **Public Land Mobile Network (PLMN)** leads to the use of smaller cell sizes, since they enable reuse of the same frequencies at a much larger scale. PMR systems are mainly used for operational control of vehicles on the road. The messages exchanged are as short as possible. The information exchanged in public systems tends to be of a completely different nature. The parties on the PSTN are used to long conversations, contrary to the more efficient commands on the PMR, so PLMN will see much longer call durations. Therefore PLMN will need more channels than PMR, and must eventually go to smaller cell sizes to cater for the required traffic volume (expressed in Erlangs).

Since cars do not stop at national frontiers and development costs of new sophisticated systems are very high, these new systems tend to be used in more than just one nation. For instance, the **Nordic Mobile Telephone** (**NMT**) system, designed for the Nordic countries (Sweden, Norway, Finland, Denmark) was implemented in Germany, Austria and The Netherlands as well. The first NMT system, the NMT 450 system, operating in the 450 MHz band, started in 1981. It was followed by the 900 MHz band system NMT 900 in 1986.

CCITT started around that time to specify a standard for worldwide application, called GSM.

7.6   Global system for mobile communications (GSM) and digital cellular system (DCS 1800)

GSM was named after the CCITT group that did the work, the Groupe Special Mobile (GSM). Later on the wish to make it a world standard was expressed by the name change to **Global System for Mobile communications** (**GSM**). GSM is accepted in Europe and several countries outside Europe as the international standard for modern public mobile systems, but the US and Japan have developed their own standards. In the USA the US Digital Cellular (USDC) standard is promoted; in Japan the Personal Digital Cellular (PDC) system is chosen. Since GSM equipment appeared earlier on the market than the Japanese and US systems several US carriers and most Asiatic countries have adopted GSM. Thus GSM has a coverage that is unsurpassed by any other system.

GSM is basically a medium distance system but has the capability to evolve to a system operating with smaller cell sizes as well. In the smaller cells, lower power is used. The smaller cells enable reuse of the same set of frequencies at a shorter distance, so are capable of handling more calls in the same area. This may be needed in dense areas. A further development of GSM, particularly for use in areas with higher density traffic, is the **Digital Cellular System DCS 1800**. It operates in the 1800 MHz frequency band instead of the 900 MHz frequency band.

The aims specified for GSM are:

- a system for both voice and data
- a system that can operate as an extension to the ISDN
- a high grade of service, a good speech quality
- a high capacity system, capable of operation in high density areas (aim 25 erlang/km^2)
- fully automatic and international roaming
- an open system; the interfaces are standardized such that, for example, handsets of one supplier should be able to operate with the infrastructure supplied by a different supplier
- a worldwide system (allowing worldwide roaming and large scale manufacturing).

Based on these aims the CCITT group decided to specify digital transmission for voice and signalling and the use of Time Division Multiplexing (TDM).

7.6.1   Digital transmission and TDM

Digital transmission offers many advantages over analogue transmission for GSM:

- Digital transmission remains unaffected by low signal-to-noise ratios as compared to analogue transmission. It allows for small reuse distances and thus high efficiency of use of the available frequencies.
- Digital transmission can be encrypted for privacy reasons.
- TDM and digital transmission fit together very well.
- For efficiency reasons a low bit rate method of voice coding (linear predictive coding) is chosen at 13 kbit/s. Later developments provide high quality coding methods operating at 6.5 kbit/s. This lower speed coding can be fitted in the TDM time frame later on without major problems. With systems using one channel per frequency, the doubling of the number of frequencies in the same frequency band would not be practicable. The width of the frequency channels is too small; it requires very high frequency stability and extremely small margins between frequency channels. It is very difficult to make such a system resistant to the frequency shifts due to the Doppler effect. GSM made the choice for a channel carrier spacing of 200 kHz. In these channels 8 TDM

speech channels of 16 kbit/s (voice + signalling) can be accommodated, or alternatively 16 channels of 8 kbit/s. For data and fax 9600 bit/s channels can be provided.

● TDM offers many channels on one frequency and thus offers a saving in the number of transmitters and receivers required in the base stations.

7.6.2   GSM characteristics

● The digital channels
  – Carrier frequency spacing 200 kHz.
  – Digital transmission bit rate 270 kbit/s.
  – Modulation: Gaussian Minimum Shift Keying (GMSK).
  – Coding of speech: linear predictive coding at 13 kbit/s or 6.5 kbit/s.
  – TDM: 8 full-rate channels of 16 kbit/s or 32 half-rate channels of 8 kbit/s.
  – Mobile station (MS) transmits in the band 890–915 MHz.
  – MS receives in the band 925–960 MHz.
  – Each pair of receive and transmit frequencies forming a full duplex channel has frequencies at a spacing of 45 MHz.

● Power saving measures
  – Voice Activity Detection/Discontinuous Transmission (VAD/ DTX): no transmission during silence or background noise only.
  – Power level control: when close to the base station the transmission power is reduced. For this facility the received power is measured and the base station is informed.
  – The use of small cells allows for low power transmissions.

● Services
  – The GSM system is designed to provide a large number of services and facilities. Not every handset will, however, be able to offer these functions to the user.

● Basic services
  – Telephony.
  – Short Message Service (SMS); a message of max. 180 characters can be transmitted in the signalling information.
  – Fax group 3 (up to 9600 bit/s).
  – Data up to 9600 bit/s.
  – Emergency calls.

- Basic features
  - Encryption on the radio channel for privacy.
  - Calling line identification provision (CLIP).
  - International roaming and automatic handover during calls.
  - Personal identification with a Subscriber Identification Module (SIM), a card that should be inserted in the GSM handset. With this card other handsets in other countries can be used; the billing is performed on the basis of the personal ID.
  - Equipment identification: this allows for blocking the use of stolen handsets.

- Supplementary services
  - Closed user groups.
  - Call forwarding.
  - Call hold.
  - Multiparty calls.
  - Advice of charge.
  - Subscriber control of call acceptance.

7.6.3   The GSM infrastructure

In the past most mobile systems were standardized by specifying the **air interface**, that is the radio interface between the mobile station and the radio base station. For GSM the CCITT went much further by specifying functional subsystems and protocols at several reference points. This is rather similar to the way the ISDN was specified. The SS No. 7 protocol plays an important role in the specifications of the GSM infrastructure. The GSM infrastructure has the task of receiving calls from mobile and regular PSTN or ISDN subscribers and providing connections to the proper destinations over the existing public networks or specialized links for mobile traffic (direct connections MSC–MSC, see Figure 7.9). This GSM infrastructure is intended to handle all future traffic between mobile and fixed subscribers. It handles traffic from person to person, not from subscriber connection to subscriber connection as the PSTN and ISDN do. It is a **Personal Communications Network** or **PCN**.

Such a network requires a special numbering plan; both persons and the extremities of the network should have an identification number. The person's number is called the **MSISDN number**; **Mobile Subscribers ISDN number**. The mobile subscriber may travel around somewhere in the home country or even abroad.

How to reach this roaming subscriber? Somewhere the knowledge of his whereabouts should be registered, otherwise reaching this subscriber is impossible. The place where the knowledge is registered is the **Home Location Register (HLR)** of this subscriber. The database system containing the HLR can maintain records for a large number of subscribers.

The first task when setting up a call is to find the proper HLR and the proper record of the wanted subscriber. This occurs on the basis of the MSISDN number. Now the HLR provides the information about the area where the subscriber can be found in the form of a (temporary) **Mobile Station Roaming Number (MSRN)**. The call is now rerouted on the basis of this MSRN and leads to the proper radio base station and a broadcast call to alert the called MS. But how did the HLR find out what MSRN to provide? The answer is that each area keeps a record of all the MSs it finds in its area in a **Visiting Location Register (VLR)**. It knows about visitors in its area when a visiting MS places a call itself, or when the MS sends a message indicating that it has passed the border of an area and has now entered this area. The MS can detect passing from one area to another or from one cell to another by reception of an identification code from a different radio base station. The VLRs update the HLRs by withdrawing the MSRN after becoming obsolete and assigning the proper new MSRN.

Figure 7.9 gives an impression of the architecture of the GSM infrastructure.

In Figure 7.9 we find the **Authentication Centre (AC)**, which verifies the identity of the subscriber to prevent unauthorized use of the system and plays a role in the encryption/decryption process. The **Equipment Identification Register (EIR)** can identify stolen or malfunctioning equipment. Very important for the GSM system is the **Operation and Maintenance System (OMS)** since this also registers the call details for later billing.

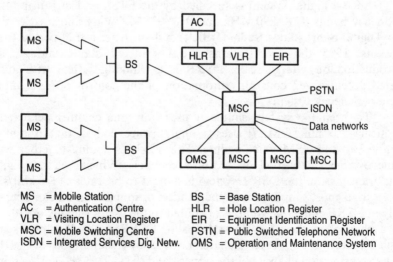

MS	= Mobile Station	BS	= Base Station
AC	= Authentication Centre	HLR	= Hole Location Register
VLR	= Visiting Location Register	EIR	= Equipment Identification Register
MSC	= Mobile Switching Centre	PSTN	= Public Switched Telephone Network
ISDN	= Integrated Services Dig. Netw.	OMS	= Operation and Maintenance System

Figure 7.9 The GSM infrastructure.

7.7   Local radio communications; Citizens' Band (CB) radio and digital short range radio (DSRR)

Private mobile radio finds its users among people from one organization who operate as a group on a common task. The operation could be restricted to a small area or in other cases a large area.

Public local radio communications finds its users among people who happen to be in the same area. In many cases local radio communications give them the possibility of helping each other in difficult situations or making appointments to meet people who are driving or living in the particular area where they are at that moment.

An important group in this category are truck drivers. Drivers of trucks of different organizations use the **Citizens' Band (CB) radio** to warn others of traffic jams, bad or blocked roads, speed control and to arrange for a stop together at the next restaurant. People living in the area may mix in the conversations to give further advice.

CB operates generally at the low end of the VHF band. CB radio uses a group of frequency channels. The human coordination of the use of the channels is simplified by the assignment of one of the channels as the control channel. The operation is **simplex** using the same frequency for sending and receiving as explained earlier (see Section 7.5.1). CB radio's main problem is the bad quality of the connection due to interference, particularly in dense areas. The analogue transmission is easily disturbed by other signals. A digital solution would cure this problem to a large extent. However, the main advantages of the system should be kept unchanged: its simplicity and thus its very low price and its easy introduction without licensing problems.

Such a digital system is specified by the ETSI, and in Europe two frequency bands (888–890 MHz and 933–935 MHz) are allocated to this new **Digital Short Range Radio (DSRR)** system. After a trial period from 1993 to 1995 the specifications are considered stable enough for introduction on a large scale. DSRR is a trunking system with auto-mated decentralized control. Automation of the control offers a much higher efficiency system.

To keep the system simple it uses only one channel per carrier frequency, so no TDM. It uses a digital voice coding that is almost identical to the GSM voice coding. This 13 kbit/s coding together with some overhead is carried on 16 kbit/s channels. When used for digital data transmission the DSRR system is limited to bit rates of 9.6 kbit/s.

In its most simple version the handset or mobile station can operate only in DSRR mode A. Mode A is limited to the use of **simplex** operation on a channel in the 933–935 MHz band. DSRR mode B allows **semi-duplex** operation on a receive channel in the lower band (888–890 MHz) and a transmission channel in the upper band (933–935 MHz). This semi-duplex mode of operation enables the use of repeater stations. Although

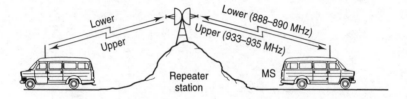

Figure 7.10   The use of a repeater station in DSRR.

repeater stations are not allowed to transmit with higher power than mobile stations (maximum 4 W), they can be equipped with higher and more sophisticated antennas. The repeater stations can therefore bridge larger distances and cover areas that are not reached by mobile transmitters. (See Figure 7.10.)

The mobile station transmits to the repeater station on a channel in the lower band. The repeater station uses a (paired) channel in the upper band. Mobile stations exclusively receive in the upper band. No mobile sets, either in mode A or in mode B, need to be capable of receiving in the lower band. This simplifies the design of the mobile station.

Mobile stations can be designed for mode A operation or for Mode B operation. Mobile stations can also be constructed for both mode A and B.

The DSRR system also allows the use of base stations, stations installed at a fixed location. They may also operate in mode A or B. Operating in mode B they will transmit on the receive frequency of the mobile stations. These base stations may offer interfaces to terrestrial (private) networks. No provisions are available in the mobile station to effect automatic handover when roaming, nor provisions for call charging.

When a mobile station initiates a call, it first searches for a free channel among the 79 **working channels**. Only after finding a free channel will the MS send a selective calling code on the **control channel**. The code may indicate a particular station, a specific type of users or all stations interested in the area. The MS will not find a free channel when the channels are fully loaded with conversations. The MS will then not access the control channel. This prevents any overload of the control system.

7.8   Short distance communication, CT, DECT and PHS

The radio communication systems discussed so far bridge distances in the order of at least a few kilometres. For the wireless extension of our telephone at home we need only to bridge distances of a few metres or, when in the garden, maybe one hundred metres. For this purpose

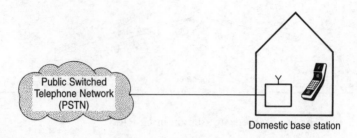

Figure 7.11   Mobile communications in the home. (Source: *Philips Telecommunication Review*, Vol. 51, No. 2.)

low powered, so-called **Cordless Telephones (CT)** are produced. (See Figure 7.11.)

The older CTs used analogue transmission and a simple design. This was adequate as long as you did not have neighbours with a CT as well. Not only could such neighbours listen to your conversations, but they also could establish calls through your base station at your expense.

Somewhat advanced CTs offered the possibility of selecting one out of a few frequencies. But this does not really cure the problems.

The real solution came with digital transmission and a sophisticated system for the automatic assignment of frequencies to new calls. Such a system needs standardization. The organization of European PTTs, CEPT, produced the standards CT1 and CT2. **CT1** offers automatic frequency assignment but is still an analogue system.

CT2 is digital and offers more privacy by encryption of the coded voice signal. CT2 is not only used as a cordless telephone at home but also promoted in several European countries for use as a 'cordless public pay phone'. In the neighbourhood of these so-called **Telepoints** the subscribers to this service can make calls on the public telephone network. The same CT used at home could be used for calls through a Telepoint.

The Telepoint service requires special provisions in the PSTN infrastructure to identify the caller and charge the subscriber for his calls. (See Figure 7.12.) Calls to Telepoint subscribers are not possible: the infrastructure does not keep track of the whereabouts of the subscriber.

The technically simple solution of adding a wide area paging receiver to the CT2 handset, supplying the number to be called back to the CT2 user, was not introduced until it was found that the growth of the Telepoint service was much slower than expected.

The CT2 system was accepted by ETSI as an interim solution until the time that the new system, **Digital European Cordless Telecommunications (DECT)**, appeared on the market. A competing system for CT2 and also for some applications of DECT is the **Japanese Personal Handyphone System (PHS)**. Outside Europe PHS is a serious competitor for DECT in a number of applications with low traffic requirements.

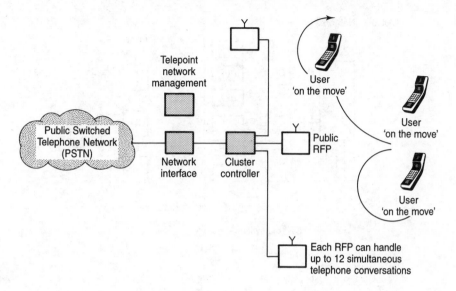

Figure 7.12   Schematic diagram of a Telepoint system. (Source: *Philips Telecommunication Review*, Vol. 51, No. 2.)

7.8.1   DECT

The DECT system is not like CT2, a system designed as a cordless telephone at home, but aims at a much wider set of applications. First, it is not designed for telephony only but for all applications proposed for the ISDN. Secondly, it covers not only the home application but also applications in the office environment (see Figure 7.13) and the Telepoint service.

The office environment can lead to severe mutual interference if the number of CTs is very high in a small area. The requirement may go up to about 10 000 erlang/km². No other system, GSM, CT2 or even PSH, comes even close to this figure, but DECT is designed to reach this. DECT is an access system; the specifications do not describe the infrastructure, like the GSM specifications do. Therefore DECT can be used to access different kinds of systems for different applications.

DECT can reach the high traffic-carrying capability by using microcells of 20–100 metres and a large number (12) of traffic channels offered per frequency channel by using time division. The frequency is further allocated dynamically from a pool of 10 frequency channels. The frequency/slot combination with the least interference is selected for a new call, but not only for a new call. When conditions change, for whatever reason, the handset initiates the changeover to a different frequency/slot combination. This so-called **handover** is generally to a different radio base station but could in certain cases be to the same radio base station. The

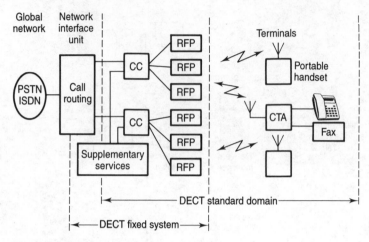

CTA = Cordless Terminal Adapter
RFP = Radio Fixed Part
CC = Cordless (Cluster) Controller

Figure 7.13   Functional concept for DECT in the office environment. (Source: *Philips Telecommunication Review*, Vol. 49, No. 3.)

DECT system takes the newly selected connection in use but does not immediately release the previous one. Temporarily two connections are used. This makes it possible to change over to the other connection, or back to the original again, without interruption of the traffic.

Other systems do not use two channels during a handover and do not provide a **seamless handover**. For systems with larger cells this is not a serious drawback, since the number of handovers will be low. In the DECT environment very frequent handovers can be expected because of the very small cell size and thus a seamless handover is essential.

In the office environment the radio waves will certainly not keep to a nice honeycomb-like cell pattern (this is true even in rural areas but in the office environment it is much worse). To lay out cells in clusters of seven, each cell with its own frequency, as is practised in rural areas for car telephony, does not provide the proper solution for the office environment. The problem of frequency and cell planning is alleviated in DECT by the dynamic assignment of frequencies. A frequency plan is not necessary, since each base station can select each frequency channel.

DECT is an FDMA/TDMA/TDD system, using 10 frequency channels and a time division scheme that offers 12 transmit channels and 12 receive channels. So DECT operates with **Time Division Duplex (TDD)**. (See Figure 7.14.)

The DECT system does not keep track of the location of the users except during a conversation in progress. When a call comes in from the network destined for a cordless set, the DECT system will broadcast

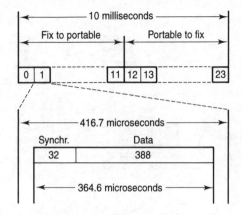

Figure 7.14 The structure of a DECT frame and time slot. (Source: *Philips Telecommunication Review*, Vol. 49, No. 3.)

the information about this call to up to 6000 users. The cordless set receiving the information will react if the call is for it. Then a path is set up to the most appropriate base station. Only for systems covering several sites will it be useful to provide a simple form of location register, keeping track of the site where the particular user is located at that moment. In an office system changes of site occur only rarely.

In countries with a low number of telephone subscribers we find few copper cables available for extension of the network. In these cases it will generally be more economic to provide new customers with mobile communication than to install new cables for the **local loop**. Both CT2 and DECT can be used in these cases. Two different solutions should be distinguished. The first solution is illustrated in Figure 7.15. The subscriber is provided with a Cordless Terminal Adapter (CTA) for connection of the telephone or data equipment in his home. A wireless connection using CT2 or DECT interfaces the CTA with the public network. By use of directional antennas in such a point-to-point

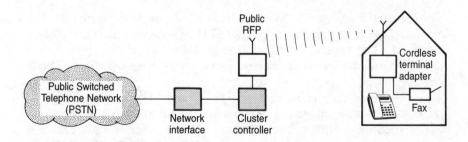

Figure 7.15 Wireless local loop without mobility. (Source: *Philips Telecommunication Review*, Vol. 51, No. 2.)

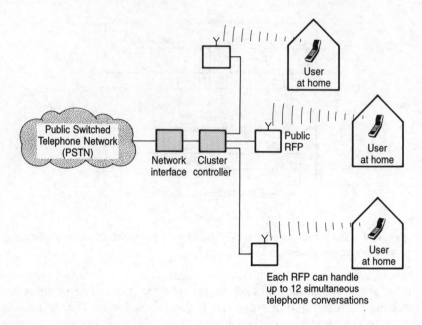

Figure 7.16   Wireless loop with mobility. (Source: *Philips Telecommunication Review*, Vol. 51, No. 2.)

case it is possible to bridge distances of over 1 kilometre with CT2 or DECT.

Particularly in areas with a large density of potential subscribers it will, however, be preferable to provide mobility to all subscribers as illustrated in Figure 7.16. In this case DECT will provide a much better grade of service than CT2, since each DECT base station or Radio Fixed Part (RFP) can handle 12 simultaneous calls instead of only one for CT2.

7.8.2   Personal Handyphone System (PHS)

The Personal Handyphone System (PHS) is a Japanese development. The air interface is standardized (RCR STD-28) as well as the network interfaces. The system is very similar to DECT in many respects, but differs considerably in some others. Table 7.4 gives an overview of these characteristics.

The main differences between DECT and PHS are the number of traffic channels per frequency channel and the more sophisticated hand-over procedure of DECT. The difference in the number of traffic channels is reflected in the required bit rate at the air interface. The lower bit rate of the PHS implies more immunity against multipath interference with large delay differences. On the other hand, DECT has a larger choice of

Table 7.4 A comparison between the characteristics of DECT and PHS.

System	DECT	PHS
Frequency band for private systems	1900 MHz	Same
Access technique	FDMA/TDMA/TDD	Same
Average power	10 mW	Same
Speech coding	ADPCM (ITU-G.721)	Same
Traffic channels per frequency channel	12	3 (+ 1 control channel)
Bit rate on air interface	1152 kbit/s	384 kbit/s
Modulation method	GMSK	$\pi/4$ QPSK
Handover latency	Up to 2200 ms	<50 ms

other channels not giving these interference problems. The number of simultaneous channels that a radio transmitter handles in the PHS system (3) is rather low. The handling of large traffic volumes results in a low probability of finding a free channel (see Section 10.4 and Figure 10.3). This is particularly annoying when it occurs during the handover of an ongoing conversation. DECT appears to be designed primarily for high density applications such as in the large office environment and for the local loop with mobility, whereas PHS appears to be designed primarily for lower density applications and very few handovers, such as at home and in the small business environment.

7.9 Wireless data

It can be useful and economically justified to connect fixed data equipment by wireless means to the infrastructure. Data equipment in remote locations far from the infrastructure and in locations where moving is not feasible are prime candidates for wireless connections. For mobile equipment wireless is the only possible method. Data equipment can be connected using wireless equipment designed for voice communication. The use of a modem and suitable error control protocols can provide a good connection for data transmission on speech connections. For some types of data transfer this may offer a satisfactory solution.

However, the infrastructure designed for speech uses circuit switching techniques and we know that for most types of data, packet switching techniques are more appropriate. The same considerations are valid in the wireless world. Systems designed for speech communication use a large overhead for signalling to enable call set-up, and for mobile operation also for handovers. This overhead is still relatively small compared to the large streams of bits needed for the coding of voice. But for short data messages this same signalling constitutes a relatively large overhead, which leads to avoidable delays and considerable waste of frequency spectrum. For interactive data communication the retention of a circuit during large intervals without any transmission demands a special solution. Modern systems like GSM try to cure this weakness of circuit switching systems but are unlikely to offer the same cost/performance as a system dedicated to data.

There exists a multitude of applications that need some form of data transmission. Some need only one-way transmissions, such as paging and alarm indications, others require full duplex operation. Many different systems are designed for the different applications. Below we describe some internationally standardized systems.

7.9.1   One-way transmission systems

In a **paging system** we find a radio transmitter broadcasting messages to a large number of paging receivers. The messages are short so the transmitter can handle a very large number of them sequentially on one frequency channel. The message carries an address identifying the paging receiver of a particular user. Only this particular receiver will react and inform this user of the arrival of the message. This can be done by flashing a light, by an audible signal or by vibration. This last option is useful during meetings or when carrying the paging receiver in a pocket. The message can be very short: a message of two bits lighting one of four lights on the pager, or producing one of four tones. Each light or tone has a meaning, prearranged by caller and paged person. Such messages could be:

(1)   call home when you can find a suitable time
(2)   call home immediately
(3)   call the office
(4)   come home a.s.a.p.

The advantage of such a simple paging system is that someone can originate the message by using an ordinary telephone set. Other pagers show messages prearranged or composed by the sender on a small display of the paging receiver.

In 1970 a group of paging system manufacturers and system operators formed an advisory group known as **POCSAG** (Post Office Codes Standardisation Advisory Group). This group produced a standard for the air interface of digital paging systems that was accepted as a global standard. In 1994 27 million pagers used this air interface. The standard leaves some freedom to implement many facilities as options. The standard describes operation with a bit rate of 512 bit/s, and can optionally operate at 1200 or 2400 bit/s. One paging receiver can have up to eight addresses for reception from different sources. The messages are protected by **forward error correction (FEC)**, using a (31, 21) BCH coding. (BCH stands for Bose, Chaudhuri, Hocquenghem.) This FEC allows the correction of two-bit random and four-bit burst errors.

A standard of much later date is the ETSI standard for the **European Radio MEssage System (ERMES)**. The European-wide ERMES network is built up from a number of paging networks connected to each other, mostly one per country or operator. It opens, in principle, the possibility of roaming to a different country with the pager. ETSI not only specified the air interface, but also the infrastructure and services. The ERMES is a more sophisticated system than systems meeting the basic POCSAG specification. ERMES may therefore not be acceptable for applications not requiring this level of sophistication. New pagers based on POCSAG are still coming on the market.

Data broadcast systems do not address specific users but send the information to everyone who is interested, or in cases of encrypted information to everyone who has a decryptor for the service. Data broadcasts are used for, for example, stock market share prices.

Also, one-way transmission systems, but systems that do not transmit from a central point to many distributed receivers but just the opposite, are used for the transmission of, for example, alarms. One specific type, the **personal alarm system**, must be very small and very reliable. Because of their size they cannot transmit with much power, but the safety of human life depends often on the reception of the alarm message. It would be logical that a special frequency band be reserved for this type of message. In most countries, in 1995 this was not yet the case.

7.9.2 Two-way transmission systems

Two-way transmission systems have the advantage that they can apply some acknowledge system and repeat packets of data if errors are detected. Such a system is called an **Automatic ReQuest (ARQ) system**. The first ARQ system was the system used on HF channels described earlier. The system is limited to bit rates of 300 bit/s. since higher bit rates suffer too much from multipath effects at HF frequencies. The GEO satellite system **Inmarsat-C** can be used for higher bit rates.

Apart from these long-range systems there are medium-range (10–200 km) **radio data systems**, generally operating on VHF or

UHF frequencies. A specification that met almost global acceptance is a manufacturer's specification. The **Mobitex** specification from L.M. Ericsson is used for data systems in the US, Australia and many countries in Europe. It could be described as the mobile X.25 system. The mobile part offers an interface to public and private X.25-based packet switching networks. It allows international roaming, provided the operators have agreed to offer this service to the user. Seamless handover is not necessary for such a packet switched system. The system has store and forward capabilities and delivers the information when the connection is restored. Most messages are rather short, so the loading of the frequency channels remains low. There is no need to go for very small cell sizes to reuse the frequencies at short distances. The maximum bit rate is 8000 bit/s. A system of log-in and log-out prevents the flow of unnecessary information on the radio channels during user absence. The terminal on a radio data system is generally a small computer, with a program dedicated to the function. The functions vary from credit card verification and provision of work instructions to automatic testing of equipment in the field.

7.10 General aspects of mobile telecommunication

7.10.1 Safety of electromagnetic radiation

With handheld telephone sets the transmission source is held extremely close to the brain of the person. The question arises, is this harmful? Several studies have been carried out on the influence of electromagnetic radiation on the human being and some knowledge gained. However, it is still not 100% certain that the use of some handheld sets for extended periods is absolutely safe. It is therefore advisable to use handsets with as little power as possible and only for short periods. The car telephone is relatively safe, particularly with the antenna on top of the vehicle since the human inside the car is well protected from the radiation. However, with the handheld pocket versions of the car telephone the transmission power has to be adjusted to the large cell size used in these networks. Because of the practical limitations of the battery weight of handhelds, the power will be lower than that of car phones. For car phones the car's battery is used, so the weight of the battery is unimportant. With cordless telephones the cells are smaller so the power can be lower.

Some safety rules are specified in most countries. Most of these rules are not too far from the radiation limits advised by the **International Radiation Protection Association (IRPA)**. The IRPA advises to keep under 0.08 W per kg body weight. Among others the following maximum field strengths were given in 1988: 0.1–1 MHz: maximum 75 V/m,

10–400 MHz: maximum 28 V/m, 1200–200 000 MHz: maximum 60 V/m. Near powerful transmitters, heat generation in the human body is harmful. The safe distance (r) is calculated by the IRPA formula:

$$E^2 = 30P/r^2$$

with E in volts/m, P in watts and r in metres.

EXAMPLE

An HF broadcast transmitter in the 25-metre band, operating on 12 GHz emits 500 kW. What is the safe distance to the antenna of this transmitter?

Answer. The maximum volt/m acceptable in this range of frequencies is 28 V/m. The formula

$$E^2 = 30P/r^2$$

can be written as

$$r^2 = 30P/E^2$$

Substituting the maximum E and P gives

$$r^2 = 15 \times 10^6/784 = 1.9 \times 10^4$$

that is

$$r = 137.8 \text{ m}$$

With higher frequencies the influence on the human body increases. When we arrive at UV frequencies, we all know about the harmful effects on the eyes. Gamma radiation is of a still higher frequency (above 10^{16} Hz) and has sufficient energy (several eV per photon) to cause chemical reactions.

Very low frequencies do not heat the body or ionize like gamma rays. However, they also are not absolutely safe. With high power and long exposure they probably have a slight impact on the immune system. This suspicion is based on statistical information regarding people professionally exposed to high-power low-frequency radiation (3–3000 Hz), but the statistics are insufficient to provide real proof of harmful effects.

Studies of the influence of UHF waves (0.3–3 GHz) on the human brain showed better brain functioning at low power radiation

($0-4\,\mu W/cm^2$). Radiation in the range $10-42\,\mu W/cm^2$ had adverse effects for some specific frequencies.

7.10.2   Electromagnetic compatibility (EMC)

To avoid interference between mobile transmitters and other electronic equipment there are basically two possibilities. The first possibility is to reduce the emitted energy of the sources to a very low level. However, the levels in mobile transmitters are generally already kept to the minimum level necessary for an acceptable quality of communications and cannot be further reduced.

So other solutions should be followed: reduce the sensitivity of all other equipment to a level where no harm is done by the emissions of mobile radio. The problem is that usually the other electronic equipment is already there and the mobile radio came later. Is present-day electronic equipment too sensitive to mobile transmissions? The answer is yes! Most electronic equipment is designed to be insensitive to electrical fields of $3\,V/m$. This standard was produced at a time when car phones did not play any serious role and corresponds to what could be done without significantly increasing the price of products. The GSM handset emits, on maximum power, $12\,V/m$. This has already caused problems with many types of equipment. Worse is that even human life has been endangered in some cases. Accidents have been caused by failing pacemakers and the ABS system in car brakes, and also by unwanted inflation of air bags. New equipment can, at a cost, be made insensitive to high electrical field strength. Existing equipment, however, may have to be replaced if a mobile transmitter can come close to it.

7.10.3   The future of mobile communications

Mobile communications is experiencing an explosive growth. This growth forces the use of higher frequencies and, in cellular systems, smaller cell sizes. The trend is that not only telephony shows a high growth but also more and more new applications become realistic. One of the new areas of mobile communications is multimedia mobile communications. Multimedia applications include not only sound and pictures but also moving pictures. The number of bits to be transferred for these applications, assuming digital handling, is enormous. New efficient coding methods have already been introduced (MPEG); more efficient ones could be needed, maybe not based on binary coding.

Two visions of the future are found in the professional literature. The first recognizes the disappearance of the large number of different systems in favour of a few well-standardized systems. It also indicates

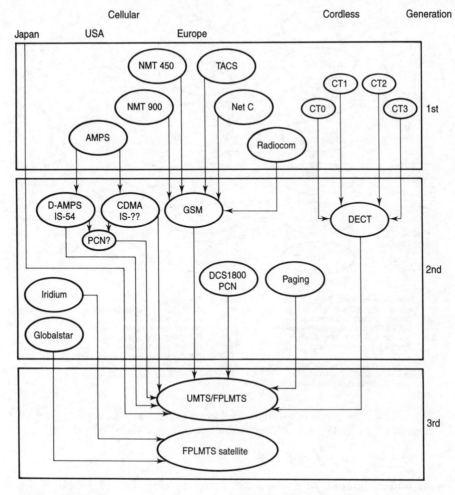

Glossary of terms

ADC: American Digital Cellular
AMPS: Advanced Mobile Phone System
CT: Cordless Telephone
ETSI: European Telecommunications
 Standards Institute
FPLMTS: Future Public Land Mobile
 Telecommunications System
GSM: Global System for Mobile
 Communications
ITU: International Telecommunica-
 tions Union
JDC: Japanese Digital Cellular
Net C: Netz C A German cellular
 network

PCN: Personal Communications Network
PCS: Personal Communication Service
PDC: Personal Digital Cellular
PHP: Personal Handy Phone
PSTN: Public Switched Telephone Network
RACE: Research and Development in
 Advanced Communications
 Technologies in Europe
TACS: Total Access Communications
 System (UK)
UMTS: Universal Mobile
 Telecommunications System
USDC: US Digital Cellular

Figure 7.17 The development towards a UMTS and a FPTMTS satellite. (Source: *Philips Telecommunication Review*, Vol. 52, No. 1, p. 64.)

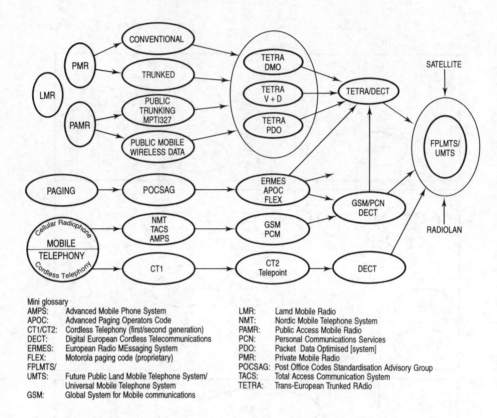

Mini glossary

AMPS:	Advanced Mobile Phone System
APOC:	Advanced Paging Operators Code
CT1/CT2:	Cordless Telephony (first/second generation)
DECT:	Digital European Cordless Telecommunications
ERMES:	European Radio MEssaging System
FLEX:	Motorola paging code (proprietary)
FPLMTS/	
UMTS:	Future Public Land Mobile Telephone System/ Universal Mobile Telephone System
GSM:	Global System for Mobile communications
LMR:	Lamd Mobile Radio
NMT:	Nordic Mobile Telephone System
PAMR:	Public Access Mobile Radio
PCN:	Personal Communications Services
PDO:	Packet Data Optimised [system]
PMR:	Private Mobile Radio
POCSAG:	Post Office Codes Standardisation Advisory Group
TACS:	Total Access Communication System
TETRA:	Trans-European Trunked RAdio

Figure 7.18   The vision of a future development of private and public systems towards a UMTS. (Source: *Philips Telecommunication Review*, Vol. 52, No. 3.)

the implementation of a worldwide infrastructure. Extrapolation of this trend leads to the conclusion that in the future we will have one standardized worldwide system, covering all the needs of mobile communications. This vision has the largest number of supporters and is perfectly in line with the dreams of many large telecommunications operators.

Figure 7.17 shows a diagram of such a development in the direction of the **Universal Mobile Telecommunications System (UMTS)** and the inclusion of satellite systems in the **Future Public Land Mobile Telecommunications System (FPLMTS)**. This last name is more restrictive than the *Universal* system and is more precise since it leaves open the possibility of non-public systems alongside it.

A second vision includes private systems and public systems in the development towards a UMTS and is given in Figure 7.18.

A third, less popular, vision realizes that public systems are always built to satisfy the needs of the largest groups of users and always have to leave certain more specific requirements to be fulfilled more efficiently by dedicated private or public systems. In this vision the continuation of many specialized dedicated systems operating alongside public systems is predicted.

The future will show which of the visions was closest to reality.

Chapter 8

Digital multiplexing

8.1 Introduction

In the OSI model description the term *multiplexing* is used where several service users in a higher layer employ the same service of the adjacent lower layer. In other words, several N + 1 layer connections use the same N layer connection. The descriptions of all the OSI layers contain this possibility of multiplexing, except that of the lowest, physical layer. Long before the OSI model was formulated, however, the layer in which multiplexing was implemented on a large scale in telecommunication networks was the physical layer.

A Time Division Multiplexed (TDM) telegraph service was introduced in Great Britain by A.C. Booth as early as 1905 (Freebody, 1958). The system could handle a maximum of six full duplex telegraph connections over a single wire. The equipment employed time-interleaving on a character basis (5 bits), using rotating contact brushes. One additional bit was used in each cycle for the synchronization of sender and receiver.

In the early 1930s these electromechanical TDM systems were replaced by **multi-channel voice frequency telegraph multiplexers** using thermionic valves. With these systems a telephone circuit was divided into a number (for example, 24) of telegraph channels, by assigning a different carrier frequency to each telegraph channel within the bandwidth of the telephone channel. By the 1960s these systems had themselves been replaced by TDM systems based on electronic components.

The same principle, **Frequency Division Multiplexing (FDM)**, was used to derive analogue telephone circuits from higher bandwidth circuits. TDM became attractive for telephony only after the development of voice coding into digital signals.

Multiplexing a number of telephone channels onto one physical circuit requires a larger transmission bandwidth to be made available. Many technical difficulties have to be solved in this area; attenuation becomes greater at higher frequencies, and crosstalk can also occur. All these problems, their theoretical basis and the solutions devised to solve them, while very interesting, fall outside the scope of this book.

Multiplexers are used not only with all types of physical circuits, that is metallic wires, coaxial cables and optical fibre, but also with radio transmission systems. Multiplexers can also be used to create additional multiplex channels, derived by multiplexing into still smaller bandwidth or lower bit-rate channels. So we can speak of a **hierarchy of multiplexers**. The use of multiplexers is common practice for trunk circuits in the present day telecommunication infrastructure of the main carriers.

The widest bandwidth channels in the infrastructure are generally used exclusively for further multiplexing. In many cases they are not directly available to users.

A significant trend is **integration** and therefore the blurring of the differentiation among switching systems, multiplexing systems and transmission systems as separately designed pieces of equipment. This is the case for digital ISDN equipment. However, regular X.25 based packet switches are examples of systems that perform switching but combine this with the use of a physical circuit for several users at the same time. So these systems perform both a digital switching and a digital multiplexing task. The term **packet transfer mode** is used in this case. A CCITT recommendation on a **transfer mode** covers the transmission, multiplexing and switching aspects as a total system. Further transfer modes specified by CCITT are the **Synchronous Transfer Mode** (STM) and the **Asynchronous Transfer Mode** (ATM); they will be described in the following sections. These transfer modes will be used in a worldwide digital infrastructure arranged according to the master plan, the **Synchronous Digital Hierarchy** (SDH).

8.2 Frequency division multiplexing (FDM) and time division multiplexing (TDM)

With Frequency Division Multiplexing (FDM) each channel has its own base frequency, its **carrier frequency**. The carrier frequencies can be modulated using several different methods to derive either digital or analogue channels. The modulation method and the characteristics of the information on the channel (for example, the bit rate) determine the bandwidth needed per channel. The circuitry to handle a channel in an FDM multiplexer is quite complicated and therefore costly. For analogue signals such as TV signals, however, FDM can still be a good choice.

Digitization of high frequency analogue signals involves extra costs and the bandwidth needed to transfer these signals in digitized form is generally much higher than for the transfer of the original analogue signals. Coding technology to reduce the number of bits required to transfer pictures is developing rapidly, and may well make the transfer of pictures in digital form cost effective in the near future. As the installed base of TV receivers is very large and still based on FDM, a complete changeover to TDM cannot be foreseen within a few years.

FDM can be used on optical fibres by using a different frequency and thus a different wavelength of the light beam for each channel. With optical systems the term **wavelength multiplexing** is used. On radio links not only different frequencies but also different polarization angles can be used.

TDM has become a cost effective method that is not only used on trunk circuits between switching centres but is today even starting to be used on local circuits to the customer. The basic interface of the ISDN is an example of this trend.

With TDM the whole bandwidth is assigned to each particular channel for a fraction of the total transmission time. This fraction can vary from one bit for **bit-interleaved multiplexers**, through a few bits for **character-interleaved multiplexers**, to a few thousand bits in the newest types of high bit-rate multiplexers, the **Synchronous Time Division Multiplexers (STDM)** designed for the synchronous transfer mode.

Time division can even be used to transfer *samples* of bits, derived by scanning the input channels with a frequency at least three times higher than the highest bit rate on these tributary channels. With this method digital signals from various sources with even unknown or changing bit rates can be multiplexed and reproduced (with a tolerable distortion) at the other end of the common channel (CCITT, 1988d).

All these TDMs are **fixed slot time division multiplexers**, in that they assign a fixed slot to each channel in a cyclic scan of all the tributary channels. The fixed position of the slot in the cycle for each channel makes it possible to identify the destination outlet for each portion of the information received over the common channel. This process requires **synchronization** in order to guarantee that the scanning of the received information at the output side runs at the same speed as the cyclic scan at the input side. All slots of one cyclic scan are arranged in a **frame**. In this frame one generally finds additional information to ensure correct synchronization and **frame alignment**, needed to prevent the information from the input channels arriving at the wrong output channels as a result of being out of phase.

TDM is less suitable for multiplexing analogue signals, particularly where these are to be communicated over long distance – as is the case in telecommunications networks. Time division has enjoyed a period of popularity in the switching of Pulse Amplitude Modulated (PAM)

Tributary circuits:

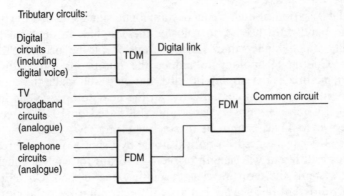

Figure 8.1   Example of FDM and TDM multiplexers arranged in a hierarchy.

signals. In today's switching systems, however, time division is only used for digital (data or PCM-coded voice) signals. This allows integration of the switching function into modern multiplexing systems which are themselves based on the time division of digital signals.

The **digital link** upon which the TDM is applied may very well consist of a circuit provided by a higher level frequency division multiplexer (see Figure 8.1) or higher order TDM. The multiplexers are then said to be arranged in a **hierarchy**.

We will not, however, discuss all these possibilities but concentrate on **digital multiplexing**. Digital multiplexing is TDM of *digital* signals from different sources over a common channel. Digital multiplexing is used on a large scale for the IDN and ISDN. Data multiplexers in private networks are generally also of the digital TDM type.

8.3   Statistical time division multiplexing/time division concentration

With fixed slot TDMs the users can use their portion of the full bit rate continuously for the whole duration of the connection. With a batch type of data transfer, or with digitally encoded voice, the full capacity of the channel will indeed be used for the whole duration. Although the transferred bit stream may not always contain really significant information, for example, during pauses in a telephone conversation, the capacity of the channel is used with a reasonably high efficiency. So for the above mentioned types of traffic the use of fixed slot TDMs is quite satisfactory.

The situation may be different for traffic types with completely different characteristics. An important example is **interactive traffic** between display terminals and computers.

Let us first examine these traffic characteristics with the help of a hypothetical example. We assume an interactive request–reply activity (text, no graphics) involving a question from the computer to the terminal operator and one answer generated by the operator. Further assumptions are as follows:

- bit rate 2400 bit/s, 8-bit characters, so 300 characters/s,
- reading speed of operator: 10 characters/s,
- typing speed of operator: 2 characters/s (120 characters/min),
- length of the question: 300 characters,
- length of the answer: 30 characters,
- the operator needs no additional time, for example, to think or to correct mistakes,
- overhead for the communication ignored.

On this basis we calculate the times needed for each phase of the activity:

- transmission of the question: 1   second
- reading of the question: 30   seconds
- typing of the answer: 15   seconds
- transmission of the answer: 0.1 second

            total: 46.1 seconds

Out of the total time of 46.1 seconds only 1.1 second is transmission time; that is 2.4%. In the direction from the terminal to the computer the duration was only 0.1 second, that is about 0.2%. If we had used a higher bit rate, for example, 9600 bit/s, a bit rate that is indeed used in many cases, the first percentage would have been about 0.6%. Other examples can be taken, but the result will always show a rather similar result with a very small percentage of the time spent actually using the circuit for communication.

The question may be asked 'was the chosen bit rate much too high?' The answer is 'no'. From a viewpoint of efficiency a lower bit rate could very well be acceptable but psychologically a longer waiting time for the transmission to be completed is unpleasant for most people. (For example 2 seconds instead of 1 second at 1200 bit/s and a total time of 47.2 seconds instead of 46.1.)

With these light loadings, sharing the use of a circuit among several terminals seems attractive from a communications cost point of view. This is only the case provided that the cost of the equipment needed to achieve the sharing is not higher than the saving on circuit costs. Sharing is not possible for the connection of rather isolated terminals. For the transfer of interactive traffic of a large group of terminals over longer distances, however, sharing becomes an attractive solution. The requirement is that, on demand, each terminal can have access for a rather short period to the total capacity (bandwidth) of the circuit or a (TDM) channel. This capacity, used during a short period, significantly exceeds the average traffic demand (in bit/s) of the terminal for the information transfer. The capacity available to one terminal thus varies from the total capacity for very short periods, to none at all for much of the time.

Obviously when two terminals want to use the common channel at the same time, one of them will have to wait. For many types of traffic this is acceptable, at least within certain limits. For interactive data traffic it is generally acceptable provided that delay times remain below a fraction of a second. The total loading of the common circuit should then stay well below 100%.

When more and more terminals are added to the flexible multiplexer and the traffic to and from the terminals increases, the loading of the common circuit may come close to 100%. Then the system will no longer operate satisfactorily; it may cause excessive delays or even lose traffic because of overflow of the buffers inside the system. The solution is either to increase the number of circuits or channels, or to use a higher capacity circuit.

Since the capacity of the common circuit is assigned to each channel on demand and the delay experienced depends on the total traffic offered within a small period, statistical rules determine the behaviour of the traffic with this type of multiplexer and of its dimensioning. This explains the name **statistical time division multiplexer**.

To stress the fact that these multiplexers can handle more (virtual) connections than would be possible with a fixed slot type of multiplexer, some people prefer to use the name **time division concentrator** (Spragins, 1991).

At the receiving end of the circuit that carries the multiplexed traffic, it must be possible to send each unit of information to its proper destination. Whereas a fixed slot multiplexer can rely on its position in the time frame in order to decide on the further handling of each unit of received information, with flexible multiplexing it is not possible to use this method. In this case we need some **addressing** for each unit of information (Figure 8.2). Because the addressing requires a part of the transmission capacity, the units should not be too small. On the other hand they must not be too large in view of the delays.

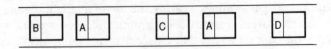

Figure 8.2   Addressed units of information flowing on the circuit.

8.3.1 Packet switches, PADs, intelligent multiplexers and LANs

Several types of system use the principle of statistical time division multiplexing. Packet switching systems inherently use it. On trunk circuits between packet switching nodes the capacity of the circuit is used for different virtual connections with varying capacity demands. Since different types of traffic may have different requirements with respect to the allowed maximum delay that can be tolerated, it may be useful to assign different handling priorities to packets of these different traffic categories.

Interactive voice is an example of traffic that cannot tolerate much delay and also requires continuous uninterrupted delivery to the receiver. Most telephone traffic is carried on circuit switched networks to satisfy these requirements. However, it may nevertheless be required to carry voice traffic on a packet switched network. This is quite possible but a number of precautions are necessary. The voice traffic should preferably be given priority over other types of traffic in order to guarantee small delays even in situations of temporary high loading of the circuits. Further, it will be necessary to introduce buffers in the system in order to be able to guarantee the uninterrupted flow at the receiving side. This introduces a fixed delay in the conversation, but is much to be preferred over a variable delay.

The **Packet Assembler/Disassembler (PAD)** is an example of a statistical time division multiplexing (and demultiplexing) system (see Figure 8.3). The input side of this system gathers the traffic from a number of circuits and buffers the traffic for each line until it is sufficient to fill a regularly sized packet or until a timeout expires (packet assembly). The packet is then offered for transmission on the common circuit connected to the first switching node of the packet switched network. In the reverse direction packets are stored temporarily in a buffer and then their content is transmitted towards the addressed terminal using the proper bit rate for the DTE terminal. (See Figure 8.4.)

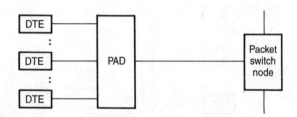

Figure 8.3 Packet Assembler/Disassembler (PAD).

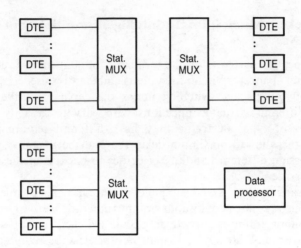

Figure 8.4   Statistical or intelligent multiplexers.

Statistical multiplexers, sometimes called **intelligent multiplexers** or time division concentrators, are similar to the PADs, but the units that are transferred on the common circuit are not packets destined to be handled by a packet switch but consist of frames with a composition specified by the particular manufacturer (see Figure 8.4). The circuit coming from the statistical multiplexer may be connected to a similar or identical multiplexer that demultiplexes the circuits. (See Figure 8.4.) Demultiplexing may also take place in a data processing system.

Statistical multiplexing is used in LAN circuits. (See Figure 8.5.) The difference from the previous systems is that the tributary circuits of the terminals do not end in a common piece of equipment but individually connect to a common circuit. Now the centralized control of the equipment is no longer available. The solution to this problem has already been discussed in Chapter 4.

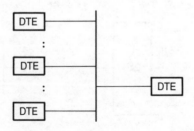

Figure 8.5   Local Area Network (LAN).

8.4   Synchronous transfer mode (STM), SONET, SDH

In modern trunk multiplexing systems two trends can be noted. The first is the trend towards a high degree of flexibility; various bit rates can be combined in one trunk circuit. The second is that towards more truly worldwide standards.

The first trend is clearly visible in the US standard for higher bit rate multiplexing on fibre optic circuits, the **Synchronous Optical NETwork (SONET)**. It offers a large choice of bit rates on the trunk circuits, the so-called **composite data rates**, as well as those of the individual channels (see Table 8.1).

The CCITT recommendations on synchronous digital hierarchy not only offer considerable flexibility but also succeed in reaching a high degree of compatibility with SONET. Although SONET offers a much larger range of composite bit rates, the SDH composite bit rates are chosen to be identical to three of the eight bit rates of SONET, so that these have become applicable bit rates worldwide. (See Table 8.2.)

In many respects, the SONET and SDH standards are fully compatible, but they are certainly not identical. A problem remains that, in Europe, there is a need for 2 Mbit/s channels and virtually no need for 1.5 Mbit/s channels, whereas the reverse is true in the USA and Japan. Therefore the subdivision of the composite bit rate into channels will be different. CCITT specifies how 2 Mbit/s channels are derived efficiently for Europe and how those at 1.5 Mbit/s are derived efficiently for other countries. In Europe the use of 1.5 Mbit/s channels will be so exceptional that no special measures will be taken for this bit rate; a 2 Mbit/s channel will be used to transfer 1.5 Mbit/s bit streams whenever necessary. CCITT also specifies this possibility. However, this method of transferring 1.5 Mbit/s bit streams was, of course, not acceptable for the US where it would constitute a significant loss of efficiency.

Table 8.1   SONET hierarchy.

SONET level (STS: Synchronous Transport Signal)	*Signal designation (OC: Optical Carrier)*	*Composite bit rate (in Mbit s)*
STS-1	OC-1	51.840
STS-3	OC-3	155.520
STS-9	OC-9	466.560
STS-12	OC-12	922.080
STS-18	OC-18	933.120
STS-24	OC-24	1244.160
STS-36	OC-36	1866.240
STS-48	OC-48	2488.320

Table 8.2   Synchronous Digital Hierarchy (SDH) compared with SONET.

SDH levels	Signal designation	Composite bit rate (in Mbit/s)	Comparable SONET level
1	STM-1	155.520	STS-3
4	STM-4	622.080	STS-12
16	STM-16	2488.320	STS-48

The aim of the SDH recommendations was certainly to reach worldwide compatibility of equipment produced by different manufacturers in different countries. In order to achieve this goal the range of basic SDH recommendations (G.707, G.708, G.709) is extended with recommendations that specify details of equipment parts such as the optical interfaces (G.957) and SDH management (G.784). These recommendations leave less freedom for the manufacturer than recommendations for more conventional multiplexing systems (G.702) have done in the past. The result should be full compatibility between systems of different manufacturers.

In the following we will describe the synchronous time division multiplexing recommended for the SDH to be used for the synchronous transfer mode. This is the transfer mode that offers a large number of channels of fixed capacity, but with flexibility in the mix of bit rates that it can transfer. In Section 8.5 we will discuss the other transfer mode that fits in with the SDH: the asynchronous transfer mode.

The **Synchronous Transport Module (STM)** uses the concept of **virtual containers**. A container can be handled as a unit, independently of its content, by a number of network elements such as repeaters and higher order multiplexers. Such a virtual container, that is, a number of bytes reappearing at regular intervals (125 μs for STM-1), is transported in a slightly larger synchronous transport module (see Figure 8.6). This module consists of 9 rows and, in the case of STM-1, of 270 columns of octets.

In addition to the virtual container the module contains the information needed at regenerators and multiplexers in a **Regenerator**

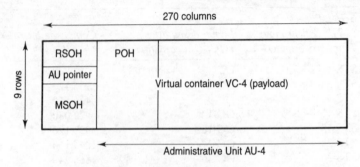

Figure 8.6   Synchronous transport module STM-1.

Section OverHead (RSOH) field and a **Multiplexer Section OverHead (MSOH)** field. The virtual container itself contains a **Path Over-Head (POH)** field, which is only analysed by the equipment at the end of a path through the network, where demultiplexing of the virtual container may be required.

The virtual container of the type VC-4 fits in the so-called **Administrative Unit (AU-4)** of the STM-1. The VC-4 container can also be filled with smaller types of containers, for instance, by three containers of the type VC-3, each consisting of 9 rows and 85 columns of octets. In that case the VC-4 will carry some additional administrative information regarding its content, in the form of a **Tributary Unit Group (TUG-3)**. This process can still go on with smaller containers of the types VC-2, and finally VC-1. The VC-1 has two versions; the VC-11 for 1.5 Mbit/s signals and the VC-12 mainly intended for 2 Mbit/s signals. This SDH concept allows the transfer of a large range of bit rates, including the bit rate that is chosen for handling ATM, 155.520 Mbit/s.

One of the advantages of SDH over the older, fixed slot, synchronized multiplexing systems of the **Plesiochronous Digital Hierarchy (PDH)** is that SDH has introduced the use of pointers that describe the position of the VCs in their respective superstructure. This allows the accommodation of VCs that are coming in faster or slower than the nominal rate. It also obviates the need for slip buffers as used in conventional systems. It makes it easy to locate the bytes of a particular bit stream by reading the pointers (at a fixed location in the STM frame), and to extract this particular part of the bit stream. This possibility is used in **Add/Drop Multiplexers (ADM)**. This type of equipment makes it attractive to use ring topology to connect switching centres: the **SDH ring** (see Figure 8.7). In an ADM one or more complete VCs are extracted from the main bit stream and/or are inserted into this bit stream

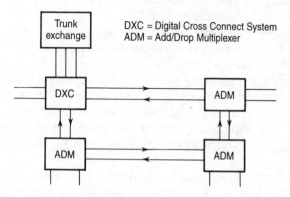

Figure 8.7 SDH ring network.

periodically. This in contrast with many older fixed slot PDH multiplexers that do not handle the same information in the form of containers but as time scattered bits (bit interleaved) or bytes (character interleaved). This last method (fixed slot) does not leave any possibility for flexibility in the handling of the main bit stream. The main disadvantage of PDH compared with SDH is that the entire hierarchy has to be traversed for every multiplexing or demultiplexing operation.

8.5   Asynchronous transfer mode (ATM)

The Asynchronous Transfer Mode (ATM) will have an important role in the future B-ISDN (Krick, 1990). Although the highest levels of multiplexing in the future infrastructure for ISDN and B-ISDN will be based on synchronous TDM within the range of bit rates specified in the SDH (and SONET in the USA), ATM is the preferred switching and multiplexing principle for the B-ISDN. The reason behind this preference is the suitability and efficiency of ATM for all types of digital traffic services.

We can classify these types of service as:

- **Constant Bit Rate (CBR) service** and
- **Variable Bit Rate (VBR) service**.

Examples of CBR traffic are the 64 kbit/s based services such as digital telephony, videophony and telefax group 4, and higher continuous bit stream based services such as present-day digital TV transmission.

A good example of VBR traffic is interactive data-, text- or image-transfer. During short periods a constant bit-rate transfer is required for this type of traffic but during the longer intervening periods no information has to be transferred at all.

When we consider the basic requirement for the information transfer of video we see a requirement for a complete new picture, say, every 5 seconds and the periodic transfer of rather small changes to this picture during the intervening period. With a refresh rate of the picture in the TV receiver of 50 per second, this boils down to the transmission of several megabits every 5 seconds, with a duration of 1/50th of a second and only a few kilobits for each of the intermediate 249 pictures. In other words, the actual requirement for bit transfer is not constant but variable.

If we base our infrastructure on fixed bandwidth multiplexers we cannot profit from the lower bit-rate transfer requirement during the relatively long intermediate periods. However, ATM is designed to enable more efficient transfer of VBR traffic (see Figure 8.8). Of course, in order to profit from the temporary lower bit-rate requirements of one traffic

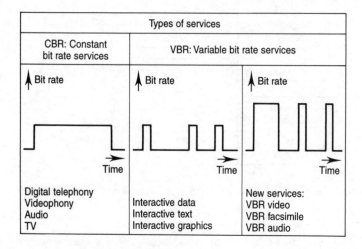

Types of services		
CBR: Constant bit rate services	VBR: Variable bit rate services	
Digital telephony Videophony Audio TV	Interactive data Interactive text Interactive graphics	New services: VBR video VBR facsimile VBR audio

Figure 8.8 Classification of types of service.

stream to handle the traffic of another, a certain risk is introduced that occasionally one of the streams will be delayed for a short period. Generally this can be tolerated provided the maximum delay remains within reasonable limits and proper measures are taken to avoid the delay being noticeable by the user. We may expect that in the future new services will be specified using this variable bit rate capability of the B-ISDN based on the use of the ATM.

The advantage of a transfer system like ATM that can handle all types of information flows is also very significant for the simplicity of the system users' connections in the future. Users at home or in smaller offices will want to be connected to low-speed data networks for data and text handling, to the telephone network, and to broadband networks for TV and HDTV, and maybe also for facsimile.

Instead of separate connections, ATM will make it possible to use just one connection to such a user. (See Figure 8.9.) For this purpose the B-ISDN provides a B-ISDN **User–Network Interface (UNI)**. The interface at the T_B reference point of the B-ISDN (comparable to the T reference point of ISDN) is defined for short distances up to 100 or possibly 200 metres as an electrical interface using two circuits, one for each direction, and for larger distances as an optical interface. The bit rate is 155.52 Mbit/s in both directions, so is symmetric. The specifications for the interface at the S_B reference point are not yet complete.

ATM is a transfer mode that uses **cells** as the means of transferring information. Asynchronous implies that the recurrence of cells containing information from an individual source is not necessarily periodic. The use of the ATM has implications for switching, multiplexing and transmission in the network.

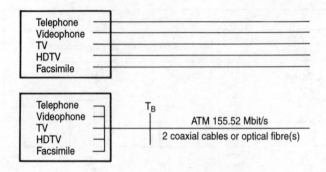

Figure 8.9   Single ATM physical connection versus connections for each service.

The cell has a fixed length of 53 octets, 48 for the information field and 5 for the **cell header**. Error control is limited to the information in the cell header. Single (detectable) errors in the header are corrected; cells with two errors in the header can be identified. The ATM layer header format at the UNI is shown in Figure 8.10.

The header format for cells within the network during the transfer from node to node, at the **Network Node Interfaces** (**NNI**), is only slightly different; the bits reserved at the UNI for the GFC are in this case available to extend the **Virtual Path Identifier** (**VPI**) with another 4 bits. The VPI and **Virtual Channel Identifier** (**VCI**) serve to identify a virtual channel. The VPI does not remain the same for a virtual connection from ATM switch to ATM switch; that is only true for the VCI. In the network we will also find ATM cross connect switches, called **virtual path switches**, that switch bundles of virtual channels as a unit. These bundles of virtual channels are identified by the VPI (see Figure 8.11). Virtual channels are only switched at ATM **virtual channel switches**.

The ATM cells are used to carry different types of information. Some VCs will carry control information, others carry user

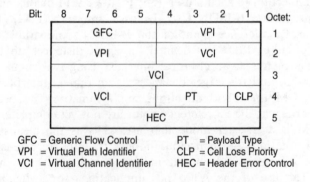

Figure 8.10   Cell header format at the user network interface.

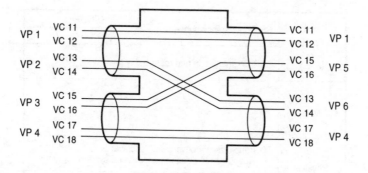

Figure 8.11   Virtual path switching of bundles of virtual channels.

information of a different nature, such as CBR or VBR. These differences lead to the need to distinguish a separate layer above the ATM layer. This layer is called the **ATM Adaptation Layer (AAL)**. (See Figure 8.12.)

Both the ATM layer and the ATM adaptation layer can provide a service to OSI model layer 2 protocols and could therefore be classified as OSI layer 1 protocols.

Below the ATM layer we find the physical layer. This layer is subdivided into two sublayers. The **Transmission Convergence (TC) sublayer** has the task of embedding cells of the ATM layer in the transmission frames of the chosen transmission medium. This choice could, depending on availability of the medium, be a transmission channel in the PDH or the new SDH. This medium is controlled in the **Physical Medium (PM) layer**. See Figure 8.13.

Further functions of the TC layer are cell delineation and the checksum calculation over the header information, for insertion in the **Header Error Control (HEC)** field. The TC sublayer passes the information received from the physical medium, to the ATM layer in a standard manner. Thus, the functions in the ATM layer are completely independent of the chosen medium.

Control plane	User plane
Higher layers	Higher layers
ATM adaption layer	
ATM layer	
Physical layer	

Figure 8.12   B-ISDN protocol reference model (simplified).

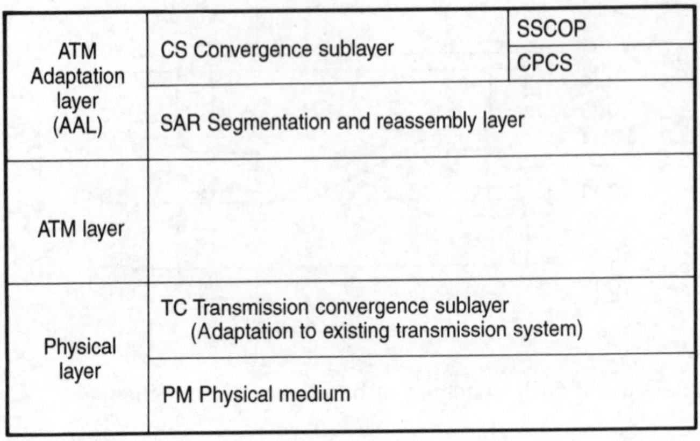

ATM Adaptation layer (AAL)	CS Convergence sublayer	SSCOP
		CPCS
	SAR Segmentation and reassembly layer	
ATM layer		
Physical layer	TC Transmission convergence sublayer (Adaptation to existing transmission system)	
	PM Physical medium	

SSCOP: Service Specific Convergence Protocol
CPCS: Common Part Convergence sublayer

Figure 8.13   ATM protocol reference model.

The AAL has a similar task, to make the ATM layer independent of the different types of transferred information. Originally five types of AAL were defined for the transfer of user information and one type for the transfer of signalling information, the **Signalling ATM Adaptation Layer (SAAL)**.

AAL Type 1 is intended for the transfer of CBR applications. An example of this traffic is telephone traffic on ISDN B-channels. Lost or erroneous data is not corrected or repeated. It is essential that the ATM network delivers the octets at the proper bit rate and at the proper moment. This requires related clock information to be transferred with the data. This clock information is passed in the AAL type 1.

AAL type 2 is designed for VBR traffic, needing a time relation between sender and receiver. Also, for this type of traffic timing information should be passed to the receiver. How this type of traffic is handled in the AAL layer is not yet specified in detail (1995).

AAL type 3 is intended for the connection oriented transfer of data packets in point-to-point and point-to-multipoint operation.

AAL type 4 is intended for the **connectionless** transfer of data packets in point-to-point and point-to-multipoint operation. During the design of AAL type 3 and AAL type 4 it was found that there is no need to distinguish between connection oriented and connectionless traffic in the AAL. AALs type 3 and type 4 were merged to type 3/4.

AAL type 3/4 handles variable-length data packets of up to 65 535 octets. One of the important tasks of the AAL type 3/4 is to segment the large packets into several ATM cells and at the receive side to reconstruct the packets. This task is performed in the **Segmentation And Reassembly (SAR)** sublayer of the AAL type 3/4. Further, AAL type 3/4 offers several

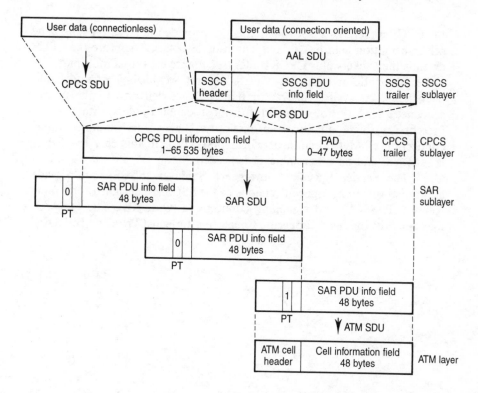

Figure 8.14 Structure of the AAL type 5 transmission frame.

modes of operation for different requirements. For further details see Kyas (1995).

AAL type 5 is a simplified version of type 3/4. Important simplifications are that type 5 does not handle point-to-multipoint traffic, nor does it allow multiplexing of data streams. We describe AAL type 5 in more detail below.

Like type 3/4, AAL type 5 is suited to handle **connection oriented** and **connectionless** transfer of data, and time synchronization between sender and receiver is not provided. The protocol reference model (see Figure 8.13) shows two sublayers in the AAL type 5.

The SAR sublayer is similar to that for type 3/4. To distinguish the beginning and end of a packet in a stream of cells the SAR sublayer (mis)uses the PT field in the cell header. All PT fields except in the last cell, containing the end of the packet, are set to 0. The cell containing the end of the packet gets the PT value 1. (See Figure 8.14.)

The **Convergence Sublayer (CS)** is split into two parts. The **Common Part Convergence Sublayer (CPCS)** is common to both connection-oriented and connectionless traffic. The CPCS performs error detection and reporting and transfers a User-to-User byte (CPCS UU) in the CPCS trailer. This last function is not provided in AAL type 3/4. The cell information field has a fixed length of 48 octets. Therefore the CPCS extends the packets plus CPCS trailer (see Figure 8.14) to a multiple of 48 octets with padding bytes. The CPCS does not provide any assurance that packets are received error-free or that they are delivered in the proper sequence. This is not required for most connectionless transfers via present-day high quality transmission systems (for example, inter-connection of Metropolitan networks or LANs). In this case the CPCS is sufficient and no other sublayer is needed.

The **Service Specific Convergence Sublayer** (**SSCS**) can provide additional functions. Special versions of the SSCS are designed for Frame Relay (FR SSCS) and signalling connections (Q.SAAL). The Q.SAAL makes use of the **Service Specific Connection-Oriented Protocol** (**SSCOP**).

Chapter 9

Sources and encoding

9.1 Introduction

In communications technology we can distinguish a wide variety of systems that produce information. Such systems are called information sources. Examples are video, sound and speech information as well as so-called discrete sources. To allow communication, that is, information transfer from source to user and vice versa, the source signals, each with its own specific technical characteristics and any associated procedures, have to be encoded. See Figure 9.1.

By encoding we mean the conversion of a given signal type by an algorithm to another signal type. The goal of this operation is to achieve a better match to the characteristics and limitations of the transmission and/or processing system. Of course the information in the input signal must be completely preserved. Examples of encoding methods are:

- *Pulse Code Modulation (PCM)*. This coding is designed to convert the information content of an analogue signal to information in digital form, so that digital signal processing and/or digital transmission is possible. PCM takes place in a so-called **codec** (coder/decoder) that is normally placed as close as possible to the signal source.

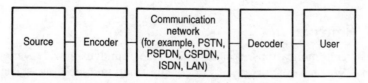

Figure 9.1 Block schematic of a simplified communication system.

- *Source encoding*. This method is designed to reduce the volume of digital data to be transmitted without loss of relevant information. Hence the redundancy, and possibly the irrelevancy, of the digital output signal after source encoding is (significantly) less than that of the digital input signal.

- *Channel encoding*. This ambiguous concept is often used to indicate encoding designed to make the digital output signal less sensitive to the limited transmission quality of the channel used. In this case it is important to use error detecting and/or correcting codes. Encoding is achieved by increasing the redundancy in the output signal compared with the input signal. Taking into account the opposite character of source and channel signalling, it is conceivable that both forms of encoding could be combined into a single operation. In practice, however, these two types of encoding are often carried out separately.

- *Line encoding*. This method is designed to adapt the signal optimally to the (physical) characteristics of the transmission route such as bandwidth, direct current, transparency and recognition of the clock frequency. Line encoding is not normally carried out in the codec but, for example, in the so-called Data Circuit-terminating Equipment (DCE), the Network Termination 1 (NT1) or the transceiver apparatus.

- *Encryption/decryption*. Designed to protect the transmitted information (by this, we mean protection against unauthorized use of the data and possibly preservation of the anonymity of the users), this protection is increasingly being applied to public communication networks with their **open** character. In order to meet protection of privacy requirements, this form of encoding is always executed as close as possible to the source.

- *Authentication*. Also intended to protect information, its function is to verify the identity of the sender and receiver and thereby the integrity of the transmitted data. It is always carried out for both ends. Although this is a different type of protection, authentication is usually carried out in combination with encryption. Since this is a form of protection with an **end-to-end** character, it must also be applied as close as possible to the source.

9.2 Sources

Within communications, sources are to be found in a wide variety of forms. We have sources of video information, such as television, videophone and facsimile; of sound information, such as speech and music; and data sources representing any other physical quantity in electrical form (**transducers**) are also very common. In the last case we usually speak of **telemetering**, and **telecommand** systems.

A very large group of sources consists of equipment for information transfer in the form of characters, such as terminals for telex, teletex and message handling systems. A special category, **discrete** sources, consists of databases from computer systems.

The signals originating from these various sources can be divided into a number of global categories as follows:

- Analogue signals: these are time-dependent signals in which both amplitude and time, within a certain range, can take an infinite number of different values. That is to say, a signal that is continuous in both amplitude and time.

- Digital signals: these are signals that can take a finite number of different values at a finite number of different points in time: discrete in both amplitude and time.

The importance of the first category is that the real world is an **analogue** world, while the second category is usually more suitable for the processing and transmission of information because of its quality and cost aspects.

9.3 Pulse code modulation (linear or uniform)

By pulse code modulation we mean encoding whereby an analogue signal is transformed to a digital signal while preserving practically the whole information content. A model of a PCM codec can be defined on the basis of the three following signal processing operations:

- **sampling** of analogue signals,
- quantizing of the time discrete samples,
- encoding of the amplitude and time discrete signals.

Note that, in any specific implementation, these three operations may not be individually recognizable nor necessarily occur in the given order.

The signal so obtained has two major advantages:

- if the bandwidth of the digital signal is smaller than or even (theoretically) equal to the channel capacity C of the transmission route then, according to Hartley–Shannon, transmission can take place over a virtually infinite distance without loss of quality (sufficient signal/noise ratio);

- the transmission route can be multiplexed by inserting bits from other signal sources: this is called **Time Division Multiplex (TDM)**.

In addition, the PCM model is often used as a reference code in order to make qualitative judgements about other codes.

9.3.1 Sampling an analogue signal

The **sampling** of an analogue source signal is shown schematically in Figure 9.2.

This diagram shows that samples of the analogue frequency are taken with a sampling frequency f_s where:

$$f_s = 1/T$$

In the system chosen in Figure 9.2, both the time τ during which the switch is closed and the sampling period T are determined by the rotational speed of the switch in rev/s (equal to f_s). In practice, the **duty cycle** $d(= \tau/T)$ is independent of T. The result of sampling can be represented by a number of time dependent functions $F_{AN}(t)$, $S(t)$ and $F_s(t)$, as shown in Figure 9.3.

$F_{AN}(t)$ is an arbitrary time-dependent analogue source signal, $S(t)$, which represents the waveform of the sampling function, and $F_s(t)$ is the sampled function. The time-discrete signal $F_s(t)$, is also called a **Pulse Amplitude Modulation (PAM)** signal. This function can be written as:

$$F_s(t) = F_{AN}(t) \cdot S(t)$$

According to Shannon's sampling theory, all the information in the analogue source signal (amplitude and argument information) will be present in the sampled PAM signal if the correct choice of sampling frequency, f_s, has been made. The relation between the frequency spectra of the analogue and the PAM signals is described in Appendix C.

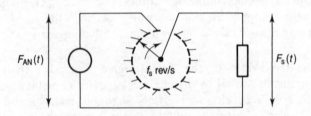

Figure 9.2 Principle of sampling of $F_{AN}(t)$.

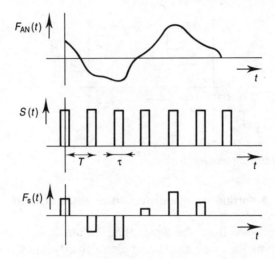

Figure 9.3 The relationship between analogue, sampling and sampled signals.

9.3.2 Quantizing the sampled signal

The task of quantizing is to convert a continuous amplitude signal – a signal within a certain range with an infinite number of possible values – to a signal with a finite number of discrete values. The result of such an operation on a time-continuous signal is made clear in Figure 9.4.

When quantizing linearly, a choice can be made of two quantizing characteristics, the **mid-rise** and the **mid-tread** characteristics, as shown in Figure 9.5.

For both characteristics, the discrete-level differences are always the same size. The difference between the two characteristics is only of consequence for the noise occurring in an otherwise empty channel.

As is evident from Figures 9.4 and 9.5, quantizing means rounding off the value of a continuous signal to discrete values. This rounding results

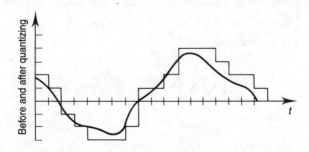

Figure 9.4 Quantizing of an analogue signal.

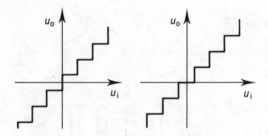

Figure 9.5   Quantizing characteristics.

in **quantizing distortion** or **quantizing noise**, illustrated for the mid-rise characteristic in Figure 9.6.

It can be seen from the figure that the maximum value this noise can take remains the same for the whole of the dynamic range of u_i. It follows that the signal to noise ratio (S/N):

$$\frac{S}{N} = \frac{u_i^2}{(u_o - u_i)^2}$$

is strongly dependent on the value of the signal u_i. For small values of u_i the S/N ratio is relatively small; for large values of u_i it is relatively large.

Summarizing, it can be stated that the S/N ratio of digitized linear PCM signals can take on low to very low values for small values of u_i. If linear quantizing is used, an improvement in the S/N ratio for small signal values can only be achieved by reducing the level differences and thereby increasing the number of levels. This signal to noise ratio is also called the **signal to quantizing noise ratio (SQR)**.

9.3.3 Encoding

Although the signal obtained by quantizing has a discrete character, the transmission and signal processing problems are hardly any less than for

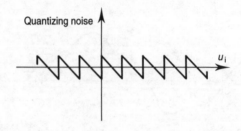

Figure 9.6   The quantizing noise $(u_o - u_i)$ as a function of u_i.

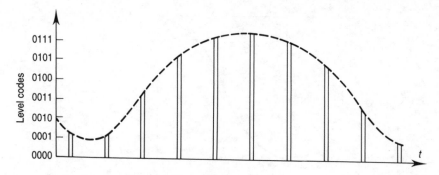

Figure 9.7 Encoding of quantized signal levels.

the original analogue signal. This is because of the large number of different levels in a high quality quantized signal. Therefore encoding is almost always used in addition to quantizing. The various discrete quantized levels are each given an individual code, making the transmission and any necessary processing of the signal as simple as possible. See Figure 9.7.

In practice, this form of encoding is usually done by means of binary codes.

9.4 Source encoding

Source encoding encompasses several types of signal processing which are intended to reduce the bit rate of the digital signal. These processes must ensure that there is almost no loss of quality compared with the original signal. Bit rate reduction is only possible if it can be realized at the cost of irrelevancy and/or redundancy in the original signal.

Source encoding is used both on analogue signals (waveform encoding), such as sound and video information, and on discrete source signals. Several important examples of source encoding are discussed below.

9.4.1 Non-linear PCM

The quantizing of a waveform (see Section 9.3.2) turned out to have the undesirable but unavoidable side effect of generating quantizing distortion or noise. This is an irreversible process in the sense that there are no technical means of eliminating noise introduced in this way.

The effect of quantizing noise can be made as small as is desired for uniform PCM by increasing the number of quantizing levels for a given

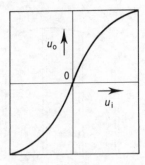

Figure 9.8   Non-linear quantizing characteristic.

dynamic range of the signal to be digitized. In this way, an acceptable value for the S/N ratio of a smaller signal can also be achieved. The disadvantage is a large increase in the bit rate.

Reduction of the bit rate while retaining the desired S/N ratio can be achieved by the use of non-linear quantizing. Here there is no longer any question of having equal level differences in the quantizing characteristic, but use is made of variable level differences, dependent on the absolute value of the waveform amplitude. See Figure 9.8. The result of non-linear quantizing is called a **compression characteristic**.

Because this process can lead to undesirable non-linear distortion on decoding, it is necessary to include a complementary non-linear characteristic, the **expansion characteristic**, in the decoder. This characteristic can be determined by reflection relative to a 45° axis as shown in Figure 9.9 (only positive values illustrated).

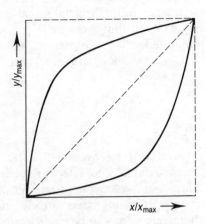

Figure 9.9   Coder and decoder characteristics.

An optimal non-linear quantizing curve should have at least the following properties:

- the discrete level differences should be proportional to the signal values in order to realize a fixed S/N ratio over the complete dynamic range; in other words, the curve should be as close as possible to logarithmic;

- the quantizing curve should pass through the origin of the axes;

- the dynamic range of the input and output signals should be the same, so that the normalized curve passes through the point (1.1);

- the amount of compression and expansion should be easily adjustable.

However, it is not possible to realize these desired properties for all signal values.

As an example of standardized compression characteristics, the standard A- and μ-laws used in the sound transmission of speech signals can be cited (Figure 9.10). Both codes utilize 8-bit PCM words.

The A-law (Europe):

$$y(x) = \frac{Ax}{1 + \ln A} \, \sin(x) \qquad \text{for } 0 < \frac{|x|}{x_{max}} < \frac{1}{A}$$

$$y(x) = \frac{1 + \ln A \, |x|/x_{max}}{1 + \ln A} \, x_{max} \cdot \sin(x) \quad \text{for } \frac{1}{A} < \frac{|x|}{x_{max}} < 1$$

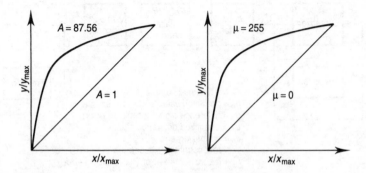

Figure 9.10   Standardized quantizing characteristics for speech.

The μ-law (USA and Japan):

$$y(x) = \frac{\ln(1 + \mu|x|/x_{max}}{\ln(1 + \mu)}\,\sin(x)$$

Both compression characteristics can be approximated as linear characteristics in a relay configuration (13 segments for the A-law and 15 segments for the μ-law).

ITU-T (CCITT) Recommendation G.711 gives full details on the implementation of this encoding system.

9.4.2 Differential PCM (DPCM)

Both with linear (or uniform) and non-linear (for example, logarithmic) PCM, the bit rate is determined by the highest frequency f_H and highest amplitude of the source signal. In the vast majority of practical cases, in both speech and video, neither the maximum amplitude nor the maximum frequency is continuously present in the signal. In the digitized signal, this results in the majority of adjacent PCM words having only small differences.

A significant reduction can be achieved in the number of bits to be transmitted – depending on the statistical properties of the source signal and the complexity of the codec – by transmitting the difference between two successive words (or the difference between the actual word and an estimated value) instead of the complete sample (PCM words).

The global design of a DPCM codec working according to this principle is shown in Figure 9.11.

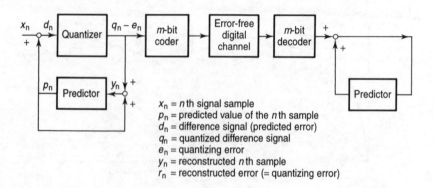

x_n = nth signal sample
p_n = predicted value of the nth sample
d_n = difference signal (predicted error)
q_n = quantized difference signal
e_n = quantizing error
y_n = reconstructed nth sample
r_n = reconstructed error (= quantizing error)

Figure 9.11 Global design of a DPCM codec.

The properties of the codec are mainly determined by:

- the design of the non-linear quantizing circuit;
- the design of the predictor circuit;
- the relative utilization of the analogue and digital parts of the system.

9.4.3 Delta modulation (DM)

Delta modulation can be considered as a special form of DPCM, in which the codeword consists of a single bit and the sampling frequency f_s is much higher than that required by the sampling theorem. For DM the bit rate is thus equal to f_s.

The block diagram of Figure 9.11 for DPCM is valid for all DM codecs. A common design of a DM codec is illustrated in Figure 9.12.

In this design, an integrator is used as a predictor. In contrast to the DPCM codec shown earlier, the input and output signals of this codec are analogue. Sampling takes place after the analogue difference signal has been quantized.

Although the predictor of a DM circuit can be complex, DM codecs are usually simpler to realize than DPCM codecs. It can also be shown that DM is principally less interference-sensitive than DPCM.

9.4.4 Voice encoding

The source coding techniques dealt with above apply to waveform coders. This means that coding and subsequent decoding results in a waveform that is as true a replica of the original source signal as possible. However, considerably more data reduction can be achieved by using the category of so-called **vocoders** (voice encoders). In using vocoders the emphasis is

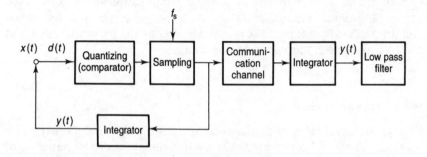

Figure 9.12 Example of a common DM codec.

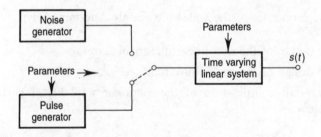

Figure 9.13   Basic model of a synthetic speech source.

on the transfer of the information content of the speech signal rather than on the preservation of the analogue waveform of the source signal.

The information content of a speech signal is essentially discrete in nature. Speech signals are composed of up to (in most languages) approximately sixty different sound symbols, called **phonemes**. These can be broadly classified as: consonants, vowels, semivowels and diphthongs. The sounds and the different transitions between them take place in accordance with specific linguistic rules peculiar to a language. A typical average speech rate is ten phonemes per second.

Thus, theoretically, the information transfer rate of speech signals can be approximated by sixty bits per second (not taking into account characteristics of the source such as identity, emotional state, loudness of the speech etc.).

Speech signals with these characteristics can be synthetically generated by an electronic analogy of the physical speech production process, as shown in Figure 9.13. Most vocoder techniques make use of synthetic speech generators more or less comparable to the basic model. The coding process then analyses the natural speech and from that analysis estimates the digital parameters required by the model.

Although a variety of analysis and estimation methods and techniques is available, the most widely used method is that of **Linear Predictive Coding (LPC)**. This is based on the assumption that a speech sample can be approximated by a linear combination of those received earlier. The digital parameter values are conveyed to the decoder, which comprises a synthetic speech source controlled by the parameters (such as the LPC parameter) provided by the coder.

9.4.5 Image encoding

Besides the advantages of digital encoding in general as mentioned under Sections 9.2 and 9.3, there may exist a requirement for digital handling of images due to one or more of the following possibilities offered by digital image data:

- easy integration with other digital media,
- easy integration with other digital services,
- easy encryption of the encoded data.

However, in digital image data handling one has to cope with huge quantities of bits. As an example, the bit rate of 1.2 Gbit/s required for the source (studio) format of **High Definition Television (HDTV)** can be mentioned. The bandwidth generally available for the transport of such data will be in the order of 140 Mbit/s. This means that the encoding of images necessarily requires source encoding algorithms with compression factors between approximately 10 and 1000, depending on the application and the characteristics of the network used for transport of the data.

The following signal processing operations can be applied in image encoding:

- *Sampling and quantization*. This operation results in digital **picture elements (pixels** or **pels)**, is usually carried out on an orthogonal grid and is very similar to the PCM or DPCM processing as described in Sections 9.3 and 9.4. The processing can be carried out as **scalar quantization** in which subsequent samples are quantized independently or **vector quantization** in which consecutive samples are quantized in combination.

- *Source encoding*. This operation results in the required compression factor and is realized by means of decorrelating tools such as **Discrete Cosine Transform (DCT)** and entropy encoding by such means as Variable Length Coding (VLC) (for example, Huffman encoding, see Section 9.5).

- *Error protection*. This processing provides a certain degree of protection against transmission errors caused by the transport network. Both error detecting and error correcting codes (see Section 9.5) are applied.

- *Encryption*. This operation is meant to protect the digital image data against unauthorized use of the data (example: Pay TV).

In the past considerable effort was invested in international standardization of the various encoding operations. With regard to the encoding of **still pictures** the collaboration between the ISO and the International Electrotechnical Commission (IEC) resulted in the forming of the **Joint Picture Expert Group (JPEG)**. This group produced the ISO International Standard IS 10918. Depending on the number of bits per pixel (between 0.25 and 2.0 bit/pixel) the quality achieved by means of this JPEG standard may vary between respectively moderate to excellent quality. There is no explicit bit rate specified by this international standard. Due to the high performance of the JPEG encoding it is frequently used as a reference standard in judging other encoding standards not mentioned in this chapter.

The encoding of **motion pictures** has different requirements and offers other encoding possibilities such as two-dimensional or three-dimensional encoding. In using **intra-frame** video encoding, the encoding is carried out on a frame-by-frame basis (still picture encoding on all video frames). In applying this **Motion-JPEG** (**M-JPEG**) it appears relatively easy to realize bit rate control. More frequently the source encoding is carried out as three-dimensional encoding. In this **inter-frame** encoding the differences between two consecutive frames are encoded.

Examples of such **hybrid encoding** can be found in the international standards produced by a further joint ISO/IEC collaboration, the **Motion Picture Expert Group** (**MPEG**), which resulted in the MPEG-1 standards (ISO IS 11172) and the MPEG-2 standards (ISO IS 13818).

Both the JPEG and the MPEG standards have a close relation to the source format as specified by ITU-R (formerly CCIR) Recommendation 601 with important characteristics as:

- number of total lines: 625 (Europe) or 525 (USA);
- number of total pixels per line (luminance): 864 (Europe) or 858 (USA);
- number of fields per second: 50 (Europe) or 59.94 (USA).

MPEG standards provide **isochronization** (see Section 11.3.5) of the image and sound data at a combined bit rate of typically 1.5 Mbit/s (and up to 30 Mbit/s). Other examples of hybrid encoding can be found in the (future) standards MPEG-4 (with a very low bit rate), US-HDTV, DVB and DVC.

9.4.6 Variable length coding (VLC)

In the codes discussed in Sections 9.3 and 9.4.1 to 9.4.3, the codewords were of standard length; for example, 8 bits for PCM and 1 bit for DM. Further bit reduction can be achieved by using codewords with a variable length, depending on the information content of the corresponding source signal, rather than the same length.

In this form of source encoding, all elements (source symbols) of the set B are converted to a set C of codewords (which may or may not be binary code symbols), the length $l(c)$ of which is dependent on the probability $p(b)$ of the corresponding source signal, as follows:

$$B = \begin{bmatrix} b_1 & b_2 & b_3 & b_4 & \cdots & b_n & \cdots & b_m \\ p(b_1) & p(b_2) & p(b_3) & p(b_4) & \cdots & p(b_n) & \cdots & p(b_m) \end{bmatrix}$$

$$C = \begin{bmatrix} c_1 & c_2 & c_3 & c_4 & \cdots & c_n & \cdots & c_m \\ I(c_1) & I(c_2) & I(c_3) & I(c_4) & \cdots & I(c_n) & \cdots & I(c_m) \end{bmatrix}$$

Here we have to interpret the concept *set B* in broad terms. Such a set can consist not only of character sets, such as the International Alphabets CCITT ITA2 and CCITT IA5, but also of the 256 possible values of an 8-bit PCM word, the possible values of video samples, the difference values occurring in DPCM or the various **run length** values of video coding vectors.

In these examples it is clear that not all source symbols exhibit the same statistical behaviour. The principle of variable length coding – the more probable the source symbol, the shorter the codeword – is based on that fact. The reduction achievable with this coding thus depends on the distribution characteristic. A useful concept here is that of **code efficiency** η, which can be defined as 'the average information content per source symbol $H(B)$ divided by the average codeword length $L(c)$'. The following holds for binary symbols.

$$\eta = \frac{H(B)}{L(c)} = \frac{-\sum_{n=1}^{m} p(b_n)^2 \log p(b_n)}{\sum_{n=1}^{m} p(b_n) I(c_n)}$$

For the redundancy R after encoding we have:

$$R = 1 - \eta$$

Of course, this reduction affects the processing of the code, because any departure from the standard word length can pose problems for decoding. In any case, coding must be such that individual codewords are recognizable as such (direct and unambiguous decodability). An acceptable condition is that no codeword *begins* with any other codeword.

Very common examples of variable length coding are the Shannon–Fano, Huffman and so-called **comma codes**. They all use the principle of shorter codewords for source symbols with higher probabilities. The **Huffman code**, which almost always guarantees optimum coding, will be considered in more detail.

The standard procedure in Huffman coding, assuming m-valued symbols, consists of the following operations:

(a)   List the set of source symbols B as a column with decreasing probability.

(b)   Combine the m lowest probabilities and re-sort in decreasing order of probability.

(c)   Repeat step (b) until the last column contains m probabilities.

(d)   Beginning with the final column of probabilities, assign the first code symbol to all source symbols associated with the highest probability. Assign the remaining $m - 1$ code symbols to the source symbols associated with the following probabilities.

(e)   Repeat step (d) for the previous column, taking account of the composite character of some probabilities, as the second code symbol of the codeword.

(f)   Repeat step (e) until all the original source symbols have been assigned a codeword.

To clarify this, an example is given of encoding with binary code symbols ($m = 2$). Let B be the set of source symbols as follows:

B	$p(b_n)$
b_1	0.30
b_2	0.25
b_3	0.20
b_4	0.15
b_5	0.10

Execution of steps (a) to (c).

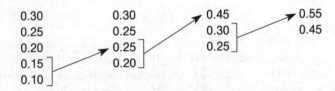

Execution of steps (d) to (f).

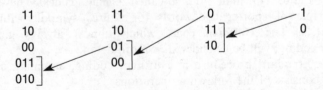

This results in the following Huffman coding:

B	C
b_1	11
b_2	10
b_3	00
b_4	011
b_5	010

It can be seen that this code can be directly and unambiguously decoded, since no codeword begins with any other codeword. The vulnerability of codes generated in this way, however, leads to preference sometimes being given to codes in which a specific code symbol is used to indicate the division between two codewords. Codes of this type are called **comma codes**.

9.5 Channel encoding

In practice, every channel used for data transmission produces errors, even when the signalling speed is lower than that given by Hartley–Shannon. These errors can be caused, for example, by switching circuits at the network nodes.

In addition, interference sources (other than the so-called **white noise** sources) on the transmission routes can cause bit errors. The number of errors is often expressed as the **Bit Error Rate (BER)**, the ratio between the number of error bits introduced and the total number of transmitted bits. Thus the BER characterizes the quality of the channel used for data transmission. Depending on the physical cause and related statistical behaviour of the bit errors, these may occur as random or grouped bit errors, the latter being known as an **error burst**. In this case, the concept **burst length** b is used, where b includes the first and the last bits in the group.

For both categories, a number of error management techniques have been developed. These either detect that an error has arisen (**error detecting code**) or correct the error (**error correcting code**).

Error detecting codes offer the following options:

- the receiver destroys the incorrectly received information and replaces it by previous codewords. This procedure can be applied, for example, to information with a real-time character such as video or sound.

- the receiver applies an **Automatic Repeat Request (ARQ)** procedure, which uses **Negative Acknowledgement (NAK)** or **Positive Acknowledgement (ACK)** signals to indicate that retransmission is or is not required. If ACK or NAK is not sent on time, this will also lead to retransmission of the code. This procedure is normally used with discrete source signals.

Error correcting codes are capable of eliminating any errors that occur, using a procedure referred to as **Forward Error Correction (FEC)**. It must be stressed that the detecting and correcting properties only apply within well-defined limits, which are dependent on the code used; if the actual number of errors exceeds the limit, the excess are called **residual errors**.

All techniques used for channel encoding are based on the principle of *adding* bits to the information to be transmitted. In other words, the redundancy of the signal is deliberately increased. Thus, this type of signal processing appears to undo, partially or totally, the results achieved with source encoding. This contradiction is only apparent: redundancy in the source signal is rarely of use in error management procedures designed to handle transmission errors.

9.5.1   Block encoding

Block encoding is a variant of channel encoding used for both error detection and error correction, usually for random errors. It is accomplished by adding to the original binary data word D, where:

$$D = d_1, d_2, d_3, d_4, \ldots, d_m$$

a number of **parity check bits**. This results in a new channel encoded codeword T for *transmission*:

$$T = t_1, t_2, t_3, t_4, \ldots, t_m, \ldots, t_n$$

The procedure is referred to as (n, m) encoding – the new codeword, T, contains n bits whereas the original dataword, D, had m bits. Thus $p = n - m$ parity bits have been added to the original codeword.

Depending on the relationship between p and m, block codes can have the following properties:

- the ability to detect one, two, three or more errors within a single codeword (single, double, ... error detecting codes).

- the ability to correct one, two, three or more errors within a single codeword (single, double, ... error correcting codes).

In general, the number of errors that can be detected is always one more than the number of errors that can be corrected. For forward error correction, the concept of **Hamming distance**, h, plays an essential role. Hamming distance is the minimum number of bits that can differ between any two channel encoded codewords U and V. In modulo-2 notation this can be written mathematically as:

$$h(U,V) = \sum_{j=1}^{n} u_j \oplus v_j$$

It follows that for a code without any redundancy the Hamming distance is given by:

$$h = 1$$

The correction capability increases as the Hamming distance increases. It would be possible to correct an incorrectly received codeword, R, by comparing it with all possible codewords and then choosing the closest match as the correct one. In practice, however, it is usual to use corresponding algorithms for encoding and decoding. It can be shown that the relationship between the number of correctable faulty databits, t, and the necessary Hamming distance, h, is given by:

$$h \geqslant 2(2t + 1)$$

9.5.2 Linear systematic block encoding

In this coding, the parity bits are generated by a specific (linear) modulo-2 summation of the original databits of the dataword, D, which is then added as the last bits of the codeword (systematic).

The coding process for this category of codes can be regarded as a linear transformation of the m-dimensional vector **D**:

$$T = D \cdot G$$

The coordinates of the vector **D** are given by the successive bits of the dataword D. The linear transformation is carried out using the **generator matrix** G. Additions are performed as modulo-2 operations.

$$G = \begin{bmatrix} g_{11} & g_{12} & \cdot & \cdot & \cdot & \cdot & \cdot & g_{1n} \\ g_{21} & \cdot & & & & & & g_{2n} \\ \cdot & \cdot & & & & & & \cdot \\ \cdot & \cdot & & & & & & \cdot \\ \cdot & \cdot & & & & & & \cdot \\ \cdot & \cdot & & & & & & \cdot \\ g_{m1} & \cdot & \cdot & \cdot & \cdot & \cdot & \cdot & g_{mn} \end{bmatrix}$$

In accordance with the definition of the category **linear systematic encoding**, the matrix G consists of a unit matrix G_1 of degree m (D is m-dimensional) and of a part G_2 that generates the parity check bits:

$$G = [G_1 \; G_2] = \begin{bmatrix} 1 & 0 & 0 & \cdot & \cdot & 0 & g_{1(m+1)} & \cdot & \cdot & \cdot & g_{1n} \\ 0 & 1 & 0 & & & \cdot & g_{2(m+1)} & & & & \cdot \\ 0 & 0 & & & & \cdot & \cdot & & & & \cdot \\ \cdot & & & & & & \cdot & & & & \cdot \\ \cdot & & & 1 & & \cdot & \cdot & & & & \cdot \\ 0 & \cdot & \cdot & \cdot & \cdot & 1 & g_{m(m+1)} & \cdot & \cdot & \cdot & g_{mn} \end{bmatrix}$$

This transformation produces an n-dimensional vector **T** as a result. The coordinates of this vector again correspond to the successive bits of the channel encoded word T that is now available for transmission.

On decoding in the receiver, the composition of the transmitted codeword T is unknown. The received signal consists of a codeword R of n bits, in other words an n-dimensional code vector **R**. Error detection can now be performed by processing the first m elements of the code vector **R** with the generator matrix G. These m bits may or may not be the same as those of the original codeword D, depending on the presence or absence of transmission errors.

If there are no errors, the parity check bits generated will be identical to those received with codeword R. If one or more errors have occurred (within the limits posed by the channel encoding) the difference will be detected. If more errors occur than can be handled by the channel code, residual errors will not be detected. Comparison of the parity check patterns is simply achieved by modulo-2 addition of both groups of check bits. With error free transmission, this summation produces the value 0. The algorithms required for error correcting operations are described in Appendix D.

9.5.3   Cyclical block codes

Cyclical block codes are so named because the set of all possible codewords of a particular channel code consists of codewords C which are derived from each other by cyclic transformations of their bit patterns. All values of the original dataword D remain possible. Cyclic block encoding can be viewed as a special case of linear systematic block encoding. When designing the encoding, special attention must be paid to keeping the code systematic so that the original dataword D is recognizable as the first m bits of the codeword C.

In the treatment of cyclic block codes it is advantageous to make use of the polynomial notation. Any codeword C, where:

$$C = c_1, c_2, \ldots, c_{n-1}, c_n$$

can then be written as an $(n-1)$ degree polynomial in x:

$$C(x) = c_1 x^{n-1}, c_2 x^{n-2}, \ldots, c_{n-1} x, c_n$$

For a cyclic rotation over k bits, the following term holds:

$$x^k C(x)(x^{n-1} + 1)$$

In a similar manner, the generator matrix can be written as:

$$
G =
\begin{bmatrix}
g_{11} x^{n-1} & g_{12} x^{n-2} & \cdots & g_{1(n-1)} x & g_{1n} \\
g_{21} x^{n-1} & \cdot & \cdots & \cdot & \cdot \\
\cdot & \cdot & & \cdot & \cdot \\
\cdot & \cdot & & \cdot & \cdot \\
\cdot & \cdot & & \cdot & \cdot \\
g_{m1} x^{n-1} & \cdot & \cdots & \cdot & g_{mn}
\end{bmatrix}
$$

For systematic cyclic codes, the matrix should take a form as shown below:

$$
G = [G_1 \; G_2] =
\begin{bmatrix}
x^{n-1} & - & - & - & - & - & \cdots \\
- & x^{n-2} & - & - & - & - & \cdots \\
- & - & & & & - & \cdot \\
- & - & & & & - & \cdot \\
- & - & & & & - & \cdot \\
- & - & - & - & - & x^{n-m} & \cdots 1
\end{bmatrix}
$$

Of importance here are the properties of the bottom row vector of this generator matrix, the **generator polynomial** $g(x)$, for which the following holds:

$$g(x) = x^{n-m} + \ldots + 1$$

The cyclic nature of the encoding occurs because all other row vectors of the matrix are determined by $g(x)$ as follows: succeeding row vectors are formed by multiplication of the generator polynomial by various powers of x, in combination with the modulo-2 summation with the preceding row vectors.

When decoding, either for error detection or error correction, use is again made of the parity matrix P which is obtained by using the procedure given for linear systematic codes.

A major advantage associated with the use of cyclic codes lies in the relative simplicity with which they can be implemented. This is because the transformation of the dataword D by the generator matrix G leads to a codeword C for which:

$$C(x) = a(x)\, g(x)$$

in other words, every codeword $C(x)$ is divisible by the generator polynomial $g(x)$.

Using this property, the parity bits of any codeword $C(x)$ can be determined by the following procedure. Assuming a dataword $D(x)$, the bits of $D(x)$ will shift over $(n - m)$ positions to the left as a result of the multiplication of x^{n-m}, thus enabling the $(n - m)$ parity check bits to be added. Modulo-2 division by $g(x)$ then results in a quotient $q(x)$ and a remainder $r(x)$:

$$\frac{x^{n-m}\, D(x)}{g(x)} = q(x) + \frac{r(x)}{g(x)}$$

By rearrangement of terms (modulo-2), it follows that the term:

$$x^{n-m}\, D(x) + r(x)$$

will be divisible by $g(x)$. The remainder, $r(x)$, forms the required group of parity check bits.

Cyclic encoding is widely used for the detection of so-called burst errors. The longest error burst, b_{max}, that can be detected with absolute certainty with this method is equal to the number $n - m$ of parity bits:

$$b_{max} = n - m$$

The proof of this assertion is omitted. However, it can be imagined that all the data bits of the codeword can be divided into groups of $n - m$ bits. The first parity check bit could then be used to give all the first bits of these groups an even (or odd) parity. In a similar way, the second, third and remaining bits of the groups of bits could be protected against errors.

This form of error control is very often used in conjunction with the transmission of relatively long blocks, usually called **frames**. The following conditions are then imposed on the generator polynomial $g(x)$:

- $g(x)$ must have a form $g(x) = x^{n-m} + \ldots + 1$;
- the number of terms of $g(x)$ must be even, that is, divisible by $x - 1$. (It can then be shown that all uneven numbers of bit errors are detectable.)
- the number of parity check bits $n - m$ must be equal to the maximum burst length b_{max} that can be detected with absolute certainty.

This application of cyclic encoding is called **Cyclic Redundancy Check (CRC)** and the $n - m$ parity check bits are called the **Frame Check Sequence (FCS)**.

However, the choice is not always made for an FCS value that makes the codeword, including the FCS, divisible. In a number of cases, it turns out that better error management is possible if a standard remainder is obtained after modulo-2 division. An example is to be found in CCITT Recommendations X.25 LAPB and Q.921 in which the binary remainder '0001110100001111' must be obtained after error free transmission.

The following are examples of standard generator polynomials:

$$\text{CRC - 12} = X^{12} + X^{11} + X^3 + X^2 + X + 1;$$
$$\text{CRC - 16} = X^{16} + X^{15} + X^2 + 1;$$
$$\text{CRC - HDLC} = X^{16} + X^{12} + X^5 + 1;$$
$$\text{CRC - 32} = X^{32} + X^{26} + X^{23} + X^{16} + X^{12} + X^{11} + X^{10} + X^8 + X^7$$
$$+ X^5 + X^4 + X^2 + X + 1$$

Chapter 10

Performance analysis

10.1 Introduction

Telecommunication systems may have all the required functions correctly implemented and still not work satisfactorily. In particular, such a situation can occur when the amount of telecommunications traffic exceeds the capacity of the system. In that case calls can be lost, for example, or there can be excessive waiting times.

In telephony, calculations were already being made at the turn of the century as to how much traffic could be carried, for example, by a trunk group. The Danish mathematician A.K. Erlang published a formula in 1917 which allowed the calculation of the probability that a call would find all lines busy. This marks the beginning of the subject of **teletraffic theory**.

After the Second World War, many calculations were performed on computer systems to allow predictions to be made, for example, about the waiting times of jobs for the CPU. This led to the creation of the subject of **performance analysis of computer systems**.

Currently, almost every telecommunication system contains one or more processors (computers), and most computer systems are equipped with some capability for telecommunication. The subjects of teletraffic theory and performance analysis of computer systems are also becoming more and more intertwined with each other. Therefore we have chosen the title of the study of the quantitative aspects of telematics (telecommunications and informatics) to be: **performance analysis of telematic systems**.

In one chapter one can do no more than discuss a few elementary concepts associated with performance analysis and give a few examples. Those examples answer the questions:

- How much traffic can be handled by a trunk group of N lines at a given blocking probability of 1%?
- What is the probability of blocking when 20 erlang traffic is generated by 80 users who move randomly through an office building with 4 base stations and 12 radio channels per base station?
- If data packets from various sources are to be transmitted over one line, at what line loading is there only a 1% probability that the waiting time will exceed 10 times the transmission time?

10.2　Inter-arrival time of calls

Typically, the load of telecommunication systems is mainly determined by external factors. For example, a subscriber takes the receiver off the hook or a message is offered to an electronic mail system. For the system these are random events that can be modelled as **stochastic variables (random variables)**.

The time that elapses between two successive calls offered to a telephone exchange is usually modelled as a continuous stochastic variable. It is often assumed that the time between successive calls has the **negative exponential probability distribution**. In Figure 10.1, the **probability density function** of a negative exponentially distributed random variable (with mean 2, by way of example) is plotted. The formula of this probability density function is:

$$f(t) = \begin{cases} \frac{1}{2} \cdot e^{-t/2} & t \geqslant 0 \\ 0 & t < 0 \end{cases} \qquad (10.1)$$

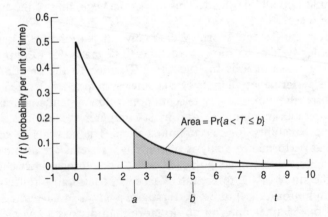

Figure 10.1　Probability density function of a negative exponentially distributed random variable with mean 2.

The probability density function can be interpreted as follows: the probability that the random variable T takes a value in the interval (a, b) is equal to the area between a and b under the curve $f(t)$. This statement can be written in the form of a formula:

$$\Pr\{a < T \leqslant b\} = \int_a^b f(t)\, \mathrm{d}t \qquad \textbf{(10.2)}$$

where $\Pr\{X\}$ (taken from Probability) is the notation for: 'the probability that event X occurs'. A negative exponential distribution is completely determined by one parameter. It is convenient to take the **mean** (also called the **expected value**) to be this parameter. In the example given in (10.2) and plotted in Figure 10.1, the mean is equal to 2.

The negative exponential distribution is closely linked with the **Poisson process**. If the arrival process is a Poisson process with intensity λ, then the inter-arrival times are negative exponentially distributed with mean $1/\lambda$. Because of the nice mathematical properties, it is usual to assume the arrival process to be a Poisson process. The greater the number of independent sources generating the arrivals, the more justified this assumption will be.

The negative exponential distribution is the only continuous probability distribution that has the **memoryless property**. This means that knowledge of the condition that for the first a time units no arrival has taken place does not tell anything about the additional time that has to be waited from time a until the first following arrival. The probability distribution of T under the condition $T > a$ is the same (only shifted a time-distance a to the right) as the original time distribution of T. This follows from the fact that the curve of Figure 10.1 to the right of a is a reduced copy of the original curve.

10.3 Number of busy lines

The number of busy lines at time t, $X(t)$, fully describes the state of a trunk group if the arrival process of telephone calls is a Poisson process and if we assume that the holding time of a call (the time that a line is kept occupied by that call) is negative exponentially distributed. If it had another distribution, then it would be necessary to specify also the arrival times of the $X(t)$ calls that are present. Because of the memoryless property, the process $X(t)$ is a **Markov chain**. For this Markov chain we want to find the equilibrium distribution; from that probability distribution we can read the probability that a call will find all lines busy.

It is helpful to draw the **state diagram** corresponding to the Markov chain. In this diagram the circles indicate states (in this case the number of busy lines) and the arrows indicate **transition intensities**. The transition

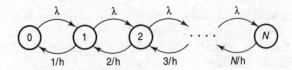

Figure 10.2   State diagram of the number of busy lines of a trunk group of N lines. The values along the arrows are transition intensities.

intensity λ from state 1 to state 2, for example, means that with probability $\lambda \Delta t$ the state will be $X(t + \Delta t) = 2$, given that at time t the state is $X(t) = 1$ (Δt should be very small, in fact, the statements are only correct in the limit case $\Delta t \to 0$). In the same way, it holds that when k lines are busy, the probability that a line becomes free in an interval of length Δt is equal to $k \, \Delta t / h$. Here h is the mean holding time of a line.

The probability that at any random moment the Markov chain is in state k, is given by ν_k. The probability distribution ν_k, $k = 0, 1, 2, \dots, N$, is called the **equilibrium distribution** of the Markov chain. The determination of the equilibrium distribution of a Markov chain with a 'one-dimensional' state diagram as in Figure 10.2 is simple if we assume the following equilibrium property: the probability of a transition from k to $k + 1$ in an interval Δt is equal to the probability of a transition from $k + 1$ to k in an equally short interval. In formula form, this implies the following property:

$$\nu_k \cdot \lambda \cdot \Delta t = \nu_{k+1} \cdot \frac{k+1}{h} \cdot \Delta t \qquad k = 0, 1, 2, \dots, N-1 \qquad \text{(10.3)}$$

From (10.3), in combination with the fact that the sum of the probabilities must be equal to 1, that is, $\nu_0 + \nu_1 + \nu_2 + \dots + \nu_N = 1$, the equilibrium distribution follows. The calculation of these probabilities is considered in the following section.

10.4   Blocking probability

A new call that finds all lines busy is blocked. A blocked call is assumed to be lost. If the arrival process is a Poisson process, then the **blocking probability** is equal to ν_N, the probability that all lines are busy.

Formula (10.3) gives the ratio between successive probabilities of the equilibrium distribution. Dividing both sides of the equation by λ, we can see that the ratio is equal to $(k + 1)/(\lambda h)$. The term λh is a measure of the amount of **offered traffic**. The amount of offered traffic is proportional to λ, the number of calls per unit of time, and to h, the holding time expressed in units of time. Therefore the unit of traffic is a dimensionless quantity, given the name **erlang**. In order to simplify the notation, we indicate offered traffic with a single letter A:

$$A = \lambda \cdot h \text{ erlang} \tag{10.4}$$

Construct the series of non-normalized probabilities $w_0, w_1, w_2, \ldots, w_N$ as follows:

$$
\begin{aligned}
w_0 &= 1 \\
w_1 &= A \\
w_2 &= A^2/2 \\
&\vdots \\
w_k &= A^k/k! \\
&\vdots \\
w_N &= A^N/N!
\end{aligned}
\tag{10.5}
$$

The ratio between two successive non-normalized probabilities is then as given in (10.3). Now we need only to normalize (divide by the sum of the non-normalized probabilities) in order to get the equilibrium distribution. The blocking probability then becomes:

$$\nu_N = \frac{w_N}{w_0 + w_1 + \cdots + w_N} \tag{10.6}$$

If we write the blocking probability for A erlangs of traffic, offered to N lines as $E_N(A)$ and fill in the expressions for w_k then we obtain the familiar form of the well-known Erlang-B formula:

$$E_N(A) = \frac{A^N/N!}{1 + A + A^2 + \cdots + A^N/N!} \tag{10.7}$$

Here we derived the Erlang-B formula on the assumption that the holding time had a negative exponential distribution. It can be proved for loss systems that the equilibrium distribution is independent of the probability distribution of the holding times. So even if the holding time is a constant (but the arrival process is still a Poisson process), then formula (10.7) remains valid. This property has contributed to the frequent application of the Erlang-B formula. Applications are not limited to the lines of a trunk group or the time slots in a TDM multiplexer, but apply to each pure loss system where the assumption of a memoryless probability distribution of inter-arrival times is not unreasonable.

EXAMPLE

What is the blocking probability if an average of one call per 40 s is offered on five lines, when the average holding time of one call is 100 s?

Answer. One call per 40 seconds implies $\lambda = 0.025$. With $h = 100$ s the traffic offered is $A = 2.5$ erlang. The non-normalized probabilities are:

$$
\begin{array}{rl}
w_0 = & 1.0 \\
w_1 = & 2.5 \\
w_2 = & 3.125 \\
w_3 = & 2.604167 \\
w_4 = & 1.627604 \\
w_5 = & \underline{0.813802} \\
 & 11.670573
\end{array}
$$

From this, it follows that the blocking probability is:

$$
E_5(2.5) = \frac{0.813802}{11.670573} \approx 7\%
$$

Thus approximately 7% of the offered traffic is lost. The **carried traffic** is then 2.325 erlang. This means that on average 2.325 lines are busy, and that 7% of the time all five lines are busy. The **loading** of the trunk group is $2.325/5 = 46.5\%$.

10.5   Computation of blocking probabilities

The direct calculation of the blocking probability is possible in simple cases, such as the previous example, but in practical cases, N is a multiple of 30 and the direct calculation of 30! ($= 265\,252\,859\,812\,191\,058\,636\,308\,480\,000\,000\,000$) is bad enough! Various businesses and institutions have published graphs and books of tables including the Erlang-B formula. Now that more people have access to a programmable computer, it is useful to take note of a robust method for calculating blocking probabilities. This method makes use of a recursive relation for the inverse of the blocking probability (V). If A and N have a value, then the execution of the following three lines of Pascal produce the value of $E_N(A)$ in the variable EnA

```
V: = 1;
for i:=1 to N do V:=V*i/A+1;          (10.8)
EnA:=1/V;
```

It is often required to know how much traffic is allowed for a given value of the blocking probability. For example, in the introduction we asked the question:

- How much traffic can be handled by a trunk group of N lines at a given blocking probability of 1%?

The required value of A can be found, for example, by a binary search method. We begin with a broad interval with 0 as the left-hand and $N \times 10$ as the right-hand boundary. We choose A in the middle of this interval. If the blocking probability is too large, we proceed with the left half of the interval, otherwise with the right. A is chosen in the middle of the new interval and after 30 repetitions, the required value of A has been found with an accuracy of $N \times 10^{-8}$. This adds a number of lines to (10.8):

```
write('N ? '); readln(N);
left:=0; right:=N*10;
for k:=1 to 30 do begin
  A:=(left+right)/2;
  V:=1;
  for i:=1 to N do V:=V*i/A+1;
  EnA:=1/V;
  if EnA > 0.01 then right:=A else left:=A;
end{for k};
writeln('A =',A:8:5);
```

$$(10.9)$$

In this way, the value of A (the offered traffic in erlangs) can be calculated for a large number of values of N. With a small modification we can also calculate this relation for other values of the blocking probability. The result can be seen in Figure 10.3.

The first part of the solid line, belonging to a blocking probability of 0.01, shows that the loading is limited for a small group of lines. For example, when N is 10, $A = 4.46$ erlang offered traffic (and 4.42 erlang carried traffic, because 1% of the traffic has been lost) gives a loading of 44.2%. For larger values of N the solid line gets steadily closer to the diagonal of the figure and the loading gets steadily closer to 100%. For $N = 100$, the loading corresponding to 1% blocking is considerably higher, namely $A = 84.06 \implies 83.22$ erlang carried traffic and hence a loading of 83.2%.

It is thus very efficient to use large trunk groups. There is also a clear associated disadvantage, namely the sensitivity to overload of efficient, large trunk groups. The convergence of the dotted lines to the

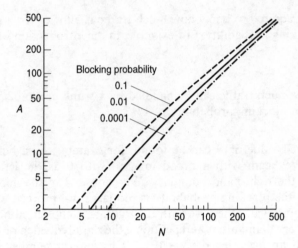

Figure 10.3 Permissible amount of traffic (A) as a function of the number of lines (N) at a given blocking probability.

solid line for increasing N shows that, at large values of N, a small relative change in the amount of offered traffic leads to a large change in the blocking probability.

10.6   Blocking probabilities in mobile systems

The blocking analysis as described in the previous sections works very well in the context of a not too small – say, 50 or more – population of fixed users. In the case of a mobile communication system, the number of users in the vicinity of one base station, or Radio Fixed Part (RFP) in DECT terminology, can be small. Moreover, the number of users who share the radio channels of an RFP is a quantity that varies randomly as opposed to the constant population size when all users have a fixed connection to the communication system. The number of users in the area that is covered by a particular RFP varies as users move from one area to another. In this section we consider the computation of blocking probabilities when the number of users is not large and also when this number is random.

As an example, consider an RFP with 12 radio channels – this corresponds to the standard for Digital European Cordless Telecommunications (DECT). The number of users that compete for those channels may be 10, 20, 30 or any other number. It will be obvious that if there are only 10 users, or whichever other number ⩽ 12, then a free radio channel will always be found. Here we consider only blocking due to limited resources; it is assumed that the radio propagation conditions are adequate. The 10 users in this example offer a certain amount of traffic; using the Erlang formula with $N = 12$ would result in a non-zero value of blocking, whereas we know that no blocking can occur. Therefore the Engset formula should be used in place of the Erlang formula.

The Engset formula is similar to the Erlang formula. It has one additional parameter, s, representing the number of sources, that is, the size of the population. Instead of the call intensity or arrival intensity λ, the call intensity per free source is specified and denoted with the symbol α. The inverse of the call intensity per free source, $1/\alpha$, is equal to the mean duration between the end of a conversation and the next call of a source, also called the idle time of a source. The formula that gives the Engset blocking probability reads:

$$G_N(s, \alpha) = \frac{\binom{s-1}{N} \cdot \left(\frac{\alpha}{\mu}\right)^N}{\sum_{i=0}^{N} \binom{s-1}{i} \cdot \left(\frac{\alpha}{\mu}\right)^i} \tag{10.10}$$

The μ in the formula is equal to the inverse of the mean holding time, that is, $\mu = 1/h$. As before, N is the number of channels. In Appendix A it is shown how the formula relates to the Markov model of the number of occupied channels (cf. Figure 10.2 and Figure E.1) and how it can be computed.

The other speciality of mobile systems is that the number of users in the vicinity of a base station is random. Consider an office building with a DECT system that has several RFPs (base stations). The users will be more or less equally distributed over the RFPs. For one RFP the probability that it serves s users will be denoted by q_s. The blocking probability at such an RFP with N radio channels is then:

$$B_N(\alpha) = \sum_{s=0}^{S} q_s \cdot G_N(s, \alpha) \tag{10.11}$$

The computation of the blocking probability $B_N(\alpha)$ is best illustrated with the graph of Figure 10.4. The solid line in the graph is a plot of the function $G_{12}(s, 0.333)$. Here we have set $\alpha = 0.333$ corresponding to an idle time of $1/0.333 = 3$ time units. The time unit can – without loss of generality – be chosen equal to the mean holding time, implying $h = 1 = \mu$. The value of $\alpha = 0.333$ corresponds to 0.25 erlang per user, approximately, as will be explained in the remainder of this paragraph. When a mobile user has an idle time of 3 time units and a mean holding time of 1 time, then it is 'on air' a fraction $1/(1+3) = 0.25$ of the time. Here the effect of blocking is neglected. This results in an approximation that is very close in the case of small blocking probabilities.

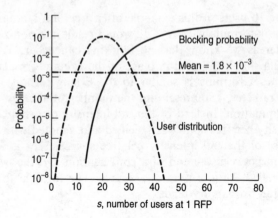

Figure 10.4 Location probability or user distribution, that is, the probability that s users are at an RFP (dashed line), and Engset blocking probability (solid line) as a function of s. The mean is an average of the solid line weighted according to the dashed line.

The dashed line in Figure 10.4 represents the probability that out of a total population of S users there are s in the vicinity of one particular RFP. In this example the total population $S = 80$ is divided over four RFPs, resulting in the following binomial distribution of the number of users at one RFP:

$$q_s = \binom{80}{s} \cdot \left(\frac{1}{4}\right)^s \cdot \left(1 - \frac{1}{4}\right)^{80-s} \tag{10.12}$$

The overall blocking probability for a mobile user is now found by applying formula (10.11), which gives the probability that the user finds all 12 radio channels of its RFP occupied. The actual blocking probability may be lower because a user can reach more than one RFP or higher because of poor radio conditions. If one RFP is consistently more popular than others then equation (10.12) must be adapted, for example, by specifying that the RFP gets more than 1/4 of all the traffic.

The parameters used in producing Figure 10.4 were such that they correspond to the second question posed in the introduction:

- What is the probability of blocking when 20 erlang traffic is generated by 80 users who move randomly through an office building with 4 base stations and 12 radio channels per base station?

As explained above $\alpha = 0.333$ corresponds to 0.25 erlang per user; the 80 users therefore generate 20 erlang. The user distribution in the figure corresponds to 80 users distributed randomly over four base stations. The Engset blocking probability (solid line) is computed for a system with 12 lines. The average of the solid line – weighted with the dashed line – is 1.8×10^{-3} which gives the answer to the question above.

Any blocking due to congestion further on in the network is additional. Moreover, when a user moves during a conversation from one RFP to another then the event of blocking at the new RFP may result in a dropped call. Therefore, the computed blocking probability is generally required to be lower than 0.01: typically 0.005 or 0.001.

10.7 ATM traffic characteristics

In Section 10.5 we saw that the efficiency of a trunk group becomes greater as the number of lines in the trunk group increases (cf. Figure 10.3). Those calculations were based on the Erlang blocking formula. Now we want to increase the efficiency further by using the fact that many sources do not offer a constant bit rate: the average bit rate can be considerably lower than the peak bit rate. ATM offers the possibility of flexible bandwidth multiplexing of such sources. The additional benefit of increased efficiency does not come for free: somehow provisions must be made to allow for stochastic fluctuations of the bit rate. This requires a method for describing the traffic characteristics of ATM sources and an extension of the Erlang theory.

The Erlang theory deals with constant bit rate sources that hold one unit of a resource (one line of a trunk group) for the whole duration of the connection. The activity of a constant bit rate source does not vary. While active, a constant bit rate source produces, for example for 64 kbit/s voice, one octet of information every 125 μs. We can contrast this with a variable bit rate source such as 'the computer' in the request reply example at the beginning of Section 8.3, where in an interval of 46.1 seconds there is only activity during 1 second. During this active period characters are transmitted at a rate of one character every 3333 μs. During one connection, many active periods (bursts) may occur. In Figure 10.5 we represent the traffic generated by a variable bit rate source at three levels. In this example the variable bit rate source is an on/off source, which has an on/off pattern at burst level.

An important feature of this representation is the distinction of different levels, each one with its own time scale. At the top we have connection level, where the line is high when the source under consideration has a connection established and low otherwise. The duration of a connection is typically measured in minutes. For variable bit rate sources the faster time scale of the burst level is necessary to describe the bursts of activity that alternate with periods of silence. For variable bit rate sources the line at burst level is high, for example, when a block

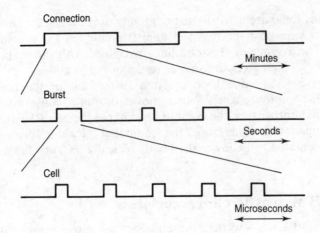

Figure 10.5 The three levels of quantification of traffic.

of text is transmitted and low during the periods of silence. The fastest time scale is at cell level; at this level the transmission of characters, octets or ATM cells takes place. The transmission of one ATM cell of 53 octets on a 155 Mbit/s link takes 2.7 μs: this sets the time scale for the cell level.

Most ATM sources are of the on/off type: when active they transmit cells at their peak rate which is, for example, determined by the processing speed of the source (or destination) or which is set otherwise. This means that during a burst of activity, cells are transmitted more or less equidistant in time (further on the transmission path intermediate buffering may cause cells to be less evenly spaced). In this context one can clearly define what is meant by mean and peak bit rate. The mean bit rate is the bit rate averaged over the duration of a connection (connection level); the peak bit rate is the bit rate averaged during a burst (burst level). The bit rate during one cell transmission is equal to the aggregate bit rate of the ATM channel (155 or 622 Mbit/s).

In some cases a source may emit cells so irregularly that each cell should be considered a burst in itself, defying the time scale of the burst level. In that case one would average the bit rate over some convenient interval corresponding to the time scale of the burst level, say, 1/25th of a second for video sources.

The most elementary variable bit rate source is one that is active during 50% of the duration of the connection and silent otherwise. If we have, say, 100 such on/off sources connected via an ATM channel, then on average 50 sources are active, but the actual number of sources that are active fluctuates around this value. The probability that more than 76 sources are active can be computed to be equal to 2.8×10^{-8}. The factor $76/50 = 1.52$ is called a **safety factor**. Multiplying the average utilization

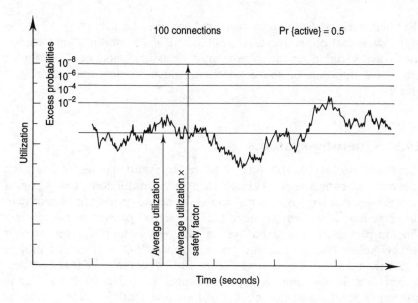

Figure 10.6   Simulation of changes in utilization of an ATM channel due to fluctuations at burst level.

of the ATM channel (at the time scale of the connection level, that is, averaging over minutes) with this safety factor gives a value of utilization that is exceeded with a very small probability. Figure 10.6 shows a simulation of the utilization of an ATM channel at the time scale of the burst level and the values of utilization that are exceeded with probabilities 10^{-2}, 10^{-4}, 10^{-6}, and 10^{-8}, respectively.

The set of rules to decide whether a new ATM connection can be accepted is generally referred to as **connection acceptance control**. From Figure 10.6 it is clear that on an ATM channel new connections may be refused, while the average utilization of the channel is below 100%. To keep a margin that allows for fluctuations at burst level, new connections are admitted only if average utilization multiplied by safety factor is not above 100%. This differs from fixed bandwidth multiplexing, where, for example, on a 2 Mbit/s channel carrying 30 'lines' of 64 kbit/s, each new connection will be accepted as long as any of the 30 'lines' is free.

To dimension a communication link we use in the first place the Erlang theory, which tells us that, for example, for 20 erlang traffic we need 30 'lines' in order to have a probability of 0.01 that a connection is not accepted (Figure 10.3). The reduction from 30 'lines' to 20 erlang, in this example, is a provision for traffic fluctuations at the connection level. When dimensioning for ATM traffic there is an additional reduction, quantified by a safety factor, to provide for fluctuations at the burst level. At first glance one could conclude that this way ATM has very low utilization. However, if flexible bandwidth multiplexing were not used, each variable bit rate source must be assigned its peak bit rate for the whole duration of the connection, which would imply really low efficiency.

10.8   Queuing systems

If a data packet of 160 bits is to be transmitted over a line with transmission capacity of 64 kbits/s then the transmission of that packet lasts 2.5 ms. If a large number of sources generate packets to be sent over the same line, it is often assumed that the arrival process of packets is a Poisson process. For a stable system the average time between arrivals will be greater than 2.5 ms, but it often happens that an inter-arrival time is less than 2.5 ms. A glance at Figure 10.1 makes it clear that an inter-arrival time in the interval $(0, 2.5)$ is more probable than one in the interval $(2.5, 5.0)$, even though it is of the same width.

A temporary pile-up of packet-arrivals can be dealt with by queuing those packets. If the buffer used to queue the packets is sufficiently large, then it is reasonable, and a simplification for the performance analysis, to assume that the buffer is infinitely large.

Such a queuing system with Poisson arrivals, a fixed service time (duration of the transmission) and one server is called an M/D/1 queue in the **Kendall notation**. The first letter refers to the inter-arrival process that has the Markov property, that is, it has inter-arrival times whose probability distribution has the memoryless property. The second letter refers to the service process, which has a deterministic length if all packets are 160 bits The third symbol refers to the single server for the packets.

We have explained the M/D/1 model for a system where packets are awaiting transmission. In fact, the M/D/1 model is a general model with many more applications: for example, the jobs of a processor (CPU) arrive as a Poisson process and all have the same processing time. The simplest queuing system is the M/M/1 queue. The second letter M indicates that the service time has the memoryless property and thus is negative exponentially distributed. The state of the M/M/1 queue is fully defined at time t by $X(t)$, the number of customers in the system (one being served, the others waiting). The process $X(t)$ is again a Markov chain.

In Section 10.3 we have already seen an example of a Markov chain. It was a loss system in which the state was defined by the number of busy lines. In the Kendall notation, this is an M/M/N/N system: Poisson arrivals/negative exponential service (holding) times/N servers (lines)/N places in the system. For M/M/1 and M/D/1 queues, no fourth parameter is given, which indicates that the number of places in the queue is assumed to be infinite.

For the M/M/1 queue, we can again make use of a state diagram (now with an infinite number of states) to set up the equilibrium equations, similar to how it was done for the M/M/N/N system. Again, from this, the equilibrium distribution and, for example, the average waiting time can be deduced. Instead of doing this exercise, in the following section, we give a general formula for the average waiting time.

10.9   Mean waiting time for an M/G/1 queue

The letter G for General in M/G/1 indicates that the formula for the mean queuing time is valid for any service time distribution. The only thing we need to know about this distribution in order to determine the mean waiting time is the mean service time (m) and the standard deviation of the service time (σ). Of course, the waiting time also depends on λ, the arrival intensity of customers (packets). Before giving the formula for the mean waiting time, we first define what is meant by loading and by coefficient of variation for the M/G/1 queue. For a queuing system with one server, the **loading** (ρ) is equal to the product of the arrival intensity and the average service time:

$$\rho = \lambda \cdot m \tag{10.13}$$

This definition looks very similar to the definition of offered traffic (10.4). The difference is that we are here concerned with a queuing system so that, in the equilibrium situation, offered traffic is equal to carried traffic (no loss). For the M/G/1 queue, the equilibrium situation is only reached provided that $\rho < 1$. We assume implicitly that this condition is met.

The **coefficient of variation** of the service time distribution (C_s) is the ratio of the standard deviation and the mean of the service time:

$$C_s = \frac{\sigma}{m} \tag{10.14}$$

The mean waiting time (w) is given by:

$$w = \frac{\rho}{2 \cdot (1 - \rho)} \cdot \left(1 + C_s^2\right) \cdot m \tag{10.15}$$

This is the **Pollaczek–Khinchine formula**. For the M/D/1 queue and the M/M/1 queue, the formula is simpler. If the service time is deterministic, then the standard deviation $\sigma = 0$ and therefore $C_s = 0$ as well. If the service time has a negative exponential distribution, then the standard deviation is equal to the mean and therefore $C_s = 1$. This gives:

$$w = \frac{\rho}{2 \cdot (1 - \rho)} \cdot m \qquad \text{M/D/1} \tag{10.16}$$

$$w = \frac{\rho}{1 - \rho} \cdot m \qquad \text{M/M/1} \tag{10.17}$$

EXAMPLE

Packets arrive at a terminal server by a Poisson process. These packets leave the server by a line with a transmission capacity of 64 kbit/s. The packet length is 160 bits. At which arrival intensity is the mean waiting time equal to the transmission time of a packet?

Answer. This is an M/D/1 queuing system. The loading of the M/D/1 queue at which $w = m$ is $\rho = 0.666667$. With $m = 2.5$ ms, the associated arrival intensity $\lambda = 266.667 \, s^{-1}$.

10.10   Percentiles of waiting time distribution

The performance of a queuing system is only partly defined by the mean waiting time. It is possible that the mean waiting time is acceptable, but that excessive waiting times occur too often. Therefore, it is usually required that a certain threshold value will only be exceeded with a small probability. Percentiles of the waiting time are such threshold values. For example, the 99th percentile has a 1% probability of being exceeded.

A slightly more precise formulation of this is: t_x, the xth percentile, is defined by:

$$\Pr\{T_w \leqslant t_x\} = x\%$$

NB. The probability distribution of T_w and the value of x are given; from these, t_x must be calculated.

Let T_w have a negative exponential distribution whose probability density is given in (10.1) (Figure 10.1 gives a graph of this probability density). Then, for the stochastic variable T_w, the 99th percentile $t_{99} = 2 \cdot \ln(100) = 9.21034$. Here we have made use of the fact that in this example:

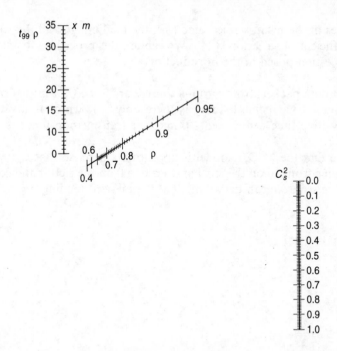

Figure 10.7 Relation between the 99th percentile (t_{99}) of the waiting time distribution for the M/G/1 queue, the loading (ρ) and the square of the coefficient of variation (C_s^2). The waiting time is expressed in multiples of the mean service time (m).

$$\Pr\{T_w \leqslant 2 \cdot \ln(100)\} = \int_0^{2 \cdot \ln(100)} \frac{1}{2} \cdot e^{-t/2} \, dt = \left|-e^{-t/2}\right|_0^{2 \cdot \ln(100)}$$

$$= 1 - e^{-\ln(100)} = 0.99$$

In terms of Figure 10.1 this can be formulated as follows. The total area under the curve is 1. Of this area 99% lies to the left and 1% to the right of the threshold value 9.21034. The probability that the threshold value is exceeded is 1%.

For the M/G/1 queue, the queuing time is not a continuous stochastic variable as in the previous example. There are no closed-form expressions (such as the Pollaczek–Khinchine formula) for the percentiles of the queuing time distribution. In Schoute (1989), however, a good asymptotic formula is given. It transpires that this formula also depends only on the loading and the coefficient of variation. With this formula, the nomogram of Figure 10.7 can be derived. From this figure, it is simple to read off the value of the 99th percentile.

By drawing a straight line cutting the three graduated scales, we can read off the relation between the 99th percentile (t_{99}), expressed in multiples of the mean service time (m), the loading (ρ) and the square of the coefficient of variation (C_s^2). We can use this procedure to answer the third question posed in the introduction:

- If data packets from various sources are to be transmitted over one line, at what line loading is there only a 1% probability that the waiting time will exceed 10 times the transmission time?

Suppose that the M/D/1 model is appropriate here, so that $C_s^2 = 0$. We draw a line from 10 on the left-hand scale to 0 on the right-hand scale. On the centre scale we can determine that the allowed loading $\rho = 0.79$.

Chapter 11

Telecommunications services

11.1 Introduction

Telecommunications services are often referred to simply as **services**. Some confusion has arisen in the telecommunications world because the International Organization for Standardization (ISO) uses the word service to mean *layer service*, a service that an OSI layer offers to the layer above. In this chapter we are concerned only with the service that an organization delivers to its users. These services usually have to be paid for, so that tariffs and conditions of supply are necessary. The user must also know with whom he can communicate and how to do that. For this, name directories and user instructions are needed, and people who can help in case of problems. All these things are part of providing a service. Finally, there are the technical facilities that make a service possible, such as transmission equipment, circuits, switching equipment and often the terminals.

A telecommunications service will only be attractive to users if they can reach the people they require, which means that they must also make use of the service. It is therefore essential for it to be accepted by a large group of users. A service is rarely very attractive to the initial users and there must be enormous advantages to persuade someone to take part. This is a simple logical fact which many enthusiastic technical people in the past have failed to realize. If a telecommunications service catches on after conquering the natural threshold, which can be very high, then the growth can be explosive and continue for several decades.

A good example of this is the **telefax** service. Facsimile was invented in 1842 and was for years only used by a very limited group, to whom it was extremely valuable (for example, meteorological offices), but did not begin its explosive growth until 1986–87 when the equipment became cheaper and more user-friendly, CCITT standards were published and almost everyone had a telephone connection that could be used for facsimile.

In the rest of this chapter, we discuss the existing telecommunications services, beginning with telegraphy as the oldest, and ending with a number of services that are planned for the future by the telecommunications organization CCITT (see also Chapter 12).

11.2   Telegraph services

Telegraphy is by far the oldest form of telecommunication. Following the ancient forms of telegraphy with smoke signals or with semaphores visible over large distances, telegraphy over electrical conductors was described as early as 1753. It was not until 1787 that the first practical telegraph link was achieved, over the considerable distance of 42 km between Madrid and Aranjuez. Telegraphy was considerably improved in 1837 when a professor of art history built a strip printer to produce the symbols in the form of dots and dashes that have acquired his name, *Morse*.

Werner Siemens' invention of machines to cover copper wire with insulation by means of a continuous process was important, and made it a practicable proposition to send the first telegram under the Atlantic Ocean. See Figure 11.1.

In 1855 the first telegraph equipment that could print letters directly was introduced by Hughes. Baudot improved this system in 1874 with the introduction of the five-unit Baudot code, which is still used today for telex, for example.

Figure 11.1   Cable ship. (Source: *From Semaphore to Satellite*, International Telecommunication Union, Geneva (1965), p. 35.)

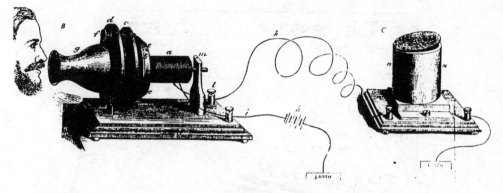

Figure 11.2 Improved version of Alexander Graham Bell's first telephone set. (Source: *From Semaphore to Satellite*, International Telecommunication Union, Geneva (1965), p. 93.)

One year after this had achieved a stable state for telegraphy, the telephone was invented by Alexander Graham Bell. See Figure 11.2.

In the course of time, telephony has taken over much of the original telegraph traffic. Nevertheless, telegraphy still has an important role in a number of applications. Data communication can also be seen as a form of telegraphy. The international telecommunications organization CCITT currently categorizes the following services as telegraphy: **public telegram**, **telex**, **radio communication**, **photo telegraphy**, **maritime mobile** and **message switching services**.

Where the telephone service still has few subscribers, for example in third world countries, the telegraph service plays a greater role than in Europe. In international traffic with people in these countries, telegraphy is sometimes the only quick form of communication. The legal value of a telegram, which is equivalent to that of a registered letter, is also a reason for the use of the telegraph service. A modern form of telegraphy, called **telemessage** (see Figure 11.3), is particularly suitable for greetings telegrams. The delivery of a telemessage from the receiving station is done by post and not by special messenger as is often the case with telegrams.

The **telex service** has about 1.5 million subscribers worldwide and therefore still plays a significant role in national and international business. The growth of facsimile (see Section 11.3) is reducing the number of telex calls.

In the example of a telex message (Figure 11.4) the received information has been underlined. In a real telex message, the information transmitted is often distinguished from that received by the use of red instead of black letters. The received information in this example consists of automatically transmitted **answerbacks** received from the network and the receiving terminal (22464 MAWNI SD). SD stands for Sudan, 437122 PHVS NL is the originator. NL indicates the Netherlands.

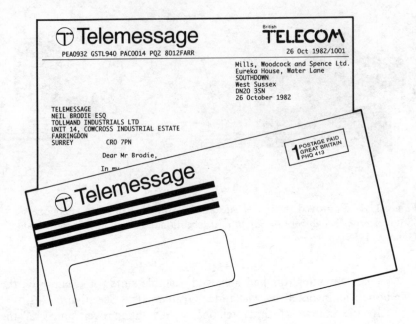

Figure 11.3   Telemessage.

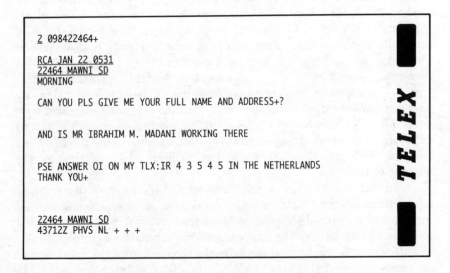

Figure 11.4   Telex message.

11.3 Telematic services

The following are regarded as **telematic services**:

- teletex service
- public facsimile service
- videotex service
- message handling service.

Telematic services are not network-specific but can, in principle, make use of:

- Public Switched Telephone Network (PSTN)
- Circuit Switched Public Data Network (CSPDN)
- Packet Switched Public Data Network (PSPDN)
- Integrated Services Digital Network (ISDN)
- Dedicated circuits (for example, leased lines).

In practice, it may be necessary to use more than one of these networks. For example, many teletex terminals in Germany use the CSPDN, while in France the PSPDN is used. By using a **gateway** connected to both networks, it is possible to offer a teletex service between the two countries.

If two telematic terminals are both connected to the ISDN network, then the term **teleservice** is used.

11.3.1 Teletex service

Teletex is an international service that enables subscribers to exchange correspondence between two teletex terminals. These operate on the basis of the transfer of data from the memory of the transmitting terminal, via a telecommunication network, to the memory of the receiving terminal. Use is made of the teletex code (CCITT Recommendation T.61) which has similarities with the CCITT IA5 8-bit code. See Figure 11.5. The latter is also referred to unofficially by the name of its American counterpart, ASCII.

Teletex uses communication protocols that conform to the ISO model, in which the higher protocol layers are independent of, and the lower protocol layers are adjusted to, the network used. In a number of countries, teletex is being promoted as the successor to telex. However, the rate of replacement of telex by teletex has been considerably lower

b.					0	0	0	0	0	0	0	0	1	1	1	1	1	1	1	1
b.					0	0	0	0	1	1	1	1	0	0	0	0	1	1	1	1
b.					0	0	1	1	0	0	1	1	0	0	1	1	0	0	1	1
b.					0	1	0	1	0	1	0	1	0	1	0	1	0	1	0	1
b.	b.	b.	b.		0	1	2	3	4	5	6	7	8	9	10	11	12	13	14	15
0	0	0	0	0			SP	0	@	P		P				°	⑤		Ω	K
0	0	0	1	1			|	1	A	Q	a	q			i	±	'		Æ	æ
0	0	1	0	2			"	2	B	R	b	r			¢	2	'		Đ	đ
0	0	1	1	3			④	3	C	S	c	s			£	3	^		▪	∂
0	1	0	0	4			④	4	D	T	d	t			$	×	~		H	h
0	1	0	1	5			%	5	E	U	e	u			¥	μ	–			ı
0	1	1	0	6			&	6	F	V	f	v			≠	¶	˘		IJ	ij
0	1	1	1	7			'	7	G	W	g	w			§	.	·		L·	l·
1	0	0	0	8			(	8	H	X	h	x			□	+	"		Ł	ł
1	0	0	1	9			)	9	I	Y	i	y					②		Ø	ø
1	0	1	0	10			*	:	J	Z	j	z				°			Œ	œ
1	0	1	1	11			+	;	K	{	k				"	"	,		º	β
1	1	0	0	12			,	<	L	L	l					¼	③		þ	ρ
1	1	0	1	13			–	=	M	}	m					½	"		Ŧ	ŧ
1	1	1	0	14			.	>	N		n					¾	¿		η	ŋ
1	1	1	1	15			/	?	O	①	o					¿	~			'n

Figure 11.5   Teletex basic character repertoire. (Source: *International Telecommunications Union.*)

than expected. Quite early on, it was realized that teletex would never get off the ground unless there was a possibility of reaching all telex subscribers from a teletex terminal. For this purpose telex–teletex converters have been provided by the service suppliers (PTTs) in many countries, which are connected between the telex network and the network used for teletex in that country.

The higher price of teletex terminals, and higher network connection costs are only compensated by lower network usage costs when large numbers of messages are to be sent. While telex is intended for the transfer of message content without placing conditions on the exact form in which the message appears on paper, teletex does impose certain constraints on this form. The symbol repertoire and the available letters, digits and symbols is also much larger. With teletex, a letter can be transmitted just as it would normally be typed; with the most modern form of teletex, diagrams can also be transmitted. **Mixed-mode** terminals have been specified by the CCITT for that purpose. Teletex operates at the standard speed of 2400 bit/s.

11.3.2 Public facsimile service

Since copying machines have become commonplace, facsimile can be described simply as a service that makes telecopying, copying at a distance, possible.

Over the course of time, several facsimile terminals have been defined by CCITT. Currently, it is mainly the **Group 3** terminal that is of interest, being used on a very large scale worldwide. This terminal operates over the public switched telephone network (PSTN), which simplified its introduction because telephone connections are available almost everywhere. The service set up for subscribers with these terminals is known internationally as **telefax 3**. The same equipment is used, for example, in post offices to send documents on behalf of persons that do not themselves have a terminal. This service is internationally called **bureaufax**.

The most modern form of telefax, called **telefax 4**, has been designed for use on data networks or ISDN. Although the service is still new, three classes of terminal have already been defined:

• Class I: a send/receive terminal for facsimile encoded documents

• Class II: can also *receive* teletex encoded documents

• Class III: can also *transmit* teletex documents. This equipment is not limited to separate telefax and teletex pages of text, but can also reproduce pages of mixed text and diagrams, so-called **mixed-mode** documents.

Telefax 4 is intended to operate at a modulation rate of 64 kbit/s and is thus extremely well suited for use on ISDN B-channels (see Chapter 6).

CCITT has also specified a store and forward facsimile switching service called **comfax**. This service is intended to make it possible to communicate between different types of facsimile terminal, in addition to the provision of such store and forward services as multiple distribution. Comfax will also accept the input from text terminals and convert the text to facsimile form for delivery to facsimile terminals – a service which already exists in Japan at national level.

11.3.3   Videotex service

The **videotex** service is an interactive service that allows users of videotex terminals to communicate with databases via telecommunications networks. The majority of videotex terminals are connected via the PSTN. With a special videotex modem, made for sending at 75 bit/s and receiving at 1200 bit/s, both text and diagrams from the database can be reproduced on a screen. With a suitable screen, reproduction can be in colour.

Videotex does not suffer from the problem that it will only become attractive when many subscribers use the service, because intercommunication is not the goal. There is, however, still an introduction problem for videotex: the service is only of interest to the *information providers* if there are sufficient subscribers, and it is only of interest to subscribers if many databases from information providers are available. Thus we have a chicken and egg problem.

In France, the problem of the initial threshold was solved by large government subsidies. It was decided completely to automate the telephone book using videotex, and terminals were supplied free to subscribers. This method removed much of the resistance of the French subscribers; there are currently several million videotex terminals in use. As a result, it has also become attractive to other information providers and the growth in the use of videotex for uses other than consulting the telephone book is very marked. Large-scale production has made it possible for French industry to produce videotex terminals very cheaply, which allows it to offer them at low prices in other countries as well. That was the basic goal of the French subsidy plan.

In spite of the efforts of CCITT, videotex systems have been started as national systems, with international compatibility a secondary consideration. The systems of the various countries are not completely compatible, although a large measure of conformance to the CCITT standards has been attempted.

11.3.4   Message handling services

Message Handling Systems (MHS) were first specified by CCITT in 1984, the specifications being significantly improved in 1988. The message protocol for use between MHS systems has become known as X.400, the name of the CCITT Recommendation specifying MHS. It concerns protocols in sublayers of the application layer (7) of the ISO/OSI model. CCITT does not specify the appearance of the MHS user interface; that is a national, or even individual, matter.

In many countries electronic mail services have been started for which the equipment was developed while X.400 was still being specified.

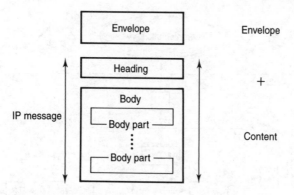

Figure 11.6 IP message structure.

Later, this equipment acquired the ability to cooperate via X.400 with other MHS systems, including **Private Computer Based Messaging Systems (CBMS)**. The MHS protocols include **message transfer layer** protocols, of which the P1 protocol is the most important. This is a message switching protocol in which the routing information is included (envelope).

The service delivered by the message transfer layer is called the **Message Transfer Service (MTS)**. There are also **user agent layer** protocols that exchange data about the transmitted document on an end-to-end basis. Currently, the main protocol in this class is the P2 protocol associated with the **Inter Personal Messaging (IPM)** service (see Figures 11.6 and 11.7). The message transfer layer protocols occur between functional units called **Message Transfer Agents (MTA)**, which are implemented in remote systems. The user layer protocols are used between the transmitting and receiving **User Agent (UA)**. A user agent is a functional entity (computer program) that communicates with the user and converts the data offered by the user into the form specified by CCITT. If the communication takes place via several switching nodes, each having its own MTA function, the P2 protocol information is passed on transparently from UA to UA.

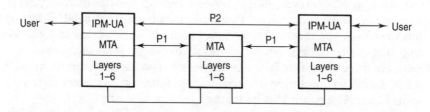

Figure 11.7 IPM-UA and MTA layers in the MHS application layer.

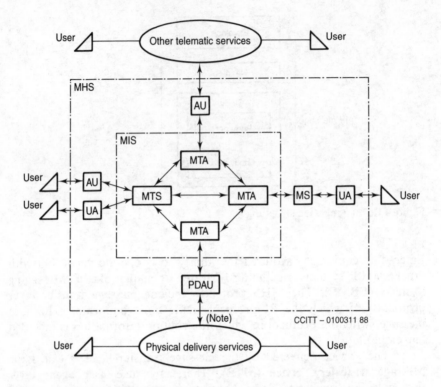

Figure 11.8   Functional model of the MHS service. (Source: International Telecommunication Union Figure 1 of Recommendation X.400 of the *Blue Book*, Volume VIII, Fascicle VIII, 7.)

CCITT has specified a model for MHS which is shown in Figure 11.8.

As with teletex, it is naturally of great importance for the IPM service to be able to reach subscribers to comparable services. Therefore functional units have been specified for IPM to make this possible.

An example is the Physical Delivery Access Unit (PDAU), which makes possible interworking with the postal services (see Figure 11.9).

It has been recognized that it is of considerable importance for the future growth of the MHS service that an electronic directory becomes available. It is, however, illogical to set this up for the relatively small number of MHS subscribers. Therefore an **international public directory** has now been specified in which all telecommunications related information about subscribers can be placed. This has a great advantage over separate directories for each service (service-specific directories) because when searching for someone's telephone number, it can immediately be seen if that person can also be reached by facsimile or possibly telex.

The first global specifications were only produced by CCITT in 1988, so it will take some years before this general directory service can

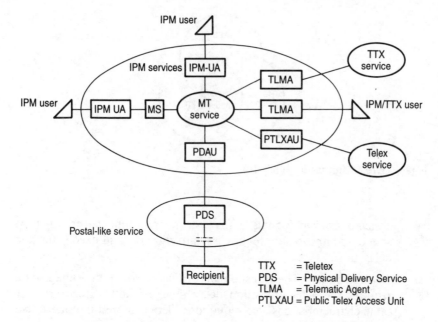

Figure 11.9   Functional model of the IPM service. (Source: International Telecommunication Union Figure 7 of Recommendation X.400 of the *Blue Book*, Volume VIII, Fascicle VIII, 7.)

get started. In addition, integration with existing service-specific systems, such as the French system based on videotex, gives rise to serious complications and limitations.

11.3.5   Multimedia mail service

MultiMedia Mail Systems (MMMS) are considerably more complex and have much higher demands than traditional mono-medium communication systems. The requirements with regard to the MMMS are determined by the various subsystems which form part of the multimedia world, both separately and in combination. See Figure 11.10.

As a result an MMMS has to provide among others, the following:

- *Large and variable bandwidth*: The simultaneous transmission of image, sound and data requires very high incidental bit rates at certain moments. It is therefore preferable to have the possibility of both low and high bit rates on demand. Networks providing in principle such facilities are, for instance, the **Fibre Distributed Data Interface (FDDI** and **FDDI II)** networks and the **Broadband-ISDN (B-ISDN)** using the asynchronous transfer mode.

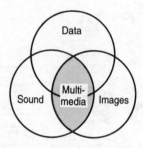

Figure 11.10 Multimedia subsystems.

- *Synchronization*: Signals with a strong real-time nature such as sound and image data require a relatively short and fixed transition delay time.

- *Isochronization*: The transmission of related sound and image data requires the *same* transition delay time for both categories. The same characteristic is also required if there is more than one sound source active in the network (multipoint configuration).

- *Dynamic configuration and re-configuration*: The application of the **Joint Viewing and Tele-Operating Service (JVTOS)** requires network facilities for call set-up and re-configuration during the session.

- *Standardization*: Mail systems require not only international standards for the transport of the data but also for the recording and the structure of the multimedia documents (hyper-documents).

11.4   Data transmission services

The telephone network, the specific data networks and, of course, the future ISDN network can all be used for data transmission

11.4.1   Data transmission on the telephone network

On the telephone network, **modems** are required to convert the digital signals into speech band frequency modem signals. The telephone network is suitable for transmitting these signals and thus few problems arise. There are, however, a few problems with systems for long distance telephone transmission which make use of the fact that most telephone users are occasionally silent. The modem continues tirelessly transmitting for long periods. Data transmission on the telephone network can hardly be called a real service; there is, for example, no special directory for data subscribers to the network. There are, however, standards for the transmission characteristics of modems and for the interface with the terminal equipment (Data Terminal Equipment, DTE).

11.4.2 Packet switched data transmission

Many countries have a national public packet switched data network for packet switched data transmission. This network is often usable internationally as well. The PSPDN has its own numbering system (X.121) and, in many countries, a directory. The **international packet switched data transmission service** is thus emerging. The DTE interface is X.25 and the network side of this interface is called the Data Circuit terminating Equipment (DCE).

11.4.3 Circuit switched data transmission

Circuit switched data transmission is only found in a few countries, of which Germany is one. There is no question of a worldwide service here. CCITT X.21 provides the interface specification.

11.4.4 Data transmission on the ISDN

The ISDN will offer both circuit switched and packet switched data transmission facilities. For the time being, of main interest are the ISDN circuit mode bearer services:

- 64 kbit/s unrestricted,
- 384 kbit/s unrestricted,
- 1920 kbit/s unrestricted (not in the USA and several other countries).

and the packet-mode bearer services:

- virtual call on B-channel or D-channel,
- permanent virtual circuit on B-channel or D-channel.

11.5   The telephone service

The present telephone service has grown from local services. While long distance traffic was of paramount importance to the telegraph and telex services, for telephony the emphasis was initially on shorter distances. International telephone traffic grew slowly; transatlantic traffic began in 1927, 69 years after this was possible by telegraphy.

The invention in 1896 of the electromagnetic selector, by the undertaker Strowger, made possible the automation of the telephone service. This began rapidly in America; in Europe it came later. The telephone network is now almost completely automated and a large part of the world can be reached without the intervention of an operator. The telephone service is unchallenged as the largest telecommunications service, especially if the broadcasting organizations are not taken into account. The service is fully organized with telephone directories, information numbers, fault reporting numbers and tariffs. The latter have become so low that almost every house in the Western world has a connection.

The transmission structure that was built up originally for telephony has made a large number of other services practicable (for example, facsimile) or assisted them (such as telegraph channels on multiplexed telephone channels).

New facilities, such as call transfer, are possible with the most modern exchanges. **Voice mail**, the store and forward method of handling speech information, is also slowly coming into use. In concept, voice mail is similar to, but has a number of advantages over, an answering machine; it is possible, for example, to register an incoming call with voice mail when the called equipment is in use for another call.

The growth of mobile telephony is spectacular. By the use of high frequency bands (800 and 900 MHz bands) and modern technology, mobile telephony is beginning to come within the reach of many people, although still almost exclusively for business traffic.

11.6   Broadband ISDN services

Although the ISDN network, already called **narrowband**, has hardly got off the ground, a serious study is being made of the possibilities of a new worldwide network that will avoid the limitations of the present ISDN. Major improvements being considered are greater bit rates and more flexibility. Fast packet switches are being looked at for its implementation, providing a fast, simple form of packet switching without error control on the link, known as **Asynchronous Transfer Mode (ATM)**.

As a transition to ATM, there is much support for the **Synchronous Transfer Mode (STM)** in which circuit switching is used on channels created with the help of Synchronous Time Division (STD). In Europe this is taking place within the framework of various **RACE** projects organized by the European Commission.

CCITT is working on **Broadband ISDN (B-ISDN)** specifications for worldwide application. The B-ISDN will have to deliver a large number of services:

- unrestricted broadband bearer service,
- high quality (HQ) broadband video telephony,
- high quality (HQ) broadband video conferencing,
- television distribution, both High Definition (HD) and Existing Quality (EQ),
- broadband videotex.

The unrestricted bearer service can be used for data transmission at high bit rates, making it possible to replace or interconnect LANs, LAN length restrictions will no longer apply. The use of fast packet switching principles means that the B-ISDN network can be efficiently employed for data transmission with a *burst* character, as is usual for interactive terminals. With circuit switching, the full transmission capacity remains reserved for the total period of the connection, although the capacity is only intermittently utilized; with packet switching the capacity available between the bursts can be utilized by other users. Especially with broadband connections, this is an extremely useful way of maintaining affordable connection charges.

The fast packet switching principle automatically leads to B-ISDNs not being tied to a fixed bit rate; a low-speed terminal can communicate effectively with a large computer system that is connected to the B-ISDN with a high-speed broadband link. Thus it is not unreasonable to allow traffic between low-speed terminals on the B-ISDN. In the longer term, we shall probably have just one ISDN that carries both narrow and broadband traffic, and allows narrowband and broadband devices to communicate both among themselves and with each other.

11.7 Electronic data interchange (EDI)

Electronic Data Interchange (EDI) is the direct transfer of data from one computer to another. EDI messages are generally transferred on communication networks between different organizations. It is necessary to make clear arrangements between the sender and receiver, not only about the protocols to be used, but also about the format of the message content. Agreements about the message format cannot be limited to defining a structure, but must extend to naming conventions, identifications and encoding.

This goes much further than message handling with its interpersonal messaging, whereby the content of the real message, the message body, is not intended to be processed by a computer but is destined to be read by a person.

There have, of course, been agreements for years about EDI. These are necessary as soon as data is exchanged between two computer systems and, indeed, when a person sends data to a computer.

In many **Lines Of Business (LOB)** standards have also been developed for the message content of standard messages that arise frequently in that particular LOB. Examples of this are messages for reservations on aircraft, trains and in hotels, messages for **Air Traffic Control (ATC)**, messages in the car industry, and messages between chemical, electronic and transport businesses. Government is also involved in this sort of message transfer, for example, in connection with customs facilities. The message content for the various LOBs is quite different. The need for a single worldwide standard for all these messages is thus not so evident.

However, if one thinks of suppliers that deliver, for example, electronic components to other businesses, these will usually be in different LOBs and thus each will follow a different standard. The supplier must thus be able to communicate in all the different message formats and 'languages'. The more electronic information exchange there is from computer to computer, the more these *islands*, each with its own standards, will be forced to communicate with each other. This is the reason for the creation of a worldwide standard for the format and content of electronic data exchange: **Edifact: Electronic Data Interchange For Administration, Commerce and Transport**.

11.7.1   Standardization of EDI

The worldwide standardization of EDI, intended for use by all LOBs, was initiated by the United Nations. ISO has already brought out standards for the structure of messages: syntax and grammar are covered by ISO 9735, and a dictionary of data elements, the **Trade Data Elements Directory (TDED)**, is the subject of ISO 7372. Work is also proceeding on standard messages for the various LOBs: **United Nations Standard Messages (UNSMs)**. The standards are published in four languages: English, French, Spanish and Russian.

These standards are all at the application level of the OSI model. For the lower communication layers, CCITT has recommended the use of the message handling protocols and described how EDI fits into this application. There were two possibilities: an EDI message could be sent as the text of an MHS-IPM message, or a special type of user agent could be defined in addition to the IPM user agent. The latter solution was the one chosen.

Although this regulates the technical possibilities for electronic message exchange, there is another aspect that is crucial to the success of EDI: agreement between those giving EDI orders and those that have to carry them out that action will be taken. That cannot of course be unlimited, because not all deliveries will be possible in the required numbers. Legal agreements and rules for these agreements will thus be necessary. The International Chamber of Commerce (ICC) has worked out these rules in the form of **UNiform rules of Conduct for Interchange of trade Data by teletransmission (UNCID)**. These rules are being studied in many countries and national legislation will probably be amended to incorporate them in the future.

We may also expect that the arrival of EDI will cause substantial changes in the affected departments of businesses. The size of orders could also be reduced significantly if everything can be carried out automatically and an extra order will thus cost little and incur little delay.

11.7.2 Practical application of EDI

A practical problem for the introduction of EDI is the presence of many fully operational LOB specific data interchange agreements and support software. It is not practicable to throw all this data interchange software away and replace it by EDI software. The latter would not fit into the structure of existing programs without creating problems, including:

- different data field lengths,
- different coding (alphanumeric versus numeric),
- different combinations of data,
- implicitly known, and therefore missing, data,
- different currencies (pounds instead of dollars, for instance),
- different measuring systems (inches instead of metres).

The result will be that existing software will continue to be used and a separate conversion program will be needed to work to the international EDI standards with organizations outside the current scope (usually LOB). This conversion program could run on the organization's own computer, but it could also be made available as a service at a special central facility. Such a service will be offered by many national telecommunications services in the future. A few large businesses may also offer such a central service to their own departments.

A second problem that arises with the introduction of the EDI standards is the need for LOB based **dialects**. For communication between LOBs it is sufficient to define a subset in the languages used by the LOBs – **a generic EDI language**. Edifact allows the existence of internal dialects within LOBs as an extension to the generic language. The dialects must, however, be specified according to the general rules of Edifact.

Third are the problems associated with EDIs being limited to only four national languages. In some countries, being restricted to English, French, Spanish or Russian can be a nuisance for some businesses; in others it could be a serious problem.

Finally, we should remember that the content of the messages is constantly evolving; new products are being invented, new order procedures being developed and new tax rules introduced. These all lead to constant extension of the rules and occasional revisions. They will always trail behind the needs.

So we can see that many problems arising with the introduction of EDI can be solved by central services that will perform the necessary conversions. The EDI service will continue to make use of a message handling system that works with CCITT X.400 series protocols; in addition, it is to be expected that other protocols will be accepted in the future.

11.8   Internet services

The **internet** is a very peculiar network. Nobody has ever designed the total network and no single organization controls the whole network. However, it is a network that shows an almost exponential growth and has attracted the attention of politicians and the press. So everyone has heard about it but almost everyone knows only a few of the facts. Some talk about the internet as if it is identical to the **electronic highway**, a subject discussed at the highest level by politicians. Whereas the electronic highway is more a hype, the internet is reality.

The internet has its roots in the **Advanced Research Projects Agency (ARPA)** network, the packet switched network of the US Defense department. The ARPA network was designed to support military research, including research on military networks for the future. With the SITA network in Europe and an airline network in the US, it was the first packet switched network in the world.

The ARPA network is designed to interconnect a large number of research computers. The protocol designed and tested for the ARPA network was a connectionless protocol, the **Internet Protocol (IP)** (see Chapter 4). In a layer above the IP protocol, the transport layer, the ARPA uses a connection oriented protocol, the **Transmission Control Protocol (TCP)**. Since most universities in the US and some outside the US did contract work for the US Defense department, nearly all universities were directly or indirectly connected to the ARPA network. Manufacturers working for the Defense department and their networks followed. This conglomerate of ARPA, university networks and other networks is called the internet. The ARPA network is paid for by the government. Newcomers have to pay for their access circuit to the network, but can use the government paid circuits free of charge. Nowadays access to the network is open to everybody who pays for his own access circuit and a small charge to one of the organizations that can provide access. This organization allows the users to use a simple protocol and provides the user with software (for example, Gopher) to guide him through the internet.

The internet offers access to an ever increasing number of databases and bulletin boards. The internet not only offers these information services but also offers the two telecommunication services, electronic mail and direct communication.

The electronic mail service resembles the MHS but the addressing is different. The internet email address consists of two parts, the person's name and the identification of the computer handling the access to the internet. The parts are separated by an **at** sign: @. For example the email address of Frits Schoute, one of the authors of this book, is F.SCHOUTE@ET.TUDELFT.NL. The email address of Peter Kastelein is PKASTEL@ET.TNT.HVU.NL.

Since the network contains dial-up lines in some parts of the world (to save money), delivery can take quite a long time. Nor is privacy guaranteed. But the internet is a cheap email network for users.

Direct communication is often established by using the UNIX program **talk**. The command: %talk allows a (typed) two-way conversation, almost in real time. Group conversations are possible with so-called, **chat** facilities. Since different talk and chat programs are used in some computers, compatibility is not always guaranteed.

The parts of the internet with high speed circuits can even enable telephone conversations.

11.9 Automatic call centres

Many private networks and several public networks offer the services of automatic call centres. The tasks of such call centres can vary from helping people with equipment or software problems (help-desks) to the acceptance of orders by mail-order organizations or even registration of votes. The application part of the call centre may consist exclusively of one or more groups of knowledgeable people (agents). It may also be a fully automated interactive voice response system without any human intervention during the call. Usually the call centres are only partly automated and are also operated by agents.

The telecommunication side of the call centre for human operated applications with a low degree of automation consists generally only of an **Automatic Call Distribution** (ACD) system. This ACD system offers optimal access to the agents for customers calling the service. As long as there is a free agent, handling the requested service, the customer will be brought in contact with him. In case all agents are occupied, the customer will be informed about the expected waiting period by a voice announcement. This spoken message is generated under the control of the ACD system. The supervisor of the ACD system receives information about excessive queues for a specific service or task. He can than decide to switch agents of a lightly loaded group, handling other services or tasks, to the overloaded group. ACD systems can also provide statistical information on agent performance and waiting times.

A further step towards automation is the coupling of the switching centre equipment (for example, the Integrated Services Private Branch eXchange, ISPBX) with the agent's computer systems. The interconnection of these systems opens the possibility to automatically set up calls from the computer. This is useful in **telemarketing outbound** applications of, for example, sales organizations. The computer tries to set up connections with telephone numbers of potential customers, stored in a database. When a connection is successfully established, the agent gets all details available on the particular potential customer on his/her screen and can start the conversation. Notes on the results of the conversation are added to the customer record by the agent.

The protocols on the interconnection are standardized by the **European Computer Manufacturers' Association** (ECMA) in a document called Services and Protocols for **Computer-Supported Telecommunications Applications** (CSTA).

Another service that makes use of the interconnection of telecommunications and computer systems is the **telemarketing inbound** application. Here the customer initiates the call. The telecommunication systems, at least for calls originated in networks that have this capability, now provide the number of the calling customer to the computer. The computer may find the name and address and other information on the caller (for example, previous transactions) in its database. This information will be helpful in the conversation with the customer. After the conversation the connection is cleared, but the ACD system prevents new calls being offered to this agent until the agent has finished the input of information on the results of the conversation.

11.10 Other services

There are several more services that are specified in greater or less detail by CCITT, but have no great significance, or are of little importance for telematics. These include the teleconferencing service, telewriting and a number of services based on radio communication. It is likely that the telecommunication (broadcast) service via satellite will become important in the future.

Chapter 12

Standards and recommendations

12.1 Standardization

Standardization can be defined as the agreement and recording of properties, sizes and qualities of products and services. The standards by which we measure the magnitudes must also be fixed in order to make our agreements worthwhile.

We probably take it for granted that many of the things we use every day have been more or less standardized. There are so many examples of how the chaos which previously existed has disappeared or been reduced thanks to standardization. An hour in Britain is just as long as an hour anywhere else in the world and a metre is a metre everywhere. The most common paper size in Europe is A4 and is accepted in Europe as standard, but that is not at all the case in the rest of the world. The plug of your razor or ladyshave fits without problem in almost any socket in almost all European countries. In Holland, you can buy American tyres that fit a Japanese or French car. Almost the whole world understands the meaning of the number 12. Very few people write XII or use binary, octal, hexadecimal or any other notation understandable only by a small group of initiated persons.

In telecommunications it is important that terminals can be connected to networks in a standard manner so that there can be efficient communication with the network. But that is not enough, because the intention is to communicate with another subscriber via the network. For telephony, it is then necessary for users to speak a common standardized language. For data, text or video terminals, there also has to be agreement about the **language usage** that covers all OSI layers.

Compatibility is not the only reason for standardization. Equipment connected to a network must also meet a number of safety requirements for the protection of both the network and the user. Testing standards are also needed, both for the test requirements and for the method of applying them.

Efficient production and stock management calls for manufacturing standards for products, subsystems and parts.

12.2   Forms of standardization

12.2.1   Standards

The **International Organization for Standardization (ISO)** is supported by governments throughout the world and therefore has great influence. The governments make adherence to many standards mandatory in areas where they have influence, such as education or supplies of equipment to government departments.

The **European Telecommunications Standards Institute (ETSI)** was set up in 1988 to set common standards for Europe, ensuring interoperability of equipment on a European basis. By relating its work to developments on the global scene, ETSI is also helping to work towards establishing telecommunications standards worldwide. Both ISO and ETSI produce **Draft Standards** that generally become **Standards** after an approval procedure. ETSI also produces **Interim European Telecommunications Standards (I-ETS)**, for systems that will be tested over a number of years, before further decisions are taken.

12.2.2   Recommendations

The word **recommendations** is used by organizations such as the International Telecommunications Union (ITU). By using the word recommendations it is stressed that the standards organization concerned recognizes the sovereign right of countries to deviate from the agreements described. It is usually expected that the countries deviating will make this known and publish their reasons. In practice this means that recommendations have almost as much authority as standards. Industry has the right of participation in the creation of recommendations, but no voice in the final decisions. This contrasts with standards, in which industry does have an influence. CCITT recommendations result from agreements solely between the PTTs and similar organizations worldwide.

12.2.3 Functional standards

Partly because standards and recommendations arise as the result of compromises, there often remains a large degree of freedom which can be exercised in the creation of products and services. In other words, the number of options is very large. This can cause problems, for example, when setting up a service for the whole of Europe. The standards which are specific to the USA, for example 1.5 Mbit/s transmission, cause even more difficulties in Europe.

As a result, a start has been made in Europe on the creation of **functional standards**. These are not new standards, but give guidelines for choosing among the options in the many standards and recommendations that could be used for a particular *application*, for example, message handling, in a certain *area*, in this case Europe.

European functional specifications in the field of telecommunications are given the name NET (Normes Européennes de Télécommunication). In 1988 the first proposals for NETs were presented. NETs are concerned with:

- user safety,
- safety for the personnel of the network proprietor,
- protection against damage to the network,
- interworking of equipment with and via the network.

12.2.4 De facto standards

Much standardization in the past has arisen more as a result of the influence of a major producer of the relevant equipment than from the efforts of the standards organizations. It was often attractive and even commercially necessary for the smaller manufacturers to ensure that the equipment to be supplied could work together with that of the most influential suppliers.

The interface and functional specifications of the most important supplier thus formed a **de facto**, internationally accepted standard. A problem could arise that a supplier would not make the interface specifications available, because he preferred to sell his own equipment for connection to his system. In practice, this problem was usually solved because the manufacturer had to provide maintenance documentation, and could not completely omit the interface specifications from it. Sometimes very powerful customers can also force publication of the interface specifications when buying equipment.

A well-known example of de facto standards is to be found in the interfaces to IBM systems, such as the interface to the IBM 3270 display system. This made it possible for non-IBM equipment to be connected to IBM mainframes. As a result, **Plug Compatible Mainframe (PCM)** equipment appeared on the market, which could take over the role of the IBM central computer and work with IBM or IBM-compatible peripherals.

In some cases the manufacturer wishes to see its interfaces accepted as a de facto standard. That is particularly true when the manufacturer is mainly interested in the equipment on just one side of the interface. The more equipment on the market that can operate with its system, the more of its own products will be sold.

One example of this is the de facto standard for the Philips audio cassette. For the successful sale of Philips cassette recorders, it was extremely important to get the cassette standard accepted by the tape suppliers. Another example is the Centronics interface for printers. Although the firm Centronics ceased to be a major manufacturer years ago, the interface used by this firm has survived as the de facto standard for parallel interfaces to personal computers. In contrast, the serial interface is based on the international CCITT Recommendation V.24, which is almost identical to the American standard RS-232-C.

12.2.5 Verification, conformance testing and certification

Meeting worldwide or European functional specifications for terminal and network interfaces is of great importance to ensure that a terminal that can be connected to the network in country A will also operate when connected to that in country B. Equipment manufacturers in Europe, the USA and Japan have taken the initiative in setting up test centres that check protocols for correctness and realizability; this is termed **verification**.

These test centres can also test equipment to ensure that the implementation of the functionally standardized protocols is correct; this is referred to as **conformance testing**. ETSI has proposed a number of NETs and regulates product **certification**. A number of test institutes chosen for this purpose are authorized to issue test certificates to manufacturers of approved products. These products are then, with the support of the European Commission, accepted as approved in all countries in the European Union (EU). A national government or PTT may then no longer ban such equipment or insist on a national acceptance test.

12.3 Standards organizations

12.3.1 ISO

The **International Organization for Standardization (ISO)** is a world-level standards organization for all subjects except electrotechnology and electronics, the latter being regulated by the IEC. The ISO issues **international standards** only after they have been available for comment for some time as **Draft International Standards (DIS)**.

Britain is a member of the ISO via the British Standards Institution (BSI). The relations between the various standards organizations are illustrated in Figure 12.1.

12.3.2 IEC

The **International Electrotechnical Commission (IEC)** complements ISO in the field of standardization for electrotechnical subjects. The IEC issues recommendations and reports, and also has provisional standards.

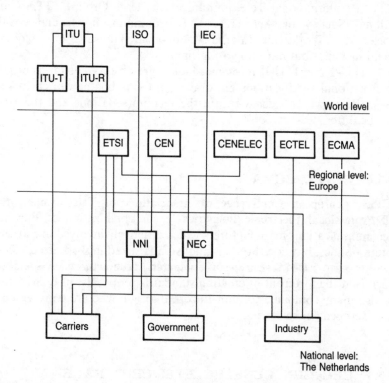

Figure 12.1 Simplified diagram of the relations between standardization organizations.

12.3.3   ITU, CCITT, CCIR

The goal of the **International Telecommunication Union (ITU)**, situated in Geneva, is not that of creating general standards, but of encouraging international cooperation in order to arrive at an efficient international telecommunications infrastructure. This includes not only the promotion of standardization, but also, for example, the creation of guidelines for tariff agreements. The ITU, a 'United Nations specialized agency dealing with telecommunications', contains two important organizations: CCITT and CCIR. **CCITT (Comité consultatif international télégraphique et téléphonique)** makes studies and recommendations in the field of wired telecommunications while **CCIR (Comité consultatif international des radiocommunications)** is oriented towards wireless communications. The names CCITT and CCIR are still found on many documents. The new names are, however, **ITU-T** and **ITU-R**.

In many countries, PTT personnel act as representatives of the government in the ITU-T and ITU-R. Scientific and industrial institutions can also become members of the ITU-T and ITU-R if given governmental permission, but they are not allowed to vote. User organizations such as INTUG (International Telecommunications User Group), SITA (International Society of Aeronautical Telecommunications) and SWIFT (Society for Worldwide Interbank Financial Transmission) may also attend meetings but have no voting rights.

ITU-T and ITU-R **recommendations** are observed as far as possible when national specifications are drawn up for public networks. In some cases, the networks existed before the recommendations and there may thus be differences.

12.3.4   ECTEL, ECMA

ECTEL (European Conference of Associations of Telecommunications and Professional Electronic Industries) is an organization of European telecommunications manufacturers which is actively involved in standardization politics, but does little original standardization work itself. This is in contrast to **ECMA (European Computer Manufacturers' Association)**, which is at the forefront of creating standards proposals. In ECMA there are also many companies of non-European origin who are represented by their European subsidiaries.

12.3.5   CEC, CEN, CENELEC, ETSI, CEPT, RACE

The **CEC (Commission of the European Communities)** in Brussels contributes in many ways to the creation of European standards. The CEC regulates the approval of apparatus, which has been approved in one country, in all other participating countries. However, the creation of the standards themselves is left to the existing European standards organizations such as **CEN (Comité européen de normalisation)** which is a body working at European level in the subject areas of ISO, **CENELEC (Comité européen normalisation électrotechnique)** working in the area of IEC and **ETSI (European Telecommunication Standards Institute)**.

ETSI was founded in 1988. Before this time all telecommunication standardization at European level was done by **CEPT (Conférence européenne des administrations des postes et des télécommunications)**. ETSI, which is based in the neighbourhood of Nice, does not limit its membership to the PTTs, as was the case with the CEPT.

CEC plays an important role in the creation of standards for the future broadband ISDN by managing and financing the **RACE project (R&D in Advanced Communications Technologies for Europe)**.

12.4 Summary of important telecommunications standards

12.4.1 Some European functional standards

NET 2:	X.25 Access
NET 3:	ISDN Basic Access
NET 6:	V.32 Modem
NET 7:	Group 3 Fax
NET 12:	Cordless Telephone
NET 21:	ISDN Primary Rate Access

12.4.2 A selection of CCITT/ITU-T recommendations

Note: CCITT/ITU-T recommendations can be obtained from the ITU Sales Section, Place des Nations, CH-1211 Geneva 20, Switzerland Tel. +41 22 730 51 11, Fax: +41 22 730 51 94.

E-series – Telephone operations

E.121:	Pictograms and symbols to assist users of the telephone service.
E.163:	Numbering plan for the international telephone service.
E.164:	Numbering plan for the ISDN era.

F-series – Operations and QOS

F1 and F31: Public telegram service.
F.111:   Principles of service for mobile systems.
F.113:   Service provision for aeronautical passenger communications supported by mobile satellite systems.
F.435:   Message handling: EDI service.
F.440:   Message handling services: The voice messaging service.
F.721:   Videotelephony teleservice for ISDN.
F.730:   Videoconference service – general.
F.811:   Broadband connection oriented bearer service.
F.812:   Broadband connectionless data bearer servicer.
F.850:   Principles of universal personal telecommunication (UPT).

G-series – Digital networks

G.174:   Transmission performance of terrestrial wireless personal communication systems.
G.701:   Vocabulary of digital transmission and multiplexing, and PCM terms.
G.702:   Digital hierarchy bit rates.
G.707:   Synchronous digital hierarchy bit rates.
G.708:   Network node interface for the SDH.
G.709:   Synchronous multiplexing structure.
G.711:   Pulse Code Modulation (PCM) of voice frequencies.
G.721:   32 kbit/s Adaptive Differential Pulse Code Modulation (ADPCM).
G.726:   40, 32, 24, 16 kbit/s Adaptive Differential Pulse Code Modulation (ADPCM).
G.728:   Coding of speech at 16 kbit/s using low-delay code excited linear prediction.
G.732:   Characteristics of primary PCM multiplex equipment operating at 2048 kbit/s.
G.764:   Voice packetization – packetized voice protocols.
G.782:   Types and general characteristics of SDH multiplexing equipment.
G.952:   Digital line systems based on the 2048 kbit/s hierarchy on symmetric pair cables.
G.954:   Digital line systems based on the 2048 kbit/s hierarchy on coaxial pair cables.
G.956:   Digital line systems based on the 2048 kbit/s hierarchy on optical fibre cables.

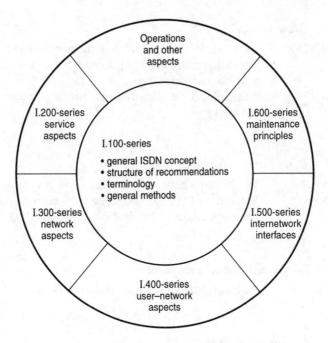

Figure 12.2 CCITT ISDN recommendations; I-series.

I-series – ISDN and B-ISDN (Figure 12.2 and Chapter 6)

I.121:	Broadband aspects of ISDN.
I.150:	Recommendation: B-ISDN ATM functional characteristics.
I.361:	Recommendation: B-ISDN ATM layer specification.
I.413:	Recommendation: B-ISDN user–network interface.

The most well-known recommendations from the I-series:

I.430:	Basic user–network interface – layer 1 specification.
I.431:	Primary rate user–network interface – layer 1 specification.

K-series – Protection against interference

K.22:	Overvoltage resistibilty of equipment connected to an ISDN T/S bus.
K.31:	Bonding configurations and earthing of telecommunication installations inside a subscriber's building.

M-series – Maintenance

M.1130:   General definitions and general principles of operation/maintenance procedures to be used in satellite mobile systems.

M.3010:   Principles for a telecommunications management network.

Q-series – Digital access signalling system

Q.931:   ISDN user–network interface layer 3 specification.

Q.1000:   Structure of the Q.1000 series of Recommendations for Public Land Mobile Networks (PLMN).

S-series – Telegraph terminal equipment

S.1:   International Telegraph Alphabet No. 2.

T-series – Telematic terminals

T.4:   Standardization of group 3 facsimile apparatus for document transmission.

T.61:   Character repertoire and coded character set for the international teletex service.

T.415:   Open Document Architecture (ODA) and Interchange Format (ODIF).

T.431:   Document Transfer And Manipulation (DTAM) – Services and protocols – introduction and general principles.

U-series – Telegraph switching

U.1:   Signalling conditions to be applied in the international telex services.

U.20:   Telex and gentex signalling on radio channels (synchronous 7-unit systems affording error correction by automatic repetition).

U.75:   Automatic called telex answerback check.

V-series – Data communication over the telephone network

V.21:   300 bit/s duplex modem standardized for use in the general switched telephone network.

V.22:	1200 bit/s duplex modem standardized for use in the general switched telephone network and on point-to-point two-wire leased telephone-type circuits.
V.22bis:	2400 bit/s duplex modem using the frequency division technique standardized for use on the general switched telephone network and on point-to-point two-wire leased telephone-type circuits.
V.23:	600/1200-baud modem standardized for use in the general switched telephone network.
V.24:	List of definitions for interchange circuits between data terminal equipment and data circuit terminating equipment.
V.32:	A family of two-wire, duplex modems operating at data signalling rates of up to 9600 bit/s for use on the general switched telephone network and on leased telephone-type circuits.
V.32 bis:	A duplex modem operating at data signalling rates of up to 14 400 bit/s for use on the general switched telephone network and on leased point-to-point two-wire telephone type circuits.
V.33:	14 400 bit/s second modem standardized for use on point-to-point four-wire leased telephone-type circuits.
V.34:	A modem operating at data signalling rates of up to 28 800 bit/s for use on the general switched telephone network and on leased point-to-point two-wire telephone type circuits.
V.42 bis:	Data compression procedures for Data Circuit Terminating Equipment (DCE) using error correcting procedures.
V.110:	Support of Data Terminal Equipment (DTEs) with V-series type interfaces by an Integrated Services Digital Network (ISDN).

X-series – Data transmission

X.4:	General structure of signals of International Alphabet No. 5 code for data transmission over public data networks.
X.25:	Interface between Data Terminal Equipment (DTE) and Data Circuit Terminating Equipment (DCE) for terminals operating in the packet mode and connected to PDNs by dedicated circuits.
X.121:	International numbering plan for public data networks.

X.200:	Reference model of Open Systems Interconnection (OSI) for CCITT applications.
X.400:	Message handling system and service overview. (See Table 12.1.)
X.500:	The directory – overview.
X.700:	Management framework for Open Systems Interconnection (OSI) for CCITT applications.
X.800:	Security architecture for OSI for CCITT applications.

Z-series – Functional Specification and Description Language (SDL)

Z.101:	Basic SDL.

12.4.3   Selected ETSI documents

ETS 300 104:	Integrated Services Digital Network (ISDN); Attachment requirements for terminal equipment to connect to an ISDN using ISDN basic access – layer 3 aspects.
I-ETS 300 168:	Digital Short Range Radio (DSRR).
ETS 300 175:	Digital European Cordless Telecommunications (DECT) common interface, part 1: overview.
ETS 300 212:	Metropolitan Area Network (MAN) media access control layer and physical layer specification.
ETS 300 217, parts 1–3:	Connectionless Broadband Data Service (CBDS).

Table 12.1   MHS recommendations and standards.

Name of recommendation/standard	Joint CCITT/ISO		CCITT only	
	CCITT	ISO	System	Service
MHS: System and Service Overview	X.400	10021-1		F.400
MHS: Overall Architecture	X.402	10021-2		
MHS: Conformance Testing			X.403	
MHS: Abstract Service Definition Conventions	X.407	10021-3		
MHS: Encoded Information Type Conversion Rules			X.408	
MHS: MTS: Abstract Service Definition and Procedures	X.411	10021-4		
MHS: MS: Abstract Service Definition	X.413	10021-5		
MHS: Protocol Specifications	X.419	10021-6		
MHS: Interpersonal Messaging System	X.420	10021-7		
Telematic Access to IPMS			T.300	
MHS: Naming and Addressing for Public MH Services				F.401
MHS: The Public Message Transfer Service				F.410
MHS: Intercommunication with Public Physical Delivery Services				F.415
MHS: The Public IPM Service				F.420
MHS: Intercommunication between IPM Service and Telex				F.421
MHS: Intercommunication between IPM Service and Telex				F.422
OSI: Basic Reference Model	X.200	7498		
OSI: Specification of Abstract Syntax Notation One (ASN.1)	X.208	8824		
OSI: Specification of Basic Encoding Rules for Abstract Syntax Notation One (ASN.1)	X.209	8825		
OSI: Association Control: Service Definition	X.217	8649		
OSI: Reliable Transfer: Model and Service Definition	X.218	9066-1		
OSI Remote Operations: Model, Notation and Service Definition	X.219	9072-1		
OSI: Association Control: Protocol Specification	X.227	8650		
OSI: Reliable Transfer: Protocol Specification	X.228	9066-2		
OSI: Remote Operations: Protocol Specification	X.229	9072-2		

Key terms

Chapter 4: Communication protocols

Chapter 5: General aspects of user equipment

Chapter 6: Integrated services digital network (ISDN)

Chapter 7: Mobile communications and cordless telephones

Chapter 8: Digital multiplexing

Chapter 9: Sources and encoding

Chapter 10: Performance analysis

Chapter 11: Telecommunications services

Chapter 12: Standards and recommendations

Appendices

References and further reading

Anonymous (1991) Memorandum of Understanding on the Implementation of a European ISDN Service by 1992. *Computer Networks and ISDN Systems*, pp. 69–74

Bigliero E. and Prato G. (eds) (1986) Digital communications. *Proceedings of Second Tirrenia International Workshop on Digital Communications.* North Holland/Elsevier

Blahut R.E. (1983) *The Theory and Practice of Error Control Codes.* Addison-Wesley

CCITT (1988a) Specification of Signalling System No. 7. Recommendations Q.700–Q.716, Fascicle VI.7, *Blue Book*

CCITT (1988b) Specification of Signalling System No. 7. Recommendations Q.721–Q.766, Fascicle VI.8, *Blue Book*

CCITT (1988c) Specification of Signalling System No. 7. Recommendations Q.771–Q.795, Fascicle VI.9, *Blue Book*

CCITT (1988d) Recommendation R.111: Code and speed independent TDM system for anisochronous telegraph and data transmission. *Blue Book*. Geneva

CCITT (1989a) Recommendations I.140, I.210, I.220, I.230 series, I.240 series and I.250 series. *Blue Book*, Vol. III – Fascicle III.7. Geneva

CCITT (1989b) Recommendation I.411. *Blue Book*, Vol. III – Fascicle III.8. Geneva

Clarke P.G. and Wadsworth C.A. (1988) CCITT Signalling System No. 7: Signalling Connection Control Part. *Brit. Telecom. Engng.*, **7**, 32–45

Collin R.E. (1985) *Antennas and Radiowave Propagation.* McGraw-Hill

Davies C.G. (1988) CCITT Signalling System No. 7: Integrated Services Digital Network User Part. *Brit. Telecom. Engng.*, **7**, 46–57

Davies D.W. and Barber D.L.A. (1973) *Communication Networks for Computers.* Wiley

Ferreira R.C. (1989) The smart card: a high security tool in EDP. *Philips Telecom. Rev.*, **47**(3), 1–19

Frank H. and Frisch I.T. (1971) *Communication, Transmission, and Transportation Networks*. Addison-Wesley

Freebody J.W. (1958) *Telegraphy*. London: Pitman, p. 42

Fretten K.G. and Davies C.G. (1988) CCITT Signalling System No. 7: Overview. *Brit. Telecom. Engng.*, **7**, 4–6.

Goldhirsch J. and Vogel W.J. (1989) Mobile satellite system fade characteristics for shadowing and multipath from roadside trees at UHF and L-band. *IEEE Trans. Ant. Prop.*, **37**(4), 189–198

Gonzales R.C. and Wintz P. *Digital Image Processing*. Addison-Wesley

Halsall F. (1988) *Data Communications, Computer Networks, and OSI*. Addison-Wesley

Holland P.M. and Walden R.R. (1989) From concept to realisation. *Trends in Telecom.*, **5**(1), 15–22

Jayant N.S. and Noll P. (1984) *Digital Coding of Waveforms*. Prentice Hall

Johnson T.W., Law B. and Anius P. (1988) CCITT Signalling System No. 7: Transaction Capabilities. *Brit. Telecom. Engng.*, **7**, 58–65

Klein M.J. (1990) The synchronous digital hierarchy: principles, variants and applications. *Philips Telecom. Rev.*, **48**(4), 20–7

Kleinrock L. (1964) *Communication Nets, Stochastic Message Flow and Delay*. McGraw-Hill

Kleinrock L. (1975) *Queueing Systems*, Vol. 1: *Theory*. Wiley

Krick W. (1990) A transfer concept not only for broadband services. *Philips Telecom. Data Systems Rev.*, **48**(2), 15–23

Kyas O. (1995) *ATM Networks*. London: ITP

Law B. and Wadsworth C.A. (1988) CCITT Signalling System No. 7: Message Transfer Part. *Brit. Telecom. Engng.*, **7**, 7–18

Lin S. and Costello D.J. (1988) *Error Control Coding: Fundamentals and Applications*. Prentice Hall

Maat J.Ph. (1987) The application of SOPHO-S2500 in fully integrated networks. *Philips Telecom. Data Systems Rev.*, **45**(3), 23–27

Mitrani I. (1987) *Modelling of Computer and Communication Systems*. Cambridge University Press

Raatgever J.F. (1989) Trends in architecture. *Trends in Telecom.*, **5**(1), 5–13

Rahnema M. (1993) Overview of the GSM system and protocol architecture. *IEEE Commun. Mag.* April, 92–100

Rikkert de Koe O.B.P. (1990) *OSI Protocollen, lagen 1 t/m 4*. Kluwer

Schoute F.C. (1989) Prestatie-analyse van telecommunicatiesystemen. Kluwer Technische Boeken, ISBN 90-201-2219-3. Out-of-print; now available on World Wide Web http://mmc.et.tudelft.nl/presan/pab

Schwartz M. (1987) *Telecommunication Networks; Protocols, Modeling and Analysis*. Addison-Wesley

Spragins J.D. (1991) *Telecommunications, Protocols and Design*. Addison-Wesley

Tanenbaum A.S. (1989) *Computer Networks*. Prentice Hall

VAN Dooren G.A.J. and Herben M.H.A.J. (1994) Electromagnetic wave diffraction by obstacles with application to field strength prediction and interference reduction. *J. Electromag. Waves Prop. (JEWA)*, **8**, 175–94

van Duuren J. (1981) The Common ICAO Data Interchange Network (CIDIN) procedures. *Philips Telecom. Rev.*, **39**(4), 201–210

Vucetic B. and Du J. (1992) Channel modelling and simulation in satellite mobile communication systems. *IEEE J. Selected Areas in Comms.*, **10**(10), 1209–18

Vervest P., van Duuren J., Preston J.M., van der Rhee J., Rikkert de Koe O.B.P., Spoon H.J. and Wissema (1985) *Electronic Mail and Message Handling.* Frances Pinter

Wade J.G. (1987) *Signal Coding and Processing.* Ellis Horwood

Technical and Mathematical Appendices

Appendix A

Basic principles of time division switching technology

The basic block diagram of a time division switch is given in Figure A.1.

The time division multiplexer A (remote or part of the switch) sends PCM samples of other 8-bit data in time slots on the common circuit to the memory. A sample from line 1 fills time slot 1, a sample of line 2 in slot 2 and so on. The transmission is serial, for example, with a bit rate of 2 Mbit/s. In the memory the samples are registered in an orderly way. Information from one of the channels, the signalling channel is processed and may lead to a new connection set-up. Such information is entered in a connection table. This table is used to transfer information from incoming time slots in to the proper time slots for the exit side. In the figure we see that information from time slot 1 is now sent

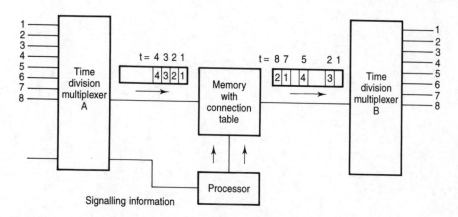

Figure A.1 Basic configuration of a time division switch.

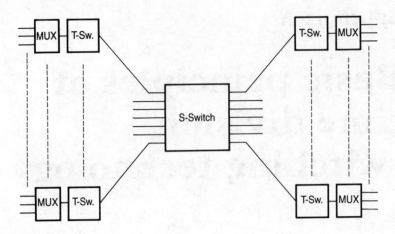

Figure A.2   A TST multistage configuration.

in time slot 7. The information in outgoing time slot 7 is delivered to circuit 7 by multiplexer B.

Limitations of technology limit the number of time slots in the TDM frame and thus the size of the Time-switch (T-switch). Therefore a certain amount of space division switching (S-switch) can increase the size of the switching system. This leads to the concept of multistage switches. Such a switching system can consist of a number of Time and Space switches, for example, TS, TST, TSSST.

As an example Figure A.2 shows a TST multistage switching system. The S-switch in this system has the task of switching the contents of individual time slots to different T-switches according to a table of connections.

Appendix B

Transmission at the physical layer of the ISDN basic user–network interface

CCITT (ITU-T) Recommendation I.430 specifies the physical layer, layer 1, at the basic user–network interface. The recommendation describes the transmission at the S or T reference point (see Figure B.1) and gives details of the primitives between layer 1 and layer 2, the wiring configurations, functional characteristics and interface procedures. The interface procedures include procedures for the access to the signalling channel (D-channel) in a multipoint configuration and activation/ deactivation procedures.

This appendix concentrates on the description of the possible configurations and the transmission at the **S or T reference point**. The interfaces at both reference points are identical. **Network Termination 2 (NT2)** is an optional function, for example, performed by an ISPABX business switching system. When NT2 is not present reference points S and T fall together.

The transmission on the transmission line (see Figure B.1) is not specified by CCITT. Generally this is a two-wire interface using echo cancelling to provide for the required two-way simultaneous (duplex) operation. The S interface is intended for the connection of *standardized* **Terminal Equipment (TE)**. The distance to be bridged from the Network Termination (NT) to the TE is assumed to be relatively small. Here two separate circuits are available for the receive and send sides of the duplex

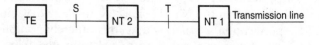

Figure B.1 Reference configuration for the basic user–network interface.

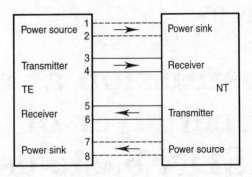

Figure B.2 The electrical connections of the interface at the S or T reference point.

operation. Economizing on wires is not efficient for these short distances. A separate circuit for the provision of power to the terminal or to the NT may be included at the interface. See Figure B.2.

Two terminal configurations are possible, a single-terminal point-to-point configuration and a point-to-multipoint configuration for up to eight terminals.

In the point-to-point configuration the source (transmitter) in the NT will send on its transmission (interchange) circuit to the sink (receiver) of the TE and the sink in the NT will receive on its receive (interchange) circuit transmission from the source in the TE. So on each interchange circuit only one sink and one source is active in a point-to-point configuration.

In the point-to-multipoint configuration the transmission is from the NT to the terminals and from the terminals to the NT. Transmission between terminals is not specified by CCITT, but the possibility is not specifically excluded by CCITT. In the point-to-multipoint configuration two modes of operation are possible:

- point-to-point operation between the NT and *one* particular TE, and
- point-to-multipoint operation between the NT and *more than one* TE.

In the latter case the sink and source pairs of the NT and of more than one terminal may be active.

The source in the NT is therefore physically connected to all sinks in the TEs and the sink in the NT is connected to all sources in the TEs. The CCITT specification *considers* that this interconnection will be provided by one continuous cable with jacks for the TEs and NT attached directly to the cable or using stubs less than 1 metre in length.

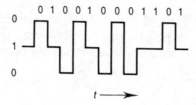

Figure B.3 Pseudo-ternary coding.

A connecting cord of the TE should not be longer than 10 metres. Only in a point-to-point configuration is it allowed to use a cord of up to 25 metres in length.

The transmission on both interchange circuits uses a pseudo-ternary line coding (see Figure B.3). No line signal (zero current) represents the binary 1, a positive or negative current represents the binary 0. Subsequent 0s alternate in polarity, in order to avoid a DC component in the frequency spectrum of the transmitted signals.

Frame synchronization is achieved by violations of this encoding rule. The signal rate, here equal to the bit rate, is 192 kbit/s. The bits are grouped into frames of 48 bits each, with a duration of 250 μs. Each 48-bit frame contains three framing bits (F, N and F_A), four bits of the D-channel, and 32 bits of the two B-channels in both directions of transmission. The remaining bits are allocated differently for the send and receive sides of the NT. From NT to TE one bit (A) is reserved for activation/deactivation of terminals. Four bits (E) are used to confirm the receipt of the last four D bits at the terminal by echoing this information back to the TE. One bit (M) indicates a multiframe sequence, one bit (S) is not yet assigned and two bits (L) are used to restore a possible imbalance of the DC component (see Figure B.4).

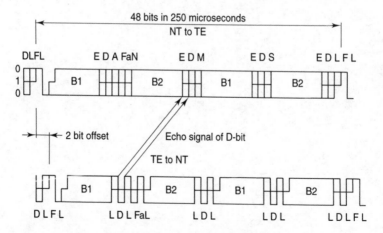

Figure B.4 Frame structure at reference points S and T.

From TE to NT, no M, E and A bits are needed. At their places we find DC balancing bits (L). The 48-bit frames in this direction of transmission start two bit times later than in the opposite direction.

Appendix C

The frequency spectrum of a PAM signal

The time-discrete signal F_s of Section 9.3.1, is also called a **Pulse Amplitude Modulation (PAM)** signal. This function can be written as:

$$F_s(t) = F_{AN}(t) \cdot S(t)$$

According to Shannon's sampling theory, all the information in the analogue source signal (amplitude and argument information) will be present in the sampled PAM signal if the correct choice of sampling frequency, f_s, has been made.

This can be shown as follows (the proof makes use of Fourier analysis and is not shown here). Assume that the following is true for the analogue signal:

$$F_{AN}(t) = \sum_{n=L}^{H} A_n \cos (2\pi f_n)t$$

For an arbitrary function $F_{AN}(t)$, a randomly chosen frequency spectrum $F_{AN}(f)$ can be drawn as shown in Figure C.1.

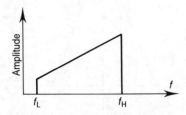

Figure C.1 Arbitrarily chosen amplitude–frequency characteristic for a signal $F_{AN}(t)$.

The form chosen for this spectrum has as its chief characteristic an amplitude that has a clear relationship to the frequency, which will increase the familiarity of several illustrations.

The time-dependent function $S(t)$ can be written as a Fourier series:

$$S(t) = \frac{A\tau}{T} + \frac{2A\tau}{T} \sum_{m=1}^{\infty} \frac{\sin\left(m\,2\pi f_s\,\tau/2\right)}{m\,2\pi f_s\,\tau/2} \cos\left(m\,2\pi f_s\,t\right)$$

$$= \frac{A\tau}{T} \sum_{m=-\infty}^{\infty} \frac{\sin\left(m\,2\pi f_s\,\tau/2\right)}{m\,2\pi f_s\,\tau/2} \cos\left(m\,2\pi f_s\,t\right)$$

The function is the product of an envelope (the so-called **sinc function**):

$$\frac{A\tau}{T}\,\frac{\sin\left(m\,2\pi f_s\,\tau/2\right)}{m\,2\pi f_s\,\tau/2}$$

and of a series of time-dependent goniometric functions (the so-called **harmonics**):

$$\sum_{m=-\infty}^{\infty} \cos\left(m\,2\pi f_s\,t\right)$$

The Fourier series can be depicted graphically as shown in Figure C.2. Using this, the PAM signal can be written as:

$$F_s(t) = \sum_{n=L}^{H} \sum_{m=-\infty}^{\infty} \frac{A_n\,A\tau}{2T} \left[\cos\left\{2\pi(mf_s + f_n)t\right\} + \cos\left\{2\pi(mf_s - f_n)t\right\}\right]$$

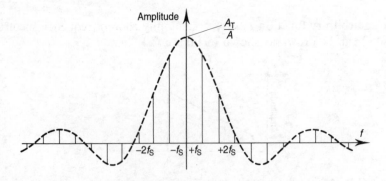

Figure C.2 Frequency spectrum of the sampling signal $S(t)$.

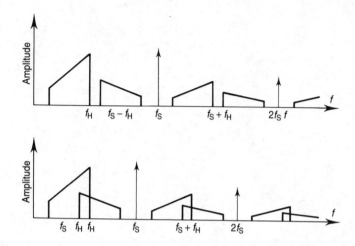

Figure C.3   Single-sided frequency spectra of the PAM signal for two values of f_s.

This time-dependent function turns out to be composed of a large number of so-called lower and upper side bands as shown in Figure C.3 (single-sided spectra).

The desired information can be obtained by processing the PAM signal through a low pass filter – but only at the correct sampling frequency of $f_s \geqslant 2f_H$.

The major advantage of using time-discrete PAM signals is the possibility of time division multiplexing (theoretically T/τ channels via one transmission or signal processing system). It has, however, the related disadvantage of TDM; account has to be taken of the distortion of the signal by intersymbol interference (whereby pulses from the various channels overlap each other as the result of the non-ideal transmission characteristics of, for example, the transmission system. A further general disadvantage of PAM is so-called **spectrum pollution**. This can be caused by unsatisfactory filter characteristics of the low pass filter used for detection and/or by **aliasing** or **foldover** distortion caused by the choice of a sampling frequency, f_s, which is too low. (See the lower half of Figure C.3.)

Appendix D

The decoding algorithm for error correction

The application of error correction (forward error correction) is similar to that of error detection, but requires extra processing of the received codeword R of Section 9.5.2. It is assumed that the difference between T and R, the transmission error, can be written as a codeword E. Each bit with a value 1 represents a bit error. Use of modulo-2 addition is also made here:

$$R = T \oplus E$$

The decoding process for error correction, as for error detection, consists of a linear transformation of the received code R by processing with a matrix P^T.

The chosen matrix ensures that the transformation of the received codeword R produces the value 0 if there are no errors $(R = T)$. This can be achieved by a transposed matrix as follows:

$$
P^T =
\begin{bmatrix}
p_{11} & p_{21} & \cdots & p_{(n-m)1} \\
p_{12} & \cdot & \cdots & \cdot \\
\cdot & \cdot & & \cdot \\
\cdot & \cdot & & \cdot \\
\cdot & \cdot & & \cdot \\
\cdot & \cdot & & \cdot \\
\cdot & \cdot & & \cdot \\
p_{1m} & \cdot & \cdots & p_{(n-m)m} \\
\cdot & \cdot & & \cdot \\
\cdot & \cdot & & \cdot \\
p_{1n} & \cdot & \cdots & p_{(n-m)n}
\end{bmatrix}
$$

$$= \begin{bmatrix} P_1^{\mathsf{T}} \\ P_2^{\mathsf{T}} \end{bmatrix} = \begin{bmatrix} p_{11} & p_{21} & \cdots & p_{(n-m)1} \\ p_{12} & \cdot & \cdots & \cdot \\ \cdot & \cdot & & \cdot \\ \cdot & \cdot & & \cdot \\ \cdot & \cdot & & \cdot \\ p_{1m} & \cdot & \cdots & p_{(n-m)m} \\ 1 & 0 & \cdots & 0 \\ 0 & 1 & \cdots & 0 \\ \cdot & \cdot & & \cdot \\ \cdot & \cdot & & \cdot \\ 0 & 0 & \cdots & 1 \end{bmatrix}$$

The partial matrix P_1^{T}, which generated the parity check bits during encoding, corresponds to the matrix G_2 of the generator matrix.

The partial matrix P_2^{T} consists of a unit matrix of degree (m, n), equal to the number of parity check bits. The modulo-2 operation used for this linear transformation ensures that the transformation produces the value 0 for $R = T$.

The matrix P, the transpose of P^{T}, is called the **parity check matrix** and can be written as follows:

$$P = \begin{bmatrix} P_1 P_2 \end{bmatrix} = \begin{bmatrix} p_{11} & p_{12} & \cdots & p_{1m} & 1 & 0 & \cdots & 0 \\ p_{21} & \cdot & \cdots & \cdot & 0 & 1 & \cdots & 0 \\ \cdot & \cdot & & \cdot & \cdot & \cdot & & \cdot \\ \cdot & \cdot & & \cdot & \cdot & \cdot & & \cdot \\ \cdot & \cdot & & \cdot & \cdot & \cdot & & \cdot \\ p_{(n-m)1} & \cdot & \cdots & \cdot & 0 & 0 & \cdots & 1 \end{bmatrix}$$

The linear transformation of $R \neq T$, taking account of the above, is equal to:

$$R \cdot P^{\mathsf{T}} = E \cdot P^{\mathsf{T}} = S$$

This only has a result not equal to the 0-vector if all elements of E are not equal to 0. So far, the procedure for error correction is similar to that for error detection as described in Section 9.5.2.

The $(n - m)$ dimensional **syndrome vector S** plays an essential part in error correction. The coordinates of the **S** vector, or the bit positions of the word S, are determined by the received bit errors (given by E) in combination with the corresponding row vector of the matrix P^{T} (in other words, with the corresponding column vector of the parity check matrix P).

From this it follows that bit errors can be detected, and their position in the codeword known, provided that the row vector of P^T (and the column vector of the parity check matrix P) meets the following conditions:

- every row vector differs from all others in the matrix,
- not all elements of the vector are 0.

This category of channel codes can thus be used to correct a bit error since the position of the faulty bit is known.

Multiple bit errors per block can also be detected and corrected. It can be shown that the following condition is sufficient:

$$2^{(n-m)} \geqslant \sum_{i=0}^{t} \frac{n!}{i!(n-i)!}$$

This term is known as the **Hamming bound**. In this expression, t is the number of error bits per block. The necessary number of parity bits is thus determined by the number of possibilities that $0, 1, 2 \ldots, t$ bit-errors can occur. This determines the dimensions of the generator matrix G and the parity check matrix P.

Appendix E

Engset blocking formula

The Engset blocking formula gives an expression for the probability that a user of a telecommunication system finds all lines busy when he/she wants to make a call. In this appendix we show how the formula follows from the state diagram of the Markov chain that models the number of busy lines. The derivation is in terms of telephone lines or radio channels that are occupied during an exponentially distributed holding time, but the formula is also valid for arbitrarily distributed holding times.

The following parameters determine the blocking probability:

N number of lines
s number of sources (users)
μ service rate $= 1/h$, where h is the mean holding time
α call intensity per free source; $1/\alpha$ is equal to the mean idle time

The state diagram of the Markov chain is given in Figure E.1.

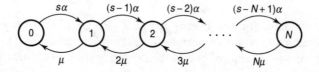

Figure E.1   State diagram of the number of busy lines when s users share N lines. The values along the arrows are transition intensities.

With the same equilibrium argument that was used in the derivation of the Erlang formula, the unnormalized state probabilities are:

$$w_i = \binom{s}{i} \cdot \left(\frac{\alpha}{\mu}\right)^i \qquad i = 0, 1, \ldots, N \tag{E.1}$$

where the binomial coefficient can be computed as:

$$\binom{s}{i} = \frac{s \cdot (s-1) \cdots (s-i+1)}{1 \cdot 2 \cdots i} \tag{E.2}$$

Just normalizing the value of w_N gives the probability that all lines are busy, but this is not the blocking probability. To see the difference, consider the special case where there are as many users as lines $(s = N)$. Then with some probability all lines will be busy, but the blocking probability is zero.

The blocking probability is equal to the call intensity while in state N divided by the overall call intensity. This ratio is equal to:

$$G_N(s, \alpha) = \frac{\alpha \cdot (s - N) \cdot w_N}{\displaystyle\sum_{i=0}^{N} \alpha \cdot (s - i) \cdot w_i} \qquad \text{for } s \geqslant N \tag{E.3}$$

This equation can be turned into a closed-form expression by substituting w_i using equation (E.1) and applying the following binomial identity that can easily be verified using equation (E.2):

$$(s - i) \cdot \binom{s}{i} = s \cdot \binom{s-1}{i} \tag{E.4}$$

This results in the Engset formula:

$$G_N(s, \alpha) = \frac{\binom{s-1}{N} \cdot \left(\frac{\alpha}{\mu}\right)^N}{\displaystyle\sum_{i=0}^{N} \binom{s-1}{i} \cdot \left(\frac{\alpha}{\mu}\right)^i} \qquad s > N \tag{E.5}$$

Just as is the case for the Erlang formula (see Sections 10.4 and 10.5), there is a recursive way to compute the value of equation (E.5). Now the recursion for the inverse of the blocking probability on i lines is started with:

$$J_0(s, \alpha) = 1 \tag{E.6}$$

and is continued, until i reaches s or N (whichever comes first), with

$$J_i(s, \alpha) = J_{i-1}(s, \alpha) \cdot \frac{i \cdot \mu}{(s - i) \cdot \alpha} + 1 \qquad \text{(E.7)}$$

The blocking probability is then:

$$G_N(s, \alpha) = \frac{1}{J_N(s, \alpha)} \qquad \text{(E.8)}$$

assuming that $N < s$, otherwise the blocking probability is zero.

Index